AF560813

Essentials of Mental Health Education

Bhujendra Nath Panda
Dipak Bhattacharya
Sanjukta Sahoo

₹ 1500
ISBN: 978-93-91978-77-8

2024
First Published in India

Essentials of Mental Health Education

Published by:
SHIPRA PUBLICATIONS
LG 18-19, Pankaj Central Market
I.P. Ext., Patparganj, Delhi 110092, India
+91 11 47322068; 96500 28065, 9810522367
info@shiprapublication.com
www.shiprapublication.com

Preface

In an era characterized by rapid change, increasing demands, and the complexities of modern life, mental health has emerged as an essential facet of our well-being. As educators and scholars dedicated to the field of psychology and mental health, we are pleased to present this comprehensive book, aptly titled "Essentials of Mental Health Education". This work represents the culmination of our collective knowledge and experience in the realm of mental health, mental hygiene, and the understanding of the human mind.

In today's world, where stressors and challenges seem to be ever-present, the importance of mental health cannot be overstated. This book is designed to provide a holistic perspective on mental health, encompassing not only the theoretical foundations but also practical insights and applications. It is our hope that this book serves as a valuable resource for students, educators, mental health professionals, and anyone interested in understanding and nurturing their own mental well-being.

This book is the result of our passion for promoting mental health and our commitment to providing a comprehensive resource that bridges theory and practice. We believe that understanding mental health is not only essential for personal well-being but also for building a more compassionate and empathetic society. We invite readers to embark on this journey with us, exploring the fascinating and multifaceted world of mental health.

Prof. B. N. Panda
Dr. Dipak Bhattacharya
Dr. Sanjukta Sahoo

Contents

1

Mental Health

Concept of Mental Health

Mental health is a crucial aspect of overall well-being, encompassing emotional, psychological, and social aspects of our lives. It is a state of mind that allows us to cope with the stresses and challenges of daily life, maintain healthy relationships, and functionsat our best. It is essential for achieving personal fulfillment and a critical component of a healthy and productive society.

There are several factors that influence mental health. Biological factors, such as genetics and brain chemistry, can impact our mental health. Environmental factors, such as trauma, stress, and social support, can also play a role. Additionally, lifestyle factors, such as exercise, nutrition, and substance use, can have a significant impact on mental health.

Mental health disorders are a significant concern, affecting millions of people worldwide. They are characterized by changes in thinking, behaviour, and mood that can significantly impact our ability to function in our daily lives. Some of the most common mental health disorders include anxiety disorders, mood disorders, psychotic disorders, eating disorders, and substance abuse disorders.

Anxiety disorders are characterized by excessive and persistent worry, fear, and avoidance behaviours. Generalized anxiety disorder, panic disorder, and obsessive-compulsive disorder are among the most common types of anxiety disorders. Mood disorders, such as depression and bipolar disorder, involve changes in mood, energy, and behaviour. Psychotic disorders, such as schizophrenia and delusional disorder, involve a loss of touch with reality. Eating disorders, such as anorexia nervosa and bulimia nervosa, involve

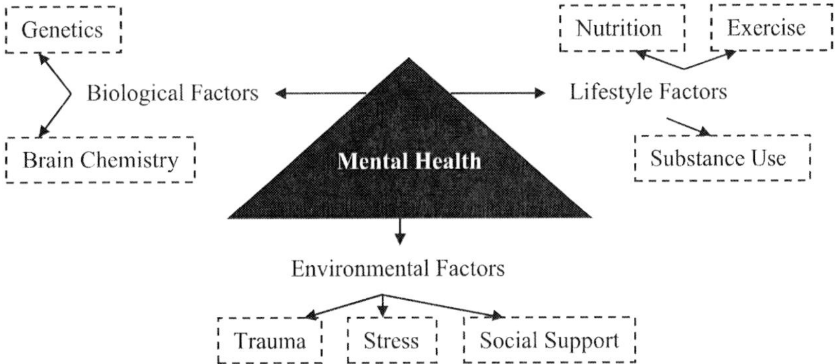

Figure 1.1: *Factors Influencing Mental Health*

distorted body image and unhealthy eating habits. Substance abuse disorders involve a dependence on alcohol or drugs.

Recognizing the signs and symptoms of mental health disorders is crucial for getting help. Symptoms can vary depending on the disorder but can include changes in mood, behaviour, and sleep patterns, as well as social withdrawal, physical symptoms, and changes in appetite or weight. It is important to seek professional help for mental health disorders, as they can significantly impact our ability to function and lead fulfilling lives.

Stigma and discrimination are significant barriers to seeking help for mental health disorders. Many people feel ashamed or embarrassed about seeking treatment, or fear being labeled as 'crazy' or 'weak'. It is important to recognize that seeking help for mental health is a sign of strength, not weakness. Mental health treatment can provide access to medication, therapy, and support from mental health professionals and peers.

Maintaining good mental health requires ongoing effort and attention. There are many strategies that can help promote mental health, including regular exercise, healthy eating habits, and stress reduction techniques such as mindfulness meditation and deep breathing exercises. Social support is also crucial for maintaining good mental health, including maintaining positive relationships and seeking out social support when needed.

Here are some key points about the concept of mental health:

- Mental health refers to a person's overall psychological well-being, including their ability to think, feel, and behave in a healthy way.
- Good mental health allows us to function well in our daily lives, maintain healthy relationships, and pursue our goals and aspirations.
- Mental health can be influenced by a range of factors, such as genetics, environment, life experiences, and lifestyle choices.
- Mental health disorders can develop when there are imbalances in our brain chemistry, emotional regulation, or cognitive functioning.
- Mental health disorders can cause significant distress, impair our ability to function, and interfere with our quality of life.
- Mental health is not a static state, but rather a continuum. We all experience ups and downs in our mental health over time.
- Seeking professional help when needed and adopting healthy coping strategies can help us maintain good mental health and well-being.

Examples of mental health disorders include anxiety disorders, mood disorders (such as depression and bipolar disorder), psychotic disorders (such as schizophrenia), eating disorders, and substance abuse disorders.

Mental health is a crucial aspect of overall well-being, impacting our emotional, psychological, and social lives. Mental health disorders can significantly impact our ability to function and lead fulfilling lives, making it essential to seek help and support when needed. By reducing stigma and promoting mental health, we can create a more supportive and compassionate society that values mental health as much as physical health.

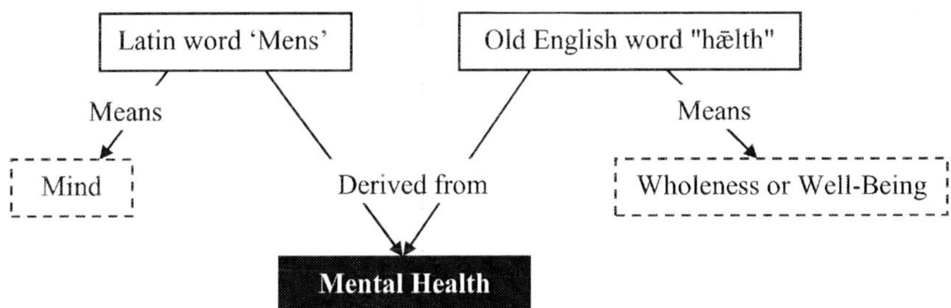

Figure 1.2: *Etymological Meaning of Mental Health*

Meaning of Mental Health

The term 'Mental Health' has its roots in the Latin word 'Mens', which means 'Mind'. The word 'Health' comes from the old English word "hǣlth", which means "wholeness" or "well-being".

The concept of mental health can be traced back to ancient civilizations such as Greece, where philosophers like Plato and Aristotle discussed the nature of the mind and its relationship to the body. In the middleages, mental health was often viewed through the lens of religion, with illnesses such as depression and anxiety seen as a result of sin or moral weakness.

It wasn't until the 19th century that the concept of mental health began to emerge as a distinct field of study. In the 1800s, psychiatrists such as Philippe Pinel and William Tuke began to advocate for more humane treatment of people with mental illness, emphasizing the importance of providing care and support rather than punishment and isolation.

As our understanding of mental health has evolved over time, so too has the language we use to describe it. Today, the term 'Mental Health' encompasses a wide range of conditions and experiences, from anxiety and depression to schizophrenia and bipolar disorder. It's a complex and multifaceted field, but at its core, it's all about promoting well-being and helping people live happy, fulfilling lives.

Mental health is an important aspect of our overall well-being. It refers to how we think, feel, and behave in our daily lives. Good mental health is essential for leading a fulfilling and productive life, and it affects everything from our relationships with others to our ability to cope with stress. When we talk about mental health, we're really talking about the health of our brain and how it functions. Our brain is responsible for a wide range of functions, including our emotions, thoughts, and behaviours. When our brain is working properly, we feel good, think clearly, and are able to cope with the ups and downs of life. But when our brain is struggling, we may experience a range of symptoms that can affect our mental health. Some common symptoms of poor mental health include feeling sad, anxious, or worried, having trouble sleeping or eating, feeling irritable or easily upset, and having difficulty concentrating or making decisions. These symptoms can be caused by a number of different factors, including genetics, life experiences, and environmental factors.

Fortunately, there are many things we can do to support our mental health and maintain good overall well-being. One of the most important things we can do is to take care of ourselves. This includes getting enough sleep, eating a healthy diet, exercising regularly, and practising relaxation techniques such as meditation or yoga. It's also important to seek support when we need it. This might mean talking to a trusted friend or family member, reaching out to a mental health professional, or joining a support group. There are many resources available to help people manage their mental health, including hotlines, online forums, and community programmes. Another important aspect of maintaining good mental health is practising healthy coping strategies. This might mean learning how to manage stress, developing problem-solving skills, or finding ways to express our emotions in a healthy way. It can also involve setting boundaries in our relationships or learning how to say no when we need to. It's important to recognize that mental health is not the same as mental illness. While mental illness is a real and serious condition that affects millions of people around the world, mental health is something that we all have to think about and take care of. Just like physical health, mental health requires ongoing attention and care. Some people may need additional support to manage their mental health. This might involve medication, therapy, or other treatments that are tailored to their specific needs. It's important to seek professional help if you're struggling with your mental health, as this can help you get the support you need to feel better.

Mental health is an essential aspect of our overall well-being. It's something that we all need to think about and take care of in order to lead fulfilling and productive lives. By taking care of ourselves, seeking support when we need it, and practising healthy coping strategies, we can support our mental health and maintain good overall well-being. Remember, mental health is just as important as physical health, and it's up to each of us to take care of ourselves in both of these areas.

Definitions of Mental Health

Mental health refers to the overall state of emotional, psychological, and social well-being of an individual. It encompasses a range of factors, including the ability to cope with stress, maintain healthy relationships, make meaningful contributions to society, and experience a sense of purpose and fulfillment in life. Good mental health is essential for individuals to function well in their personal and professional lives, and to lead happy, productive, and fulfilling lives.

Mental health can be affected by a variety of factors, such as genetic predisposition, life experiences, and environmental influences. Mental health problems can range from mild, temporary issues such as stress and anxiety to more severe and long-term conditions such as depression, bipolar disorder, and schizophrenia.

Mental health is an important aspect of overall health and well-being, and is increasingly recognized as a critical public health issue. A growing body of research shows that mental health promotion, prevention, and treatment can have significant positive impacts on individuals, families, and communities. As such, mental health is an area of focus for healthcare providers, policymakers, and individuals alike.

Here are some definitions of mental health put forth by famous organisation or educationists:

- According to the World Health Organization (WHO), mental health is "a state of well-being in which the individual realizes his or her own abilities, can cope with the normal stresses of life, can work productively and fruitfully, and is able to make a contribution to his or her community."
- Abraham Maslow, a psychologist and humanistic theorist, defined mental health as "the capacity to feel fully alive and to be aware of all the processes and feelings operating within oneself as well as in the world outside."
- Carl Rogers, another humanistic psychologist, described mental health as "the ongoing process of a person becoming more fully themselves."
- Erik Erikson, a developmental psychologist, saw mental health as "the capacity of the individual to live with a maximum of inner security and a minimum of hostility to others."
- Jean Piaget, a cognitive psychologist, described mental health as "the ability to adapt to one's environment and to successfully cope with its challenges."
- Sigmund Freud, the founder of psychoanalysis, defined mental health as "the ability to love and work."
- Albert Bandura, a social cognitive psychologist, saw mental health as "the ability to exercise a measure of control over one's life within the constraints of society."
- B.F. Skinner, a behaviourist psychologist, defined mental health as "the ability to engage in a wide range of adaptive behaviours that meet the demands of one's environment."
- William Glasser, a psychiatrist, described mental health as "the ability to establish and maintain quality relationships, to experience and express emotions, to function productively, and to make realistic and meaningful choices."
- Masaru Emoto, a Japanese author and researcher, defined mental health as "the condition where the spirit and soul are at peace and the body is in harmony with its environment."

These definitions illustrate the diversity of perspectives on mental health and the range of factors that contribute to it. They emphasize the importance of social connections, personal agency, adaptive behaviours, emotional expression, and spiritual well-being in achieving and maintaining good mental health.

Nature of Mental Health

The nature of mental health refers to a person's psychological, emotional, and social well-being. It encompasses how individuals think, feel, and behave in various situations, how they interact with others, and their ability to handle stress and cope with adversity. Mental health is essential to overall well-being, and poor mental health can have a profound impact on an individual's physical, social, and emotional health.

One of the key aspects of the nature of mental health is its complexity. Mental health is influenced by a range of biological, environmental, and social factors. For example, genetics can play a significant role in determining an individual's mental health. Certain genetic factors may increase the risk of developing certain mental health disorders, such as depression, anxiety, bipolar disorder, and schizophrenia.

Brain chemistry can also affect mental health, as imbalances in neurotransmitters such as serotonin, dopamine, and nor epinephrine can lead to various mental health issues. Additionally, life experiences and environmental stressors can impact mental health. Traumatic events, such as abuse, neglect, or violence, can cause long-term psychological and emotional harm. Chronic stress, such as financial difficulties or relationship problems, can also lead to mental health problems.

Social factors such as social support, culture, and socio-economic status can also impact mental health. Social support from friends and family can help buffer against the negative effects of stress and adversity, while social isolation can increase the risk of mental health issues. Culture can also play a role in mental health, as different cultural norms and values can affect how individuals view and cope with mental health issues. Socio-economic status can also influence mental health, as individuals with lower income or educational levels may face greater stress and adversity.

Another key aspect of the nature of mental health is the various mental health disorders that individuals may experience. These can range from mood disorders such as depression and bipolar disorder, to anxiety disorders such as generalized anxiety disorder and panic disorder, to psychotic disorders such as schizophrenia. Eating disorders, substance abuse disorders, and personality disorders are also common types of mental health disorders.

The symptoms of mental health disorders can vary widely depending on the specific disorder, but some common symptoms include changes in mood, difficulty concentrating, changes in sleep or appetite, social withdrawal, and changes in behaviour or thought patterns. These symptoms can significantly impact an individual's ability to function in their daily life, leading to problems at work, school, or in relationships.

Treatment for mental health disorders can also vary depending on the specific disorder and the individual's needs. Some common treatment options include psychotherapy, medication, lifestyle changes, and alternative therapies such as meditation or yoga. Treatment can help individuals manage their symptoms, improve their quality of life, and prevent relapse.

Here are some key points about the nature of mental health:

1. Mental health refers to a person's psychological, emotional, and social well-being.
2. Mental health is complex and influenced by a range of biological, environmental, and social factors.

3. Genetics can play a significant role in determining an individual's mental health.
4. Brain chemistry can also affect mental health, as imbalances in neurotransmitters can lead to various mental health issues.
5. Life experiences and environmental stressors can impact mental health, such as trauma or chronic stress.
6. Social factors such as social support, culture, and socio-economic status can also impact mental health.
7. Mental health disorders can range from mood disorders, anxiety disorders, psychotic disorders, eating disorders, substance abuse disorders, and personality disorders.
8. Symptoms of mental health disorders can significantly impact an individual's ability to function in their daily life.
9. Treatment options for mental health disorders vary depending on the specific disorder and individual needs.
10. Understanding the nature of mental health is critical to promoting good mental health and providing effective treatment for mental health disorders.
11. Mental health is essential to overall well-being, and poor mental health can have a profound impact on an individual's physical, social, and emotional health.
12. Mental health is not just the absence of mental illness, but also includes positive mental health, such as resilience, self-esteem, and a positive outlook on life.
13. Mental health can impact an individual's ability to learn, work, and form relationships with others.
14. Stigma surrounding mental health can prevent individuals from seeking help or receiving appropriate treatment.
15. Mental health can change throughout an individual's life, with some people experiencing mental health issues at different stages of their life, such as during adolescence, pregnancy, or menopause.
16. Mental health can also be impacted by cultural or societal attitudes towards mental health and seeking help for mental health issues.
17. Prevention and early intervention are important in promoting good mental health and preventing the development of mental health disorders.
18. Mental health can also impact physical health, with mental health issues linked to an increased risk of physical health problems, such as heart disease, obesity, and diabetes.
19. Effective mental health treatment can improve an individual's quality of life, reduce the risk of suicide, and help prevent the development of other health problems.
20. Mental health promotion and treatment should be accessible, equitable, and culturally appropriate for all individuals.

The nature of mental health is complex and multifaceted, influenced by a range of biological, environmental, and social factors. Mental health disorders

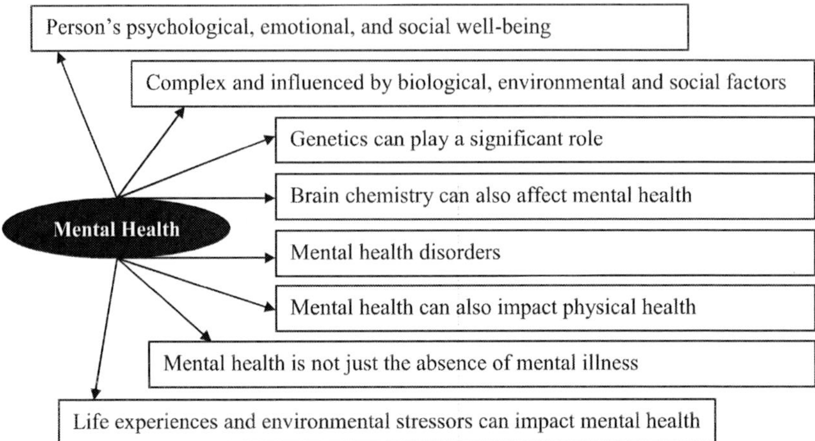

Figure 1.3: *Nature of Mental Health*

can have a profound impact on an individual's physical, social, and emotional health, and treatment options vary depending on the specific disorder and individual needs. Understanding the nature of mental health is critical to promoting good mental health and providing effective treatment for mental health disorders.

Factors Affecting Mental Health

Maintaining good mental health is crucial for overall well-being and quality of life. Mental health refers to a person's emotional, psychological, and social well-being, and it is essential to pay attention to it just like we do to our physical health. Mental health disorders can have a profound impact on a person's life, affecting their relationships, work, and daily functioning. Various factors contribute to the development of mental health disorders, such as genetic predisposition, environmental factors, and lifestyle choices. It is crucial to recognize and address these factors early on to prevent the progression of mental health disorders. Seeking appropriate treatment and support can also help individuals recover from mental health disorders and maintain better mental health. Therefore, understanding the factors that affect mental health is vital to identify potential risk factors and develop interventions to promote and maintain good mental health. There are many factors that can affect mental health, including:

1. *Genetics*: Mental health disorders can be passed down from generation to generation through genetics.
2. *Environment*: Environmental factors such as stress, trauma, abuse, and neglect can all contribute to the development of mental health disorders.
3. *Physical Health*: Physical health problems, such as chronic pain, illnesses, or injuries can impact mental health.

4. *Lifestyle*: Certain lifestyle choices, such as drug and alcohol use, poor nutrition, lack of sleep, and lack of exercise, can have negative effects on mental health.
5. *Social Support*: Social isolation and lack of social support can contribute to the development of mental health disorders.
6. *Trauma*: Traumatic experiences, such as abuse, neglect, violence, and accidents can impact mental health.
7. *Life Events*: Major life events, such as the loss of a loved one, divorce, or job loss, can contribute to mental health problems.
8. *Financial Stress*: Financial problems, such as debt and job loss, can increase stress and anxiety, which can negatively impact mental health.
9. *Discrimination*: Discrimination based on race, gender, sexuality, or other factors can contribute to mental health problems.
10. *Stigma*: The stigma surrounding mental health can prevent people from seeking help and can worsen mental health conditions.
11. *Childhood Experiences*: Childhood experiences, such as abuse, neglect, or adverse childhood events, can have lasting effects on mental health.
12. *Medications*: Certain medications, including some antidepressants and antipsychotics, can have side effects that affect mental health.
13. *Substance Abuse*: Substance abuse can lead to addiction and other mental health problems, including depression, anxiety, and psychosis.
14. *Work Stress*: Job-related stress, such as high workload, long working hours, job insecurity, and conflicts with colleagues, can contribute to the development of mental health disorders.
15. *Lack of Purpose or Meaning*: A sense of purpose or meaning in life can have a significant impact on mental health. Feeling unfulfilled or lacking direction can lead to feelings of anxiety or depression.
16. *Chronic Illness or Disability*: Chronic illness or disability can affect mental health by causing physical pain, limitations on daily activities, and social isolation.
17. *Lack of Sleep*: Sleep deprivation can contribute to the development of mental health disorders, including anxiety and depression.
18. *Personality Traits*: Certain personality traits, such as perfectionism, pessimism, or low self-esteem, can make a person more susceptible to mental health disorders.
19. *Hormonal Changes*: Hormonal changes, such as those that occur during pregnancy, menopause, or menstruation, can affect mental health.
20. *Cultural and Religious Beliefs*: Cultural and religious beliefs can impact mental health by affecting attitudes towards seeking treatment or discussing mental health issues openly.
21. *Technology Use*: Excessive use of technology, such as social media, gaming, or internet addiction, can have negative effects on mental health, including anxiety and depression.

22. *Nutrition*: Poor nutrition, including a diet high in sugar, processed foods, and saturated fats, can impact mental health.
23. *Exposure to Violence*: Exposure to violence, either in person or through the media, can contribute to the development of mental health disorders.
24. *Lack of Access to Healthcare*: Limited access to healthcare services, including mental health services, can prevent people from getting the help they need.
25. *Lack of Access to Resources*: Lack of access to resources, such as housing, food, and transportation, can contribute to stress and anxiety, which can negatively impact mental health.
26. *Seasonal Changes*: Seasonal changes, such as seasonal affective disorder, can have an impact on mental health.
27. *Medical Conditions*: Chronic medical conditions, such as cancer, heart disease, or HIV/AIDS, can have an impact on mental health.
28. *Aging*: Aging can bring its own unique mental health challenges, including loneliness, isolation, and physical health problems.
29. *Traumatic Brain Injury*: Traumatic brain injury, either from a single incident or repeated head trauma, can lead to the development of mental health disorders.
30. *Migration and Acculturation:* The process of migrating to a new country and adjusting to a new culture can be stressful and can contribute to mental health problems.

To sum up, mental health is a vital component of overall health and well-being, and mental health disorders can have a profound impact on a person's life. The development of mental health disorders is multifaceted and can be influenced by several factors, including genetics, environment, and lifestyle. Early identification and appropriate management of these factors can help prevent the onset and progression of mental health disorders. Seeking the right treatment and support is also critical in promoting and maintaining good mental health. It is essential to understand the factors that can affect mental health to take the necessary steps to mitigate their effects. By prioritizing mental health and taking proactive measures to maintain it, individuals can enhance their quality of life and overall well-being.

Symptoms of Good Mental Health

Good mental health is a state of emotional, psychological, and social well-being that allows individuals to function effectively in their daily lives. It is a state of mind that is characterized by positive emotions, healthy coping mechanisms, and an overall sense of balance and well-being. Good mental health is not just the absence of mental illness or disorders, but it is also about having the ability to adapt to changes, manage stress, and maintain healthy relationships.

In today's fast-paced and stressful world, good mental health is essential for individuals to lead a fulfilling and productive life. People who are mentally healthy tend to be more resilient and better equipped to manage challenges and setbacks in life. They are also better able to establish and maintain positive relationships, pursue their goals, and maintain a healthy work-life balance.

Good mental health is not a static state, but rather a continuum that requires ongoing attention and care. It involves developing healthy habits, such as practising mindfulness, regular exercise, maintaining a healthy diet, and seeking support when needed. By prioritizing mental health, individuals can improve their overall quality of life, enhance their resilience, and experience greater fulfillment and happiness in their personal and professional lives.

There are several symptoms that are indicative of good mental health. These include:

1. *Positive Mood*: Good mental health is often associated with a positive and optimistic mood. Individuals with good mental health tend to have a more positive outlook on life and are able to manage their emotions effectively.
2. *Resilience*: Good mental health involves the ability to bounce back from difficult situations and cope with stress effectively. Individuals with good mental health are often able to adapt to changing circumstances and maintain a sense of balance and stability.
3. *Self-awareness*: Good mental health involves having a clear understanding of one's own emotions, thoughts, and behaviours. Individuals with good mental health are often able to identify and manage their emotions effectively, and are aware of their strengths and weaknesses.
4. *Healthy Relationships*: Good mental health involves having positive and healthy relationships with others. Individuals with good mental health tend to be supportive and empathetic, and are able to maintain strong relationships with family, friends, and colleagues.
5. *Productivity*: Good mental health involves being able to focus, set goals, and accomplish tasks effectively. Individuals with good mental health are often able to stay organized, manage their time well, and achieve their objectives.
6. *Good Physical Health*: Good mental health is closely linked to physical health. Individuals with good mental health tend to prioritize their physical well-being, eat a healthy diet, exercise regularly, and get enough sleep.
7. *Sense of Purpose*: Good mental health involves having a sense of purpose and direction in life. Individuals with good mental health often have a clear understanding of their values and goals, and are motivated to pursue them.
8. *Self-esteem*: Good mental health involves having a positive sense of self-worth and self-esteem. Individuals with good mental health tend to have a healthy level of confidence in their abilities and are able to recognize and appreciate their own strengths and achievements.
9. *Empathy*: Good mental health involves the ability to understand and relate to the experiences and emotions of others. Individuals with good mental

health tend to be empathetic and compassionate, and are able to connect with others on a deeper level.

10. *Flexibility*: Good mental health involves being open and flexible to new ideas and experiences. Individuals with good mental health tend to have a growth mindset and are able to adapt to changes and new situations.
11. *Sense of Humor*: Good mental health involves the ability to maintain a positive outlook and find humor in everyday life. Individuals with good mental health tend to have a good sense of humor and are able to laugh at themselves and the situations they encounter.
12. *Mindfulness*: Good mental health involves being present and aware of the present moment. Individuals with good mental health tend to practise mindfulness techniques, such as meditation or deep breathing, to reduce stress and improve their overall well-being.
13. *Purposeful Engagement*: Good mental health involves engaging in activities and pursuits that bring a sense of purpose and fulfillment. Individuals with good mental health tend to pursue hobbies and interests that align with their values and passions, which helps to cultivate a sense of meaning and purpose in life.
14. *Openness to Help*: Good mental health involves being open and willing to seek help when needed. Individuals with good mental health tend to be proactive in addressing their mental health needs, whether that involves seeking therapy or support from friends and family. They recognize that seeking help is a sign of strength, not weakness.
15. *Self-care*: Good mental health involves taking care of oneself physically, emotionally, and mentally. Individuals with good mental health prioritize self-care activities, such as getting enough rest, engaging in regular exercise, and practising stress-reducing techniques.
16. *Respecting Boundaries*: Good mental health involves respecting one's own boundaries and the boundaries of others. Individuals with good mental health recognize the importance of setting healthy boundaries to protect their own well-being and to maintain healthy relationships with others.
17. *Effective Communication*: Good mental health involves the ability to communicate effectively with others. Individuals with good mental health are able to express their needs and emotions clearly and respectfully, and they are able to listen actively and empathetically to others.
18. *Personal Growth*: Good mental health involves a desire for personal growth and development. Individuals with good mental health tend to be motivated to learn and grow, and they are willing to take risks and try new things to achieve personal growth.
19. *Positive Self-talk*: Good mental health involves having a positive and optimistic inner dialogue. Individuals with good mental health tend to practise positive self-talk, which helps to build self-confidence and a sense of self-worth.

20. *Empowerment*: Good mental health involves feeling empowered and in control of one's life. Individuals with good mental health tend to have a sense of agency and autonomy, and they feel empowered to make positive changes in their lives.

Good mental health is characterized by a range of positive symptoms that contribute to an overall sense of well-being and resilience. These symptoms include a sense of purpose and meaning in life, the ability to manage stress and regulate emotions effectively, a positive self-image and healthy self-esteem, the ability to establish and maintain positive relationships with others, a sense of autonomy and control over one's own life, and a general sense of happiness and contentment. While everyone experiences challenges and setbacks in life, those with good mental health are better equipped to handle these challenges and maintain a positive outlook on life. By prioritizing our mental health and taking steps to maintain and improve it, we can lead fulfilling, meaningful lives and contribute to the greater good of our communities and society as a whole.

Importance of Mental Health

Mental health is a fundamental aspect of our overall well-being that encompasses our emotional, psychological, and social health. It plays a critical role in how we think, feel, and behave, affecting every aspect of our daily lives. Good mental health is essential for leading a fulfilling and meaningful life, and it is crucial to address mental health issues promptly to prevent them from having a negative impact on our physical health, relationships, work, and personal goals. Mental health is important due to following reasons.

1. *Affects Physical Health*: Poor mental health can lead to a range of physical health problems, including high blood pressure, heart disease, and obesity.
2. *Impacts Daily Life*: Mental health issues can impact our ability to function in daily life, affecting our work, relationships, and personal goals.
3. *Contributes to Self-esteem*: Good mental health is linked to high self-esteem, which helps us feel good about ourselves and our abilities.
4. *Promotes Resilience*: Good mental health helps us cope with life's challenges and bounce back from difficult situations.
5. *Enhances Social Relationships*: Good mental health helps us build positive relationships with others, which can have a positive impact on our overall well-being.
6. *Increases Productivity*: Good mental health can increase productivity, creativity, and innovation, making it easier to achieve personal and professional goals.
7. *Reduces Healthcare Costs*: Investing in mental health can lead to lower healthcare costs in the long run, as mental health issues can be addressed early on and prevent more serious problems from developing.

8. *Improves Cognitive Function*: Good mental health is linked to better cognitive function, including improved memory, attention, and decision-making skills.
9. *Reduces the Risk of Substance Abuse*: Good mental health can help reduce the risk of substance abuse, as people with good mental health are better able to cope with stress and other triggers that may lead to substance use.
10. *Enhances Overall Quality of Life*: Good mental health is strongly linked to higher levels of life satisfaction and happiness, as well as a greater sense of purpose and fulfillment.
11. *Boosts Immune Function*: Good mental health can also have a positive impact on immune function, reducing the risk of illness and disease.
12. *Prevents Chronic Conditions*: Addressing mental health issues early on can help prevent the development of chronic conditions such as depression, anxiety, and PTSD.
13. *Promotes Healthy Lifestyle Choices*: People with good mental health are more likely to engage in healthy behaviours such as regular exercise, healthy eating, and getting enough sleep.
14. *Improves Social Connectedness*: Good mental health is associated with stronger social connections and a greater sense of community, which can improve overall well-being.
15. *Increases Resilience to Stress*: Good mental health can help people better manage stress and adversity, increasing their resilience and ability to cope with life's challenges.
16. *Reduces the Risk of Suicide*: Good mental health is a key protective factor against suicide, which is a significant public health concern worldwide.
17. *Enhances Creativity*: Good mental health can enhance creativity, which can be beneficial for individuals in a wide range of professions.
18. *Promotes Empathy and Compassion*: Good mental health can promote empathy and compassion, making it easier for people to connect with and support others.
19. *Reduces Stigma*: Prioritizing mental health can help reduce the stigma associated with mental illness, making it easier for people to seek help when needed.
20. *Improves Academic Performance*: Good mental health is associated with improved academic performance, as well as higher levels of motivation and engagement in school.
21. *Increases Job Satisfaction*: Good mental health can increase job satisfaction, leading to greater levels of productivity, commitment, and overall success in the workplace.
22. *Promotes Healthy Aging*: Good mental health is a critical component of healthy aging, helping older adults maintains independence and quality of life.
23. *Fosters Personal Growth*: Good mental health can facilitate personal growth and self-discovery, allowing individuals to explore their values, beliefs, and goals more deeply.

24. *Promotes a Sense of Purpose*: Good mental health can help people find meaning and purpose in their lives, leading to a greater sense of fulfillment and satisfaction.

The importance of mental health cannot be overstated. It is a fundamental aspect of our overall well-being, affecting every aspect of our lives from our physical health to our relationships, work, and personal goals. Prioritizing mental health can lead to a range of benefits, including improved physical health, greater social connectedness, increased productivity, and a greater sense of purpose and fulfillment. By addressing mental health issues early on and seeking support when needed, individuals can lead happier, healthier lives and contribute to stronger, more resilient communities. It is crucial to continue to raise awareness about the importance of mental health and to reduce the stigma associated with mental illness, ensuring that everyone has access to the support and resources they need to thrive.

Educational Implications of Mental Health

Mental health has important implications for education, both in terms of the challenges it can present for students and the impact it can have on their academic performance. Some of the educational implications of mental health include:

1. *Increased Risk of Academic Difficulties*: Students who struggle with mental health issues may experience difficulties with concentration, memory, and motivation, which can impact their ability to learn and succeed academically.
2. *Increased Risk of Dropping Out*: Mental health issues can also contribute to higher rates of school dropout, particularly among students who feel unsupported or stigmatized.
3. *Need for Specialized Support*: Students with mental health issues may require specialized support, such as counseling services or accommodations like extra time on exams, in order to succeed in school.
4. *Importance of Promoting Mental Health*: Educators have a key role to play in promoting mental health and well-being among their students. This can include creating a positive and supportive classroom environment, offering resources and support for students who may be struggling, and educating students about mental health and wellness.
5. *Addressing Stigma*: Reducing the stigma surrounding mental health can also have important educational implications, as students who feel comfortable seeking help and talking openly about their mental health are more likely to receive the support they need to succeed in school.
6. *Impact on Socialization*: Mental health issues can also impact students' socialization and ability to interact with peers. Students with mental health issues may struggle with social skills, making it difficult for them to form friendships and engage in social activities. This can lead to feelings of isolation and further exacerbate mental health issues.

7. *Need for Early Intervention*: Early identification and intervention for mental health issues is critical for academic success. School staff, including teachers and counselors, should be trained to recognize the signs of mental health issues and provide appropriate support and referrals to mental health professionals.
8. *Role of Parents*: Parents also play a critical role in supporting their children's mental health and academic success. They can work with school staff to ensure their child's needs are being met, advocate for their child's mental health, and provide support and encouragement at home.
9. *Impact on Teachers*: Teachers may also experience mental health issues, which can impact their ability to effectively teach and support their students. Providing support and resources for teachers' mental health can help to improve overall classroom environments and student outcomes.
10. *Importance of Self-care*: Finally, promoting self-care among students and educators is crucial for maintaining good mental health and academic success. Encouraging healthy habits like exercise, mindfulness, and time management can help students and educators to manage stress and stay focused on their academic goals.
11. *Impact on Attendance*: Mental health issues can also lead to increased absenteeism and tardiness among students. Students who are experiencing mental health issues may struggle to get out of bed or may feel overwhelmed by the idea of going to school. This can result in missed classes and falling behind academically.
12. *Impact on Standardized Testing*: Mental health issues can also impact performance on standardized tests. Students with mental health issues may struggle with test anxiety or have difficulty concentrating during exams, which can impact their scores and future academic opportunities.
13. *Impact on Post-secondary Education*: Mental health issues can also impact students' ability to pursue post-secondary education. Students who experience mental health issues in high school may struggle to meet the academic and social demands of college or university, leading to difficulties with enrollment, retention, and completion.
14. *Impact on Future Employment*: Mental health issues can also impact students' future employment opportunities. Employers may discriminate against individuals with mental health issues or may be hesitant to hire them due to concerns about their ability to perform the job.
15. *Importance of Promoting Mental Health Literacy*: Finally, promoting mental health literacy among students, educators, and parents is critical for addressing the educational implications of mental health. By educating individuals about mental health, reducing stigma, and promoting early identification and intervention, we can help to ensure that all students have the support they need to succeed academically and beyond.
16. *Impact on Learning Environment*: Mental health issues can have a negative impact on the learning environment for all students. Students

with mental health issues may struggle with disruptive behaviours, which can be distracting and disruptive to other students. By addressing mental health issues can help to create a more positive and supportive learning environment for everyone.

17. *Importance of Community Partnerships*: School communities can benefit from partnerships with local mental health providers and organizations. These partnerships can provide access to additional resources and support services for students and families, including counseling, therapy, and support groups.
18. *Role of School Counselors*: School counselors play a critical role in addressing the educational implications of mental health. Counselors can provide individual and group counseling services, conduct mental health screenings, and make referrals to mental health professionals as needed.
19. *Importance of Trauma-informed Approaches*: Trauma can have a significant impact on mental health and academic success. Adopting trauma-informed approaches to education can help to create a safe and supportive environment for students who have experienced trauma, and support their overall mental health and academic success.
20. *Importance of Ongoing Support*: Finally, addressing the educational implications of mental health requires ongoing support and attention. Schools should prioritize ongoing training for staff and ongoing communication with families to ensure that students receive the support they need to succeed academically and beyond.
21. *Impact of COVID-19*: The COVID-19 pandemic has had a significant impact on mental health, particularly among students. The disruption to routine, social isolation, and uncertainty about the future have all contributed to increased rates of anxiety and depression among students. Educators must be aware of these challenges and prioritize mental health support for students during this time.
22. *Intersectional Issues*: Mental health intersects with other aspects of students' identities, including race, gender, sexuality, and socio-economic status. Students who experience multiple forms of marginalization may be at a higher risk for mental health issues, and may face additional barriers to accessing support. Educators must be aware of these intersectional issues and work to provide inclusive and equitable support for all students.
23. *Importance of Parent and Community Involvement*: Parents and community members can play an important role in addressing the educational implications of mental health. By providing support and resources for families, schools can help to promote positive mental health outcomes for students both inside and outside of the classroom.
24. *Importance of Student Voice*: Students should be encouraged to share their experiences and perspectives on mental health and the educational environment. By involving students in the conversation, educators can gain valuable insights into the challenges that students are facing, and

develop more effective strategies for supporting mental health and academic success.

25. *Need for Ongoing Research*: Finally, ongoing research is critical for advancing our understanding of the educational implications of mental health. By studying the impact of mental health on academic success and identifying effective strategies for promoting positive mental health outcomes, we can better support the academic and personal success of all students.
26. *Importance of Early Intervention*: Early identification and intervention is key for addressing mental health issues among students. Educators must be trained to recognize the signs and symptoms of mental health issues and work with families and mental health professionals to provide appropriate support as early as possible.
27. *Role of Social and Emotional Learning (SEL)*: Social and emotional learning can play a significant role in promoting positive mental health outcomes among students. By developing skills such as self-awareness, self-regulation, and empathy, students can better manage their emotions, build positive relationships, and achieve academic success.
28. *Importance of Restorative Practices*: Restorative practices can be an effective alternative to traditional discipline practices, particularly for students who are experiencing mental health issues. By prioritizing relationships, communication, accountability, and restorative practices can help to create a more positive and supportive learning environment for all students.
29. *Importance of Self-care for Educators*: Educators are also at risk for experiencing mental health issues, particularly during times of stress and crisis. By prioritizing self-care practices such as exercise, mindfulness, and connection with colleagues and mental health professionals, educators can better support their own mental health and well-being, and in turn, support the mental health of their students.
30. *Need for Ongoing Evaluation and Improvement*: Finally, addressing the educational implications of mental health requires ongoing evaluation and improvement. Schools should regularly assess the effectiveness of their mental health support services, and make adjustments as needed to ensure that all students have access to the support they need to succeed academically and beyond.

Overall, mental health is a critical component of students' academic success, and educators can play an important role in supporting the mental health and well-being of their student.

2

Mental Hygiene

Concept of Mental Hygiene

Mental hygiene refers to the practice of maintaining good mental health and preventing mental illness by adopting healthy habits, attitudes, and behaviours. It involves taking care of one's emotional, psychological, and social well-being to promote mental wellness and prevent mental health problems. The concept of mental hygiene originated in the early 20th century, when psychologists and social reformers sought to improve public health by promoting mental health. The term 'Mental Hygiene' was coined by William James, a renowned psychologist, in 1902, and it was later popularized by Clifford Beers, an American mental health advocate. Mental hygiene involves various practices such as developing positive attitudes towards oneself and others, maintaining a healthy lifestyle by eating well, getting enough sleep, and exercising regularly, practising relaxation techniques like meditation, deep breathing, or yoga, building and maintaining healthy relationships, and seeking professional help when necessary. Mental hygiene is important because poor mental health can have a significant impact on a person's quality of life, relationships, and overall well-being. By practising good mental hygiene, individuals can reduce the risk of developing mental health problems and increase their resilience in the face of adversity. Mental hygiene is based on the principles of prevention and self-care. By adopting healthy habits and behaviours, we can reduce the risk of developing mental health problems, and taking care of ourselves emotionally, psychologically, and socially can help us manage stress, increase our resilience, and improve our overall well-being.

Mental hygiene is not a one-size-fits-all approach. What works for one person may not work for another and mental health needs can vary depending on individual circumstances. Seeking professional help when necessary is an important aspect of mental hygiene, as it can provide individuals with the support and resources they need to manage mental health problems effectively. Mental hygiene is essential for maintaining overall health and well-being, and it should be a priority for everyone, regardless of age, gender, or background. Mental hygiene is a lifelong practice that requires ongoing effort and commitment. By incorporating healthy habits and behaviours into our daily lives, we can promote good mental health and prevent mental illness.

Here are some key points about the concept of mental hygiene:

- Mental hygiene involves developing self-awareness and self-reflection skills. By understanding our thoughts, feelings, and behaviours, we can identify areas that need improvement and take steps to address them.

- Mental hygiene requires us to pay attention to our emotional needs and take steps to meet them. This can involve expressing our emotions in a healthy way, seeking social support when needed, and engaging in activities that bring us joy and fulfillment.
- Mental hygiene involves setting healthy boundaries and saying no to activities or relationships that are harmful or stressful.
- Mental hygiene also includes developing coping skills that can help us manage stress and adversity. This can involve strategies like problem-solving, reframing negative thoughts, and practising mindfulness.
- Mental hygiene can help prevent burnout and compassion fatigue among individuals who work in high-stress professions like healthcare, social work, or counseling.
- Mental hygiene is important for promoting positive mental health outcomes among children and adolescents. Parents, caregivers, and educators can help young people develop healthy habits and attitudes that promote mental wellness.
- Mental hygiene is not a substitute for professional mental health treatment. Individuals who are struggling with mental health problems should seek help from a licensed mental health professional.
- Mental hygiene can be integrated into workplace wellness programmes, helping employers promote good mental health among their employees and reduce the negative impact of stress on productivity and job satisfaction.
- Mental hygiene is closely linked to physical health. Adopting healthy lifestyle habits like regular exercise, good nutrition, and adequate sleep can promote good mental health and reduce the risk of mental illness.
- Mental hygiene is a dynamic and evolving concept that reflects changing attitudes and beliefs about mental health. Ongoing research and education can help promote awareness of mental hygiene and improve access to effective mental health services.
- Mental hygiene involves promoting a positive self-image and building self-esteem. This can be achieved by practising self-compassion, positive self-talk and setting achievable goals.
- Mental hygiene includes recognizing the impact of social and cultural factors on mental health. This can involve addressing issues like stigma, discrimination, and social inequality that can contribute to mental health problems.
- Mental hygiene is a holistic approach to mental health that considers the interconnectedness of mental, emotional, and physical well-being. It recognizes that factors like sleep, nutrition, and exercise can all have an impact on mental health.
- Mental hygiene involves cultivating a sense of purpose and meaning in life. This can involve pursuing hobbies or interests that bring us joy, volunteering or helping others, and finding ways to contribute to society.

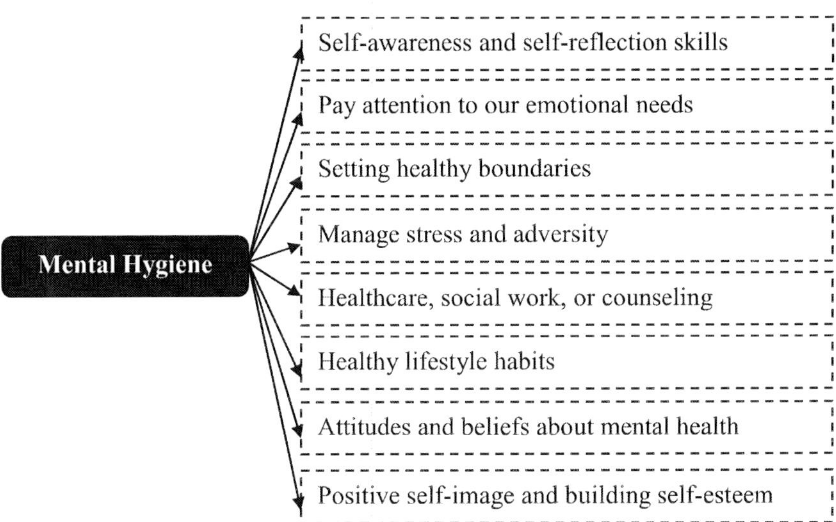

Figure 2.1: *Concept of Mental Hygiene*

- Mental hygiene requires us to be proactive in addressing mental health issues. This can involve seeking professional help when needed, participating in therapy or counseling, and engaging in self-care practices.
- Mental hygiene involves creating a supportive and positive environment for mental health. This can involve promoting mental health awareness and education, reducing stigma around mental illness, and providing resources for individuals who need help.
- Mental hygiene includes promoting good mental health in the workplace. This can involve implementing policies that promote work-life balance, reducing job stress, and providing mental health resources and support.
- Mental hygiene is important for promoting healthy aging. As we age, maintaining good mental health becomes increasingly important. Mental hygiene practices like staying socially connected, engaging in physical activity, and maintaining cognitive function can all contribute to healthy aging.
- Mental hygiene includes promoting resilience and coping skills in the face of adversity. This can involve developing problem-solving skills, practising mindfulness and relaxation techniques, and seeking social support when needed.
- Mental hygiene is an ongoing process that requires continuous effort and attention. It involves making choices that promote mental health and well-being and being mindful of our thoughts, feelings, and behaviours.

Meaning of Mental Hygiene

The word 'Hygiene' comes from the Greek word 'Hygieine' which means 'Healthy'. It was originally used in reference to practices that promote physical health and cleanliness, such as washing, exercising, and maintaining a healthy diet.

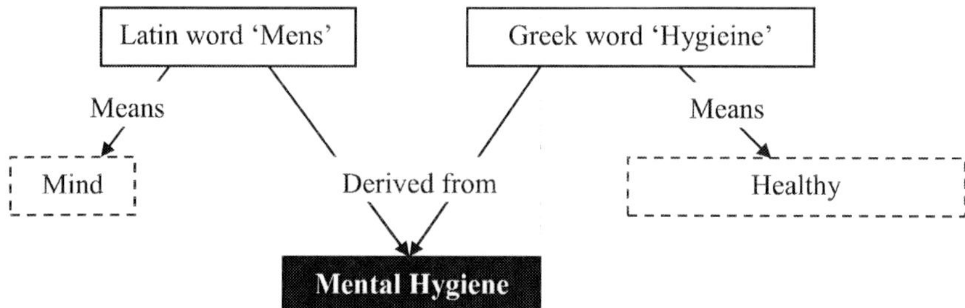

Figure 2.2: *Etymological Meaning of Mental Hygiene*

The prefix 'Mental' refers to the mind or intellect, and so 'Mental Hygiene' specifically relates to the promotion of mental health and well-being. The concept of mental hygiene gained popularity in the early 20th century, as psychologists and psychiatrists began to focus more on preventing mental illness rather than just treating it.

Here are some key points that explain the meaning of mental hygiene:

- Mental hygiene refers to practices and behaviours that promote good mental health and prevent mental illness.
- It involves developing positive habits and coping strategies that help individuals manage stress, regulate their emotions, and maintain a positive outlook on life.
- Mental hygiene includes a range of activities, such as exercise, healthy eating, adequate sleep, practising mindfulness, and seeking professional help when needed.
- Mental hygiene is important for maintaining optimal mental health and well-being, and can help individuals lead happier, more productive lives.
- Neglecting mental hygiene can increase the risk of developing mental health problems, such as anxiety, depression, and substance abuse.
- Just as we take care of our physical health, we need to prioritize our mental health by practising good mental hygiene.
- Mental hygiene practices can vary from person to person, and it's essential to find the strategies that work best for each individual's needs.

'Mental Hygiene' refers to the promotion of mental health and well-being through healthy habits and practices, similar to how 'Hygiene' refers to practices that promote physical health and cleanliness.

Definitions of Mental Hygiene

Mental hygiene refers to the practices and strategies that promote and maintain mental health and well-being. It involves taking care of one's own mental health as well as the mental health of others, through a range of activities and behaviours such as exercise, healthy eating, socializing, stress management, and seeking professional help when needed. Mental hygiene aims to prevent the development of mental health problems and disorders by promoting positive mental health habits and addressing negative mental health conditions as early as possible. It also emphasizes the importance of reducing stigma associated with mental illness and promoting awareness of the importance of mental health in overall well-being.

Mental hygiene is important for everyone because mental health problems can affect anyone at any time. Just as we take care of our physical health by eating well, exercising, and getting enough sleep, we also need to take care of our mental health by engaging in activities that promote well-being, reducing stress, and seeking help when we need it. Through mental hygiene, we can cultivate healthy attitudes and behaviours that promote resilience, personal growth, and a sense of purpose in life.

Here are some definitions of mental hygiene put forth by famous educationists:

John Dewey, an American philosopher and education reformer, defined mental hygiene as "the art of preserving the normality of mental life and of introducing that process of adjustment which is necessary to make a readjustment to the demands of the environment."

Maria Montessori, an Italian physician and educator, described mental hygiene as "the science of cultivating mental health, whereby the individual becomes a harmonious and productive member of society."

G. Stanley Hall, an American psychologist and educator, defined mental hygiene as "the science of promoting and preserving mental health, and preventing mental illness, through the organized efforts of society."

Alfred Adler, an Austrian psychotherapist and founder of individual psychology, characterized mental hygiene as "the practice of cultivating positive mental attitudes and behaviours that promote a healthy, well-adjusted personality."

Abraham Maslow, an American psychologist and founder of humanistic psychology, viewed mental hygiene as "the cultivation of a healthy, self-actualizing personality, characterized by a strong sense of purpose, creativity, and personal fulfillment."

Carl Rogers, an American psychologist and founder of client-centered therapy, described mental hygiene as "the process of achieving psychological well-being through self-awareness, self-acceptance, and self-expression."

Erich Fromm, a German-American psychoanalyst and social philosopher, viewed mental hygiene as "the cultivation of an integrated personality that is able to transcend cultural and social limitations, and to realize its full potential as a creative, compassionate, and ethical human being."

Jean Piaget, a Swiss psychologist and founder of genetic epistemology, characterized mental hygiene as "the process of developing cognitive and moral structures that enable individuals to adapt to their environment and to function effectively in society."

Lev Vygotsky, a Soviet psychologist and founder of socio-cultural theory, defined mental hygiene as "the cultivation of cultural tools and practices that facilitate mental development and support the achievement of individual and collective goals."

B.F. Skinner, an American psychologist and founder of behaviourism, described mental hygiene as "the systematic application of Behavioural principles to promote mental health and well-being, and to address maladaptive patterns of Behaviour and thought."

Mental hygiene is an important aspect of overall health and well-being. It involves taking care of our own mental health as well as supporting others in maintaining positive mental health habits. Mental hygiene practices, such as exercise, healthy eating, socializing, and stress management, can help prevent the development of mental health problems and promote resilience and personal growth. By promoting awareness and reducing stigma associated with mental health, we can create a society that values and prioritizes mental well-being. Ultimately, taking care of our mental health through mental hygiene is essential for living a happy, healthy, and fulfilling life.

Origin and Development of Mental Hygiene

Mental hygiene is a concept that refers to the practice of maintaining and promoting mental health and well-being. It encompasses a range of strategies and approaches designed to prevent mental illness, promote emotional resilience, and support mental well-being. The origins and development of mental hygiene can be traced back to several key historical moments and movements.

1. *Enlightenment Era (17th and 18th Centuries):* During the Enlightenment Era, there was a growing interest in the human mind and the nature of mental illness. This period saw the rise of scientific inquiry and empirical observation, which led to the development of new theories and treatments for mental illness. Many Enlightenment thinkers believed that mental illness was caused by environmental factors, such as poor living conditions and social inequality.
2. *Moral Treatment Movement (Late 18th and Early 19th Centuries):* The Moral Treatment Movement emerged as a response to the harsh and inhumane conditions in mental asylums. Advocates of this movement believed that mental illness was the result of social and environmental factors, rather than moral weakness or sin. They believed that people with mental illness could be treated with compassion and dignity, and that they could recover with the right care and support.
3. *Psychiatric Reform Movement (Mid-19th Century):* The Psychiatric Reform Movement emerged as a response to the abuses and neglect that were still prevalent in mental asylums. Advocates of this movement called for better living conditions, more humane treatment, and the development of new treatments for mental illness. They believed that

mental illness was a medical condition that could be treated with drugs and other therapies.

4. *Emergence of Psychology as a Field (Late 19th and Early 20th Centuries)*: The emergence of psychology as a field of study provided new insights into the workings of the human mind and the causes of mental illness. Psychologists such as Sigmund Freud and Carl Jung developed new theories of psychotherapy that emphasized the importance of addressing unconscious conflicts and childhood experiences in the treatment of mental illness.
5. *Mental Hygiene Movement (Early 20th Century)*: The Mental Hygiene Movement emerged as a response to the growing awareness of the social and environmental factors that contribute to mental illness. Advocates of this movement believed that mental illness could be prevented through education and public health initiatives. They believed that mental hygiene was just as important as physical hygiene, and that everyone had a responsibility to maintain their own mental health and well-being.
6. *Community Mental Health Movement (Mid-20th Century)*: The Community Mental Health Movement emerged as a response to the limitations of institutional care for people with mental illness. Advocates of this movement called for the development of community-based services and support, such as outpatient clinics and crisis hotlines. They believed that people with mental illness could live and thrive in their communities with the right care and support.
7. *Deinstitutionalization Movement (Late 20th Century)*:The Deinstitutionalization Movement emerged as a response to the overcrowding and abuses that were still prevalent in mental asylums in the mid-20th century. Advocates of this movement called for the closure of large institutions and the development of community-based care and support services. While deinstitutionalization has had many benefits, such as reducing the stigma associated with mental illness and improving access to care, it has also posed challenges, such as a lack of funding for community-based services and a shortage of mental health professionals.
8. *Rise of Positive Psychology (Late 20th and Early 21st Centuries)*: The rise of positive psychology has emphasized the importance of promoting mental wellness and resilience, rather than just treating mental illness. Positive psychology focuses on building strengths and cultivating positive emotions, and has led to the development of new approaches to mental health, such as mindfulness meditation and gratitude practices.
9. *Integration of Mental Health and Physical Health Care (21st Century)*: In recent years, there has been a growing recognition of the importance of integrating mental health and physical health care. This integration has led to the development of new models of care, such as collaborative care and integrated behavioural health, which seek to address both the physical and mental health needs of patients. This approach has been shown to improve health outcomes and reduce health care costs.

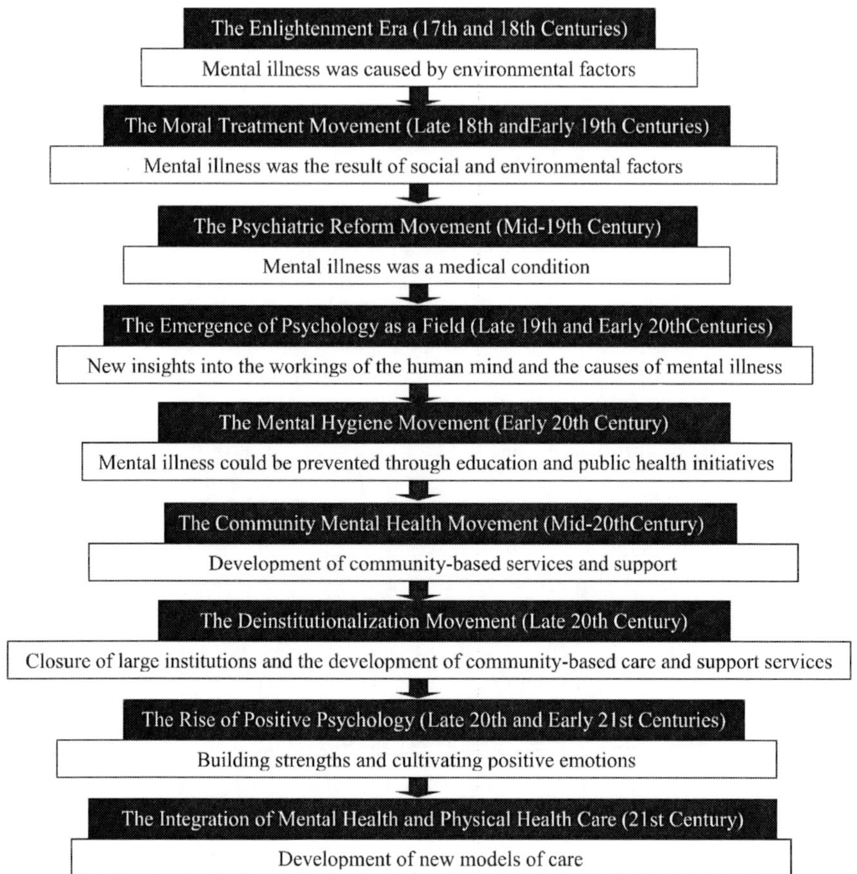

Figure 2.3: *Origin and Development of Mental Hygiene*

Overall, the origin and development of mental hygiene is a complex and ongoing process that reflects changing attitudes and understanding of mental illness and its treatment. Mental hygiene continues to be an important focus of research and public health initiatives, as we seek to improve mental health outcomes for individuals and communities around the world.

Aims of Mental Hygiene

The aims of mental hygiene include promoting and maintaining good mental health, preventing the development of mental health problems, and supporting the recovery of those who experience mental health issues.

Some specific aims of mental hygiene may include:

1. Encouraging individuals to engage in positive mental health practices, such as regular exercise, healthy eating, stress reduction techniques, and seeking social support.

2. Reducing negative stressors and promoting resilience to stress.
3. Increasing awareness of the signs and symptoms of mental health problems, and encouraging early intervention and treatment.
4. Reducing stigma surrounding mental health issues and promoting a culture of acceptance and support.
5. Providing access to resources and support for individuals who experience mental health problems, including counseling, therapy, and medication if necessary.
6. Promoting a sense of community and connection which can support positive mental health and prevent social isolation.
7. Encouraging individuals to develop a positive self-image and a sense of purpose in life.
8. Providing education and information about mental health issues, including risk factors, warning signs, and treatment options.
9. Supporting individuals in managing chronic mental health conditions, such as bipolar disorder or schizophrenia.
10. Promoting a healthy work-life balance which can reduce stress and improve overall well-being.
11. Supporting individuals who have experienced trauma, and helping them to develop healthy coping mechanisms.
12. Providing support for families and caregivers of individuals who experience mental health issues.
13. Promoting the use of evidence-based practices and treatments for mental health problems.
14. Addressing social determinants of mental health, such as poverty and discrimination, which can contribute to the development of mental health problems.

Overall, the aims of mental hygiene are focused on promoting and maintaining good mental health, preventing the development of mental health problems, and providing support and resources for individuals who experience mental health issues. Mental hygiene recognizes the importance of taking a proactive approach to mental health, and provides a framework for individuals and society to promote resilience and well-being.

Objectives of Mental Hygiene

The objectives of mental hygiene are to promote and maintain mental health and well-being, prevent mental illness and emotional distress, and provide effective treatment and rehabilitation services for those who experience mental health challenges. Some of the specific objectives of mental hygiene include:

1. *Promoting Positive Mental Health*: Mental hygiene aims to promote mental health by encouraging positive coping strategies, stress management techniques, and social support.

2. *Preventing Mental Illness*: Mental hygiene strategies are designed to identify and address risk factors for mental illness, such as trauma, substance abuse, and social isolation.
3. *Early Detection and Intervention*: Mental hygiene programmes aim to detect mental health problems early and provide appropriate intervention to prevent further deterioration of mental health.
4. *Providing Effective Treatment*: Mental hygiene programmes strive to provide effective treatment for individuals with mental health conditions, including medication, psychotherapy, and support services.
5. *Rehabilitation*: Mental hygiene services aim to support individuals in their recovery and rehabilitation, helping them to manage their symptoms and maintain their mental health.
6. *Addressing Stigma*: Mental hygiene efforts are also directed at addressing social stigma and discrimination associated with mental illness, in order to improve access to care and support for those affected.
7. *Increasing Awareness and Education*: Mental hygiene programmes aim to increase awareness and understanding of mental health issues through education and outreach. This includes providing information about mental health, promoting mental health literacy, and reducing the stigma associated with mental illness.
8. *Empowering Individuals*: Mental hygiene efforts seek to empower individuals to take an active role in their mental health and well-being. This includes providing resources and support to help individuals develop coping skills, make informed decisions about their mental health care, and advocate for themselves.
9. *Addressing Social Determinants of Mental Health*: Mental hygiene programmes recognize that social and environmental factors can impact mental health, and therefore seek to address social determinants of mental health, such as poverty, discrimination, and lack of access to health care.
10. *Supporting Families and Communities*: Mental hygiene efforts aim to support families and communities in promoting mental health and well-being. This includes providing resources and support to caregivers, promoting community engagement and social connectedness, and addressing the impact of trauma on families and communities.
11. *Collaborating with Other Systems*: Mental hygiene programmes recognize that mental health is connected to other systems, such as healthcare, education, and social services. Therefore, mental hygiene efforts aim to collaborate with these systems to promote mental health and well-being.
12. *Improving Access to Care*: Mental hygiene efforts aim to improve access to mental health care and services for all individuals, regardless of their background or circumstances. This includes increasing the availability of mental health services in underserved areas, reducing barriers to care, and promoting the integration of mental health services into primary care.

13. *Addressing Co-occurring Conditions*: Mental hygiene programmes recognize that individuals with mental health conditions often have co-occurring conditions, such as substance abuse or physical health problems. Therefore, mental hygiene efforts aim to address these co-occurring conditions in order to provide comprehensive care.
14. *Fostering Resilience*: Mental hygiene programmes aim to foster resilience in individuals and communities, helping them to cope with stress, adversity, and trauma. This includes promoting positive coping strategies, building social support networks, and providing resources and support to help individuals and communities recover from trauma.
15. *Promoting Evidence-based Practices*: Mental hygiene efforts seek to promote evidence-based practices in the prevention, diagnosis, and treatment of mental health conditions. This includes promoting the use of evidence-based screening tools, interventions, and therapies, as well as supporting research to advance our understanding of mental health and well-being.
16. *Advocating for Policy Change*: Mental hygiene programmes recognize that policy and system-level changes are needed to promote mental health and well-being. Therefore, mental hygiene efforts aim to advocate for policy change and system-level interventions that promote mental health and reduce mental health disparities.
17. *Promoting Cultural Competence*: Mental hygiene efforts aim to promote cultural competence among mental health professionals and service providers. This includes recognizing and addressing cultural factors that can impact mental health, as well as providing culturally sensitive care to individuals from diverse backgrounds.
18. *Enhancing the Quality of Care*: Mental hygiene programmes aim to enhance the quality of mental health care by promoting best practices in service delivery, improving the training and education of mental health professionals, and ensuring the availability of quality services and resources.
19. *Addressing the Needs of Vulnerable Populations*: Mental hygiene efforts seek to address the unique mental health needs of vulnerable populations, such as children, older adults, and individuals with disabilities. This includes providing targeted interventions and services to address their specific needs.
20. *Promoting Public Health Approaches*: Mental hygiene programmes aim to promote public health approaches to mental health, which focus on prevention, early intervention, and population-level strategies to improve mental health and prevent mental illness.
21. *Addressing the Impact of Trauma*: Mental hygiene efforts recognize the impact of trauma on mental health and seek to address the needs of individuals and communities affected by trauma. This includes providing

trauma-informed care and promoting resilience-building strategies to help individuals and communities recover from trauma.

22. *Promoting Recovery and Well-being*: Mental hygiene programmes aim to promote recovery and well-being among individuals with mental health conditions, supporting them in their efforts to achieve their goals and live fulfilling lives.

Overall, the objectives of mental hygiene are diverse and wide-ranging, encompassing a range of strategies and interventions aimed at promoting mental health and well-being, preventing mental illness, and supporting individuals and communities affected by mental health challenges.

Aspects of Mental Hygiene

In today's fast-paced world, it's important to prioritize our mental health and well-being. Just as we take care of our physical health through exercise and healthy eating, we must also take care of our mental health through practices and habits that promote mental hygiene. Mental hygiene refers to the set of practices and habits that promote mental health and well-being, and it can be broken down into three main aspects: conservative, preventive, and curative.

1. ***Conservative Mental Hygiene***: Conservative mental hygiene refers to practices and habits that help maintain an already existing state of mental health. This aspect involves avoiding potential stressors and maintaining a healthy lifestyle. Some features of conservative mental hygiene include:
    - Maintaining healthy relationships with family, friends, and colleagues.
    - Avoiding substance abuse, including alcohol and drugs.
    - Setting healthy boundaries and practising self-care regularly.
    - Seeking professional help when needed and maintaining a regular check-up with mental health professionals.
    - Regularly engaging in hobbies or activities that bring joy and promote relaxation.
    - Avoiding negative or toxic relationships that can drain emotional energy and cause unnecessary stress.
    - Maintaining healthy boundaries by saying no to commitments or obligations that may lead to burnout or exhaustion.
    - Practising good time management and prioritizing tasks to reduce feelings of overwhelm and anxiety.
    - Developing healthy coping strategies for managing difficult emotions, such as journaling, creative expression, or talking to a trusted friend or family member.
    - Setting realistic goals and breaking them down into manageable steps to reduce feelings of overwhelm and improve motivation.
    - Engaging in regular self-reflection to identify areas of personal growth and development.

- Building a positive support system of friends and family who offer encouragement and validation.
- Practising healthy communication skills to improve relationships and reduce conflicts.
- Avoiding excessive use of social media and other digital devices which can contribute to feelings of stress and anxiety.
- Developing a self-care routine that includes activities such as taking a relaxing bath, practising yoga, or reading a book.
- Practising healthy stress-reduction techniques, such as taking breaks throughout the day, going for a walk, or practising deep breathing.
- Incorporating a healthy diet and avoiding excessive alcohol consumption, which can negatively impact mental health.
- Developing healthy coping mechanisms for dealing with stress and difficult emotions, such as meditation, creative expression, or talking to a trusted friend or family member.
- Seeking support from a mental health professional when needed, such as during times of stress or life changes.

2. ***Preventive Mental Hygiene*:** Preventive mental hygiene involves taking proactive steps to prevent mental health problems from arising. This aspect is focused on addressing potential risk factors and building resilience. Some features of preventive mental hygiene include:
   - Developing good coping skills and practising mindfulness techniques.
   - Building strong support systems and social networks.
   - Developing a positive self-image and practising self-compassion.
   - Identifying and addressing potential sources of stress, such as work, school, or relationships.
   - Practising gratitude and mindfulness to cultivate a positive mindset and reduce negative self-talk.
   - Building healthy habits and routines, such as a regular sleep schedule, balanced meals, and regular exercise.
   - Establishing healthy communication patterns and conflict resolution strategies with loved ones.
   - Seeking therapy or counseling before a mental health problem becomes severe or unmanageable.
   - Learning stress-management techniques, such as deep breathing or meditation, and incorporating them into daily life.
   - Learning and practising effective stress-management techniques, such as progressive muscle relaxation or guided imagery.
   - Incorporating humour and laughter into daily life to reduce stress and improve mood.
   - Engaging in volunteer work or community service to build a sense of purpose and connection with others.
   - Learning to recognize and challenge negative thought patterns, such as self-criticism etc.

- Seeking out new experiences and challenges to promote personal growth and development.
- Building a strong support network of friends and family members who can provide emotional support and encouragement.
- Practising self-compassion and acceptance of oneself and one's imperfections.
- Engaging in regular self-care activities, such as getting enough sleep and exercise, to reduce the risk of mental health problems.
- Practising stress-management techniques such as relaxation exercises, yoga, or meditation to prevent burnout and exhaustion.
- Learning and practising assertiveness skills to set boundaries and communicate effectively with others.

3. ***Curative Mental Hygiene*:** Curative mental hygiene refers to practices and treatments that are focused on addressing mental health problems that already exist. This aspect is focused on identifying and treating the underlying causes of mental health problems. Some features of curative mental hygiene include:
   - Seeking professional help from mental health professionals, such as therapists, counselors, or psychiatrists.
   - Participating in group therapy or support groups.
   - Using medications when prescribed by a qualified medical professional.
   - Practising self-care and stress-management techniques as part of ongoing treatment.
   - Engaging in therapy or counseling to address underlying mental health concerns, such as anxiety or depression.
   - Participating in group therapy or support groups to connect with others who share similar experiences.
   - Seeking medication management from a qualified medical professional when necessary.
   - Practising self-compassion and developing a positive self-image to improve self-esteem and self-worth.
   - Developing an aftercare plan to maintain progress and prevent relapse, such as ongoing therapy, support groups, or medication management.
   - Building a strong therapeutic relationship with a mental health professional to facilitate healing and growth.
   - Developing a crisis plan to manage intense emotions or difficult situations, such as a list of emergency contacts or coping strategies.
   - Exploring alternative therapies, such as art therapy or music therapy, to supplement traditional talk therapy.
   - Building a strong social support system to provide encouragement and motivation during recovery.
   - Practising self-compassion and forgiveness to reduce feelings of guilt or shame related to mental health struggles.

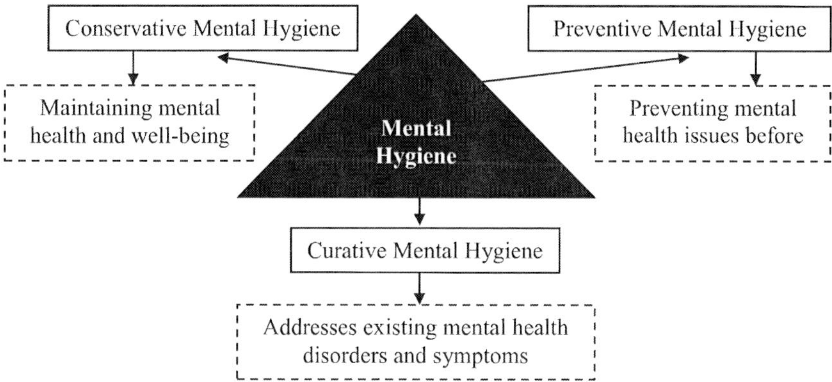

Figure 2.4: *Aspects of Mental Hygiene*

- Developing a personalized treatment plan with a mental health professional, including medication management and therapy.
- Learning and practising healthy coping mechanisms, such as journaling, deep breathing, or mindfulness, to manage difficult emotions.
- Incorporating positive self-talk and building self-esteem to improve overall mental health and well-being.
- Practising forgiveness and letting go of grudges or resentments that may be contributing to negative emotions.
- Building a support network of peers who have gone through similar experiences to provide encouragement and support during recovery.

In summary, mental hygiene is an essential part of maintaining good mental health and well-being. By focusing on the three aspects of conservative, preventive, and curative mental hygiene, as well as incorporating additional strategies such as mindfulness, good sleep routine, physical activity, and stress management, individuals can build resilience and promote mental well-being throughout their lives. Remember that mental hygiene is an ongoing process, and it's important to prioritize self-care and seek professional help when needed to ensure that our mental health remains a top priority.

Scope of Mental Hygiene

The scope of mental hygiene is broad and encompasses various aspects of mental health and well-being. It includes prevention, early intervention, treatment, and recovery support for mental health problems.

Some areas within the scope of mental hygiene include:

1. *Promotion of Positive Mental Health Practices*: This includes promoting healthy habits such as regular exercise, healthy eating, stress management, and social support, which can help prevent mental health problems.
2. *Education and Awareness*: Mental hygiene aims to increase public awareness of mental health issues, reduce stigma, and educate individuals on the signs and symptoms of mental health problems and how to seek help.

3. *Prevention of Mental Health Problems*: Mental hygiene promotes strategies to prevent the development of mental health problems, such as reducing stressors and increasing resilience.
4. *Early Intervention and Treatment*: Mental hygiene supports early intervention and treatment for mental health problems, such as counseling, therapy, and medication when necessary.
5. *Recovery Support*: Mental hygiene provides support and resources for individuals who are in recovery from mental health problems, including peer support groups and other community-based services.
6. *Advocacy and Policy*: Mental hygiene advocates for policies and programmes that support mental health and well-being, including access to mental health services, reducing stigma, and improving social determinants of mental health.
7. *Assessment and Diagnosis*: Mental hygiene involves assessing and diagnosing mental health problems, such as depression, anxiety, and bipolar disorder, through evidence-based methods such as clinical interviews and standardized assessments.
8. *Trauma-informed Care*: Mental hygiene recognizes the impact of trauma on mental health and promotes trauma-informed care approaches that prioritize safety, trustworthiness, choice, collaboration, and empowerment.
9. *Diversity and Cultural Competence*: Mental hygiene acknowledges the importance of cultural competence and inclusivity in promoting mental health and reducing health disparities across diverse populations.
10. *Research and Evaluation*: Mental hygiene promotes the use of evidence-based practices in mental health care, as well as research and evaluation to improve the effectiveness and efficiency of mental health interventions.
11. Crisis Intervention: Mental hygiene provides support and resources for individuals in crisis, such as hotlines, crisis centres, and emergency mental health services.
12. *Integration with Physical Health*: Mental hygiene recognizes the interdependence of physical and mental health and promotes integrated care approaches that address both physical and mental health needs.
13. *Workplace Mental Health*: Mental hygiene addresses mental health in the workplace by promoting supportive work environments, reducing stressors, and increasing access to mental health resources and support.
14. *Community-based Mental Health*: Mental hygiene recognizes the importance of community-based mental health services and programmes that provide accessible and culturally appropriate support for individuals with mental health problems.
15. *Prevention and Early Intervention for Children and Youth*: Mental hygiene promotes early intervention and prevention for children and youth through programmes that promote social and emotional learning, positive parenting, and school-based mental health services.

16. *Collaboration with Other Disciplines*: Mental hygiene recognizes the importance of collaboration with other disciplines, such as medicine, psychology, social work, and public health, to provide comprehensive and integrated mental health care.
17. *Mental Health Policy*: Mental hygiene advocates for mental health policy and legislative changes that promote mental health, reduce stigma, and increase access to mental health services.
18. *Technology and Mental Health*: Mental hygiene recognizes the potential of technology, such as teletherapy and digital health tools, in improving access to mental health care and supporting mental health self-management.

Overall, the scope of mental hygiene is diverse and dynamic, encompassing various areas of mental health promotion, prevention, diagnosis, treatment, recovery, advocacy, and innovation. Mental hygiene provides a holistic framework for addressing mental health across the lifespan and in diverse populations, and emphasizes the importance of collaboration, evidence-based practice, and social justice.

Relationship between Mental Health and Mental Hygiene

Mental health refers to a person's overall psychological well-being, including their emotional, social, and cognitive functioning. Mental hygiene, on the other hand, refers to the practice of maintaining and promoting mental health through various measures such as proper nutrition, exercise, stress management, and therapy. Here are some key points that explain the relationship between mental health and mental hygiene:

1. Mental hygiene refers to the strategies and habits that a person can adopt to promote their mental health and well-being. It includes practices like getting enough sleep, maintaining healthy relationships, managing stress, and seeking professional help when needed.
2. Good mental hygiene can help prevent mental health problems such as anxiety, depression, and substance abuse, and can also help people cope with and recover from these issues if they do arise. Conversely, poor mental hygiene can contribute to the development of mental health problems and make it more difficult to manage them.
3. Mental health is the overall state of a person's psychological well-being, including their emotions, thoughts, and behaviours. Mental hygiene is a set of practices that can help promote and maintain good mental health.
4. Mental hygiene practices include activities such as self-care, stress management, proper nutrition, exercise, and getting enough sleep. These practices are essential for good mental health and can help prevent the development of mental health problems.
5. Good mental hygiene practices can also help people cope with mental health issues such as anxiety, depression, and addiction. For example, engaging in regular exercise, practising mindfulness, or seeking therapy

can help alleviate symptoms of mental illness. Conversely, poor mental hygiene practices such as neglecting self-care, not getting enough sleep, or engaging in harmful behaviours like substance abuse can contribute to the development of mental health problems. Therefore, the relationship between mental health and mental hygiene is reciprocal. Good mental hygiene practices can help promote good mental health, while poor mental hygiene practices can contribute to the development of mental health problems.

6. Mental health is a complex and multifaceted concept that is influenced by a variety of factors, including genetics, environment, and life experiences. However, adopting good mental hygiene practices can help mitigate some of these factors and promote better mental health overall.
7. Mental hygiene is not only important for individuals but also for communities and societies as a whole. Promoting mental hygiene can help reduce the stigma around mental health and encourage more people to seek help when they need it.
8. Mental hygiene practices can vary depending on individual needs and preferences. What works for one person may not work for another and it may take some trial and error to find the right combination of practices that work best.
9. Mental hygiene practices can also be influenced by cultural, social, and economic factors. For example, some people may have limited access to mental health resources, making it harder to practise good mental hygiene.
10. Good mental hygiene practices can be preventative, meaning they can help prevent the onset of mental health problems. This can be especially important for individuals who have a family history of mental illness or other risk factors.
11. Practising good mental hygiene is not a guarantee against mental health problems. Mental illness can affect anyone, regardless of their mental hygiene practices.
12. Mental hygiene practices should be viewed as part of a broader approach to mental health care that includes professional treatment when necessary. Sometimes, despite one's best efforts to maintain good mental hygiene, professional help may still be needed.
13. Mental hygiene practices can help improve not only mental health but also physical health. For example, engaging in regular exercise can help improve mood and reduce the risk of developing chronic health conditions such as heart disease and diabetes.
14. Mental hygiene practices can also improve productivity and performance in various aspects of life, such as work, school, and personal relationships. When individuals take care of their mental health, they are better equipped to handle the challenges of daily life.
15. Practising good mental hygiene can also help build resilience, the ability to bounce back from adversity. This can be especially important during times of stress and uncertainty.

16. Mental hygiene practices can vary depending on age and developmental stage. Children, adolescents, and adults may have different needs when it comes to maintaining good mental hygiene.
17. Some mental hygiene practices, such as social support and meaningful engagement in activities, are more effective when done in a group or community setting. Joining a support group or participating in community activities can help promote good mental hygiene.
18. Mental hygiene practices can also include seeking help when needed. Many people are hesitant to seek professional help for mental health concerns, but doing so can be a crucial component of maintaining good mental hygiene.
19. Mental hygiene practices can be integrated into daily routines and habits, making them more sustainable in the long term. This can include things like setting aside time for self-care, incorporating mindfulness practices into daily activities, and prioritizing rest and relaxation.
20. Good mental hygiene practices can also help prevent burnout, a state of emotional, physical, and mental exhaustion often caused by prolonged stress. Burnout can be a significant risk factor for developing mental health problems, and practising good mental hygiene can help prevent it.
21. Mental hygiene practices can be especially important during times of significant life changes, such as the loss of a loved one, a job change, or a move to a new city. These changes can be stressful and disrupt mental health, making it especially important to prioritize good mental hygiene during these times.
22. Mental hygiene practices can also be tailored to address specific mental health conditions. For example, cognitive-behavioural therapy (CBT) can be an effective mental hygiene practice for individuals with anxiety disorders, while interpersonal therapy (IPT) can be beneficial for individuals with depression.
23. Practising good mental hygiene can also help reduce the risk of developing co-morbidities, which are the simultaneous presence of two or more chronic conditions. For example, individuals with depression are at higher risk for developing chronic physical conditions such as heart disease and diabetes, and practising good mental hygiene can help reduce this risk.
24. Mental hygiene practices can also include setting boundaries and saying no to activities or commitments that may negatively impact mental health. This can be especially important for individuals who struggle with people-pleasing or prioritizing others' needs over their own.

In summary, mental health and mental hygiene are closely related concepts, and practising good mental hygiene is essential for maintaining good mental health. By adopting healthy habits and seeking professional help when needed, individuals can promote their own mental well-being and prevent the development of mental health problems.

3

Mental Illness

Concept of Mental Illness

The concept of mental illness has evolved over time, and its introduction can be traced back to the early civilizations of Greece and Rome. In ancient times, mental illness was believed to be caused by the influence of gods and demons. People with mental illnesses were often ostracized and excluded from society, and they were sometimes subjected to brutal treatments, such as being chained or beaten.

In the MiddleAges, the dominant view was that mental illness was caused by possession by evil spirits or the result of sinful behaviour. This led to the rise of exorcism and other religious rituals as methods of treatment. It wasn't until the Enlightenment era in the 18th century that the concept of mental illness as a medical condition began to emerge. The French physician Philippe Pinel is often credited with leading this change. He believed that mental illness was caused by imbalances in the brain and advocated for humane treatment of people with mental illnesses. Philippe Pinel also introduced the idea of categorizing mental illnesses based on symptoms, a precursor to the modern system of psychiatric diagnosis. The 19th century saw significant advancements in the understanding and treatment of mental illness. Sigmund Freud's theories of psychoanalysis revolutionized the field of psychology, introducing the idea of the unconscious mind and the role of childhood experiences in shaping behaviour. This led to the development of psychotherapy as a treatment for mental illness. In the 20th century, the introduction of new drugs such as antipsychotics and antidepressants revolutionized the treatment of mental illness, allowing many people to lead more normal lives. The development of community-based mental health care also helped reduce the stigma associated with mental illness and improve access to treatment.

Today, the concept of mental illness is well-established in medical and scientific communities. Mental illnesses are recognized as medical conditions that can be diagnosed and treated with a combination of therapy, medication, and other interventions. However, there is still a significant amount of stigma surrounding mental illness, and many people with mental health conditions continue to face discrimination and barriers to treatment.

The concept of mental illness refers to a wide range of conditions that affect a person's thoughts, feelings, and behaviours. Mental illnesses are typically diagnosed using criteria outlined in the Diagnostic and Statistical Manual of Mental Disorders (DSM), which is produced by the American Psychiatric Association. Here are some key points about the concept of mental illness:

1. *Mental illness is a medical condition*: Mental illnesses are recognized as medical conditions that are caused by a combination of genetic, environmental, and biological factors. They are not a personal weakness or a choice, and people with mental illnesses should not be blamed for their conditions.
2. *Mental illness is common*: Mental illnesses are very common, affecting millions of people around the world. According to the World Health Organization, one in four people will experience a mental health problem at some point in their lives.
3. *Mental illness can affect anyone*: Mental illnesses can affect people of all ages, genders, races, and socio-economic backgrounds. They do not discriminate based on these factors.
4. *Mental illness can be treated*: Many mental illnesses can be effectively treated with a combination of therapy, medication, and other interventions. It is important for people with mental illnesses to seek treatment as soon as possible to improve their outcomes.
5. *Mental illness can cause significant impairment*: Mental illnesses can cause significant impairment in a person's ability to function in daily life. They can affect a person's work, school, relationships, and overall quality of life.
6. *Mental illness is stigmatized*: Despite advances in understanding and treating mental illness, there is still a significant amount of stigma surrounding these conditions. This can make it difficult for people with mental illnesses to seek treatment and can contribute to social isolation and discrimination.
7. *Mental illness requires a holistic approach*: Treating mental illness requires a holistic approach that addresses a person's physical, psychological, and social needs. This may involve a combination of medication, therapy, lifestyle changes, and support from family and friends.
8. *Mental illness can be acute or chronic*: Mental illnesses can range from acute conditions that are short-term and episodic, to chronic conditions that may last for many years or even a lifetime. Some examples of acute conditions include panic attacks or acute stress disorder, while chronic conditions may include depression, bipolar disorder, or schizophrenia.
9. *Mental illness can co-occur with other conditions*: Mental illnesses often co-occur with other medical conditions such as diabetes, heart disease, or substance abuse. These conditions can interact with mental illness and affect treatment outcomes.
10. *Mental illness can be diagnosed using specific criteria*: Mental illnesses are typically diagnosed using specific criteria outlined in the DSM. These criteria include symptoms, duration, and impact on daily functioning. Diagnostic tools such as psychological tests and imaging studies may also be used to aid in diagnosis.
11. *Mental illness can be prevented*: While not all mental illnesses can be prevented, there are steps people can take to reduce their risk of developing these conditions. This may include maintaining a healthy

lifestyle, managing stress, seeking support from family and friends, and seeking treatment for mental health problems as soon as they arise.

12. *Mental illness affects the brain*: Mental illnesses are associated with changes in brain chemistry, structure, and function. These changes can affect the way a person thinks, feels, and behaves.
13. *Mental illness is a global issue*: Mental illness affects people all around the world, and access to mental health care varies greatly depending on the country and region. The World Health Organization estimates that around 75% of people with mental health conditions in low-income countries do not receive treatment.
14. *Mental illness can be a source of creativity and innovation*: While mental illness can be a source of significant distress, some researchers have also suggested that it may be associated with certain positive qualities such as creativity and innovation.
15. *Mental illness is an area of active research*: Mental illness is an active area of research, with scientists investigating new treatments, risk factors, and biological mechanisms involved in these conditions. Advances in technology and brain imaging are helping to shed new light on the underlying causes of mental illness, which may lead to more effective treatments in the future.
16. *Mental illness can run in families*: Mental illnesses can be hereditary, meaning they can run in families. This suggests that genetics play a role in the development of some mental health conditions.
17. *Mental illness can affect children and adolescents*: Mental health problems can begin in childhood or adolescence, and early intervention is critical for improving outcomes. Common mental health conditions in children and adolescents include anxiety disorders, depression, and attention-deficit/hyperactivity disorder (ADHD).
18. *Mental illness can be a risk factor for suicide*: Mental illness is a major risk factor for suicide, and it is estimated that up to 90% of people who die by suicide have a diagnosable mental health condition. Suicide prevention efforts often focus on identifying and treating mental health conditions.

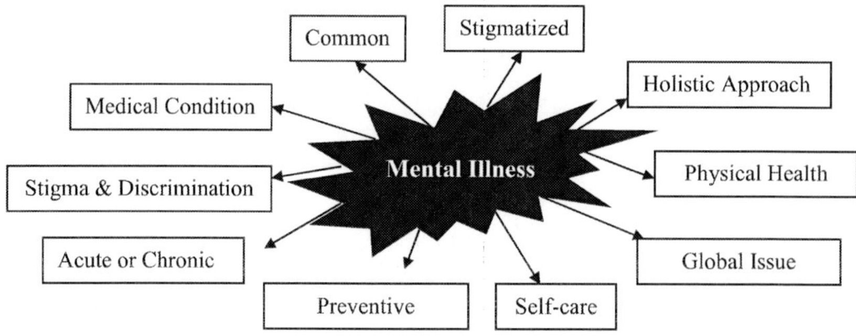

Figure 3.1: *Concept of Mental Illness*

19. *Mental illness can affect physical health*: Mental illness can also affect physical health, and people with mental health conditions may be at increased risk for certain medical conditions such as heart disease or diabetes. This underscores the importance of treating mental health problems in a holistic way.
20. *Mental illness can be associated with stigma and discrimination*: Mental illness is often stigmatized and discriminated against, leading to social isolation, poor treatment outcomes, and reduced quality of life. It is important to challenge these stereotypes and promote understanding and acceptance of mental health conditions.
21. *Mental illness can affect different aspects of life*: Mental illness can affect different aspects of a person's life, including their ability to work, study, socialize, and maintain relationships. It is important to tailor treatment approaches to the individual's unique needs and circumstances.
22. *Mental illness can be managed with self-care*: People with mental health conditions can take steps to manage their symptoms and improve their quality of life through self-care practices such as exercise, healthy eating, relaxation techniques, and social support.
23. *Mental illness can have economic costs*: Mental illness can have significant economic costs, including lost productivity, increased health care costs, and decreased quality of life. Addressing mental health problems can have positive economic impacts on both individuals and society as a whole.
24. *Mental illness can be associated with trauma*: Mental illness can be associated with experiences of trauma, such as physical or sexual abuse, neglect, or violence. Treating trauma-related mental health problems often involves specialized approaches such as trauma-focused therapy.

Overall, the concept of mental illness is multifaceted and complex, with a wide range of factors influencing the development, diagnosis, and treatment of these conditions. A comprehensive approach that addresses the biological, psychological, and social aspects of mental health is the key to improving outcomes for people with mental health conditions.

Causes of Mental Illness

Mental health refers to a person's overall psychological well-being. It encompasses emotional, social, and cognitive aspects of a person's life and influences how they think, feel, and behave. Good mental health is essential for individuals to function effectively in their daily lives, maintain healthy relationships, and achieve their goals.

However, mental health problems are common, affecting millions of people worldwide. Mental health disorders can be challenging to diagnose and treat, and they can have a significant impact on an individual's quality of life, including their ability to work, maintain relationships, and carry out daily tasks.

There are many different factors that can contribute to poor mental health, and often it is a complex interplay between different factors. Understanding the causes of mental health disorders is essential for preventing and treating them effectively. In this context, it is important to note that seeking help from a mental health professional can be beneficial in identifying and addressing the underlying causes of mental health issues.

There are many factors that can contribute to ill mental health, and often it is a complex interplay between different factors. Here are some of the most common causes:

1. *Genetics*: Mental health disorders can run in families, and research has identified a number of genes that are associated with various mental health conditions.
2. *Trauma*: Experiencing traumatic events such as abuse, neglect, violence, or accidents can have a lasting impact on mental health and increase the risk of developing mental health conditions.
3. *Stress*: Chronic stress from work, relationships, financial difficulties, or other sources can lead to anxiety, depression, and other mental health issues.
4. *Substance Abuse*: Substance abuse can lead to changes in brain chemistry that can contribute to mental health disorders, as well as exacerbate existing conditions.
5. *Medical Conditions*: Certain medical conditions, such as thyroid disorders or neurological conditions, can affect mental health.
6. *Environmental Factors*: Living in a stressful or unsafe environment can contribute to mental health problems, as can exposure to pollution or toxins.
7. *Social Factors*: Social isolation, discrimination, and other social factors can contribute to mental health issues.
8. *Childhood Experiences*: Adverse childhood experiences (ACEs) such as abuse, neglect, household dysfunction, and separation from parents or caregivers can have long-term effects on mental health.
9. *Personality Traits*: Certain personality traits, such as perfectionism, low self-esteem, or pessimism, can increase the risk of developing mental health disorders.
10. *Life Changes or Transitions*: Major life changes such as divorce, retirement, or the death of a loved one can be stressful and trigger mental health issues.
11. *Sleep Disturbances*: Sleep disorders such as insomnia or sleep apnea can affect mental health by disrupting circadian rhythms and increasing stress levels.
12. *Nutrition and Physical Activity*: Poor nutrition and lack of physical activity can affect brain function and contribute to mental health issues.
13. *Medications*: Certain medications, such as those used to treat high blood pressure or corticosteroids, can have side effects that affect mental health.

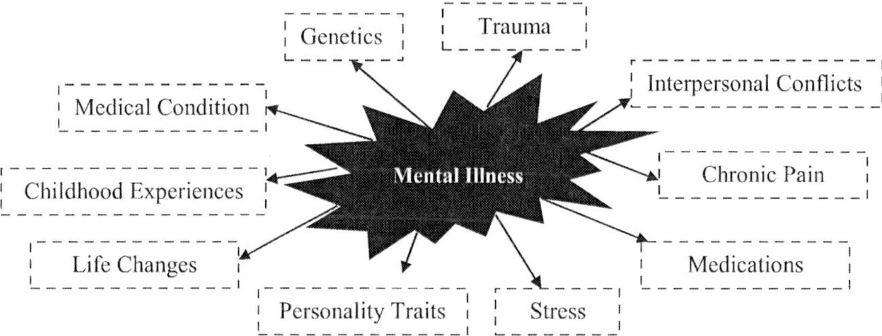

Figure 3.2: *Causes of Mental Illness*

14. *Cultural and Societal Factors*: Cultural attitudes towards mental health, social stigma, and discrimination can prevent individuals from seeking help and contribute to mental health issues.
15. *Financial Stress*: Financial difficulties, such as debt or unemployment, can cause stress and anxiety, which can lead to mental health issues.
16. *Chronic Illness*: Living with a chronic illness can be challenging and increase the risk of developing mental health issues.
17. *Traumatic Brain Injury*: A traumatic brain injury (TBI) can affect brain function and increase the risk of developing mental health disorders.
18. *Interpersonal Conflicts*: Conflicts with family members, friends, or colleagues can cause stress and impact mental health.
19. *Substance Withdrawal*: Withdrawal from certain substances, such as alcohol or opioids, can cause physical and psychological symptoms that affect mental health.
20. *Lack of Social Support*: Isolation and a lack of social support can contribute to mental health issues and exacerbate existing conditions.
21. *Chronic Pain*: Living with chronic pain can impact mental health and increase the risk of developing depression or anxiety.
22. *Seasonal Changes*: Seasonal affective disorder (SAD) is a type of depression that is linked to changes in the seasons and can occur during the winter months when there is less natural light.

Mental health is an essential aspect of a person's overall well-being, and poor mental health can have a significant impact on an individual's quality of life. There are many factors that can contribute to the development of mental health disorders, including genetics, trauma, stress, substance abuse, medical conditions, environmental factors, and social factors. Additionally, personal experiences such as childhood trauma, personality traits, life changes or transitions, sleep disturbances, and lack of social support can also contribute to mental health issues. It's important to remember that mental health disorders are not caused by any one factor, but rather a combination of multiple factors. Seeking help from a mental health professional is an important step towards identifying and addressing the underlying causes of mental health issues. With proper care and support, many individuals with mental health disorders can manage their symptoms effectively and lead fulfilling lives.

Korchin's Five Levels of Dysfunction

Korchin's five levels of dysfunction are a framework used to assess the severity of a person's psychological distress or problems. They were developed by psychologist Seymour Korchin in the 1970s and are still widely used today. This framework is used to determine the appropriate forms of treatment that people with different levels of dysfunction require.

Level-1: Mild Dysfunction

People at this level experience mild symptom of anxiety or depression, occasional sleep disturbances, and mild social or occupational impairment. They may have difficulty coping with stress but are still able to function reasonably well in their daily lives. For example, they may still be able to go to work or school, maintain relationships, and engage in hobbies or leisure activities. Treatment at this level may involve self-help strategies, such as exercise or relaxation techniques, or brief counseling or therapy.

Level-2: Moderate Dysfunction

People at this level experience more severe symptoms of anxiety or depression, frequent sleep disturbances, and greater social or occupational impairment. They may have difficulty functioning at work or in social situations and may require some form of treatment, such as counseling or medication. Treatment may also involve addressing any underlying issues or stressors that may be contributing to the person's symptoms.

Level-3: Severe Dysfunction

People at this level experience severe symptom of anxiety or depression, chronic sleep disturbances, and significant social or occupational impairment. They may be unable to work or carry out daily activities and may require intensive treatment such as hospitalization or more specialized forms of therapy. Treatment may involve addressing any underlying issues or stressors that may be contributing to the person's symptoms.

Level-4: Chronic Dysfunction

People at this level experience long-term, persistent symptoms of anxiety or depression that significantly impair their ability to function in daily life. They may have difficulty maintaining relationships, holding down a job, or participating in normal activities and may require ongoing treatment and support. Treatment may involve a combination of counseling or therapy, medication, and support from family and friends.

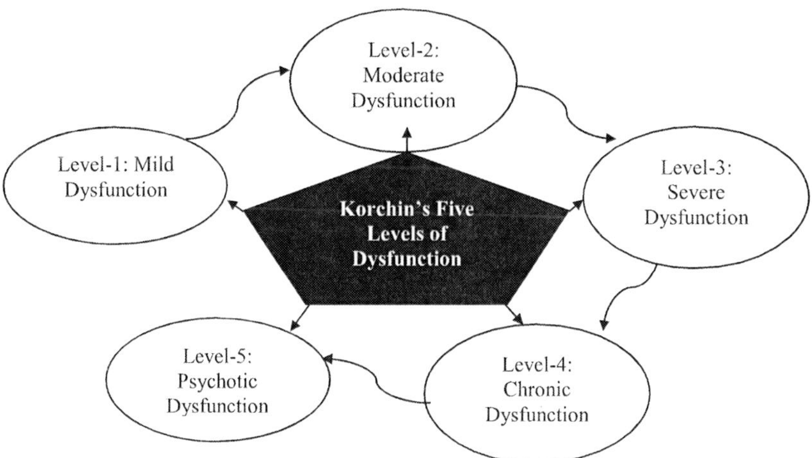

Figure 3.3: *Korchin's Five Levels of Dysfunction*

Level-5: Psychotic Dysfunction

This is the most severe level of dysfunction, characterized by psychotic symptoms such as delusions, hallucinations, and disorganized thinking. People at this level may be unable to distinguish reality from fantasy and may require hospitalization and intensive treatment to manage their symptoms. Treatment may involve medication and therapy, as well as support from family and friends.

Significance of Korchin's Five Levels of Dysfunction

Korchin's five levels of dysfunction are significant for several reasons. Here are some key points to consider.

1. *Early Identification of Symptoms*: Korchin's levels provide a framework for mental health professionals to identify symptoms of psychological distress at an early stage. By recognizing mild dysfunction, for example, mental health professionals can provide interventions that can prevent the symptoms from becoming more severe.
2. *Tailored Treatment*: Different levels of dysfunction require different treatment approaches. By accurately identifying a person's level of dysfunction, mental health professionals can develop tailored treatment plans that address the person's specific needs. This can improve the effectiveness of treatment and improve the person's overall quality of life.
3. *Communication among Professionals*: Korchin's levels provide a common language for mental health professionals to communicate about a person's level of functioning. This can facilitate communication among mental health professionals who may be working with the same person and ensure that all professionals are on the same page regarding the person's level of distress and the appropriate interventions.

4. *Preventing Further Deterioration*: By identifying people with mild to moderate dysfunction, mental health professionals can provide appropriate interventions that prevent symptoms from worsening. This can prevent a person's condition from deteriorating to the point where they require hospitalization or more intensive forms of treatment.
5. *Improved Outcomes*: Using Korchin's levels to guide treatment can lead to improved outcomes for people with psychological distress. By providing the appropriate interventions at the appropriate level of dysfunction, mental health professionals can help people manage their symptoms and improve their daily functioning.
6. *Screening and Prevention*: Korchin's levels can be used to screen for symptoms of psychological distress and provide preventative interventions to individuals who may be at risk for developing more severe levels of dysfunction. This can help identify individuals who may benefit from interventions such as stress reduction techniques, counseling, or psychoeducation.
7. *Resource Allocation*: Korchin's levels can help mental health professionals allocate resources more efficiently. For example, individuals with mild dysfunction may not require intensive treatment and can benefit from self-help strategies or low-intensity interventions, freeing up resources for individuals with more severe levels of dysfunction who require more intensive treatment.
8. *Stigma Reduction*: By providing a framework for identifying different levels of dysfunction, Korchin's levels can help reduce stigma surrounding mental health. By acknowledging that there are different levels of dysfunction and that it is normal to experience psychological distress, mental health professionals can help reduce shame and encourage individuals to seek help.
9. *Treatment Planning*: Korchin's levels can be used to develop treatment plans that are specific to the person's level of dysfunction. For example, individuals with moderate dysfunction may require a combination of medication and therapy, while individuals with severe dysfunction may require hospitalization and specialized forms of therapy. Using Korchin's levels can help mental health professionals develop treatment plans that are tailored to the individual's needs.
10. *Holistic Assessment*: Korchin's levels of dysfunction help mental health professionals to conduct a holistic assessment of a person's mental health status. By examining various domains of functioning, such as emotions, behaviours, and cognitive abilities, mental health professionals can develop a comprehensive understanding of a person's level of dysfunction and design interventions that address the person's unique needs.
11. *Cross-cultural Applications*: Korchin's levels of dysfunction have cross-cultural applicability, as they do not rely on specific cultural norms

or values. Mental health professionals can use this framework to identify and address different levels of dysfunction in people from diverse cultural backgrounds, which can help reduce disparities in mental health care.

12. *Facilitating Communication with Clients*: Korchin's levels of dysfunction can facilitate communication between mental health professionals and clients. By using a common language, mental health professionals can explain to clients the severity of their symptoms, the recommended interventions, and the expected outcomes. This can help clients understand their mental health status and become more engaged in their treatment.
13. *Prevention of Long-term Disabilities*: Korchin's levels of dysfunction can help prevent long-term disabilities that may arise from untreated psychological distress. For example, individuals with severe dysfunction may experience impairments in social and occupational functioning that can lead to long-term disability. By providing early interventions, mental health professionals can prevent these disabilities from occurring and help individuals to maintain their daily functioning.
14. *Public Health Policy*: Korchin's levels of dysfunction can inform public health policy decisions related to mental health. By identifying different levels of dysfunction, policymakers can allocate resources for mental health care in a way that addresses the needs of individuals with different levels of severity. This can help improve access to mental health care for individuals with psychological distress and promote population mental health.
15. *Continuum of Care*: Korchin's levels of dysfunction represent a continuum of care, from mild to severe. Mental health professionals can use this framework to design interventions that are appropriate for each level of dysfunction. For example, individuals with mild dysfunction may benefit from self-help strategies, while individuals with severe dysfunction may require more intensive and long-term interventions. By providing a continuum of care, mental health professionals can ensure that individuals receive appropriate care at each stage of their mental health journey.
16. *Empowering Individuals*: Korchin's levels of dysfunction can empower individuals to take an active role in their mental health care. By providing information about different levels of dysfunction, mental health professionals can help individuals understand their symptoms and the available interventions. This can help individuals make informed decisions about their mental health care and become more engaged in their treatment.
17. *Collaborative Care*: Korchin's levels of dysfunction can facilitate collaborative care between mental health professionals and other healthcare providers. For example, individuals with severe dysfunction may require medical interventions in addition to psychotherapy. By providing a framework for identifying different levels of dysfunction, mental health professionals can collaborate with other healthcare providers to provide integrated and coordinated care.

18. *Research and Evaluation*: Korchin's levels of dysfunction can facilitate research and evaluation of mental health interventions. By using a standardized framework to identify different levels of dysfunction, researchers can evaluate the effectiveness of interventions at different levels of severity. This can help improve the quality of care for individuals with psychological distress and inform future research.

Korchin's five levels of dysfunction provide a useful framework for mental health professionals to assess the severity of a person's psychological problems and the appropriate forms of treatment. By accurately assessing a person's level of dysfunction, mental health professionals can provide targeted interventions that can help people improve their quality of life and achieve their goals. It's important to note that these levels are not static, and a person's level of dysfunction may change over time based on various factors such as life events, stressors, and treatment. Additionally, some mental health disorders may not fit neatly into this framework and may require a more individualized approach to treatment.

Concept of Normality

Normality in mental health refers to behaviours, thoughts, and emotions that are considered typical or expected within a given society or cultural context. Normality is often defined by statistical norms, such as the average or standard deviation of a particular behaviour or thought in a given population. The word "Normality" comes from the Latin word 'Normalis', which means 'according to the square'.

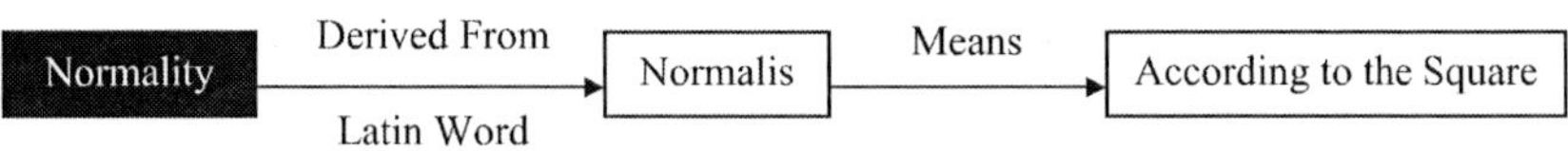

Figure 3.4: *Etymological Meaning of Normality*

In mental health, the concept of normality is used to define what is typical or expected behaviour, thoughts, or emotions, based on societal or cultural norms. It is often determined by statistical norms, such as the average or standard deviation of a particular behaviour or thought in a given population. Sigmund Freud, a pioneer of psychoanalysis, believed that normality involves a balance between the conscious and unconscious mind. He believed that repressed or unresolved unconscious conflicts could lead to psychological distress, while individuals with a healthy psyche are able to manage their unconscious desires and impulses. The concept of normality in mental health is a complex and controversial topic that has been the subject of much debate among mental health professionals. Below are some key points that help to understand the concept of normality in mental health:

1. *Normality is a Relative Concept*: What is considered normal in one society or culture may not be considered normal in another. For example,

some cultures may view hearing voices or seeing visions as a normal part of spiritual experience, while other cultures may view these experiences as symptoms of mental illness.

2. *Normality is a Statistical Concept*: Normality is often determined based on statistical norms, such as the average or standard deviation of a particular behaviour, thought, or emotion in a given population. However, statistical norms do not necessarily reflect what is healthy or optimal.
3. *Normality is a Functional Concept*: Normality is also determined by how well an individual can function in their social and cultural environments. If an individual's behaviour, thoughts, or emotions interfere with their ability to function effectively, it may be considered abnormal.
4. *Normality is Influenced by Individual Differences*: Normality is also influenced by individual differences such as age, gender, personality, and life experiences. For example, the considered normal behaviour for a child may not be considered normal behaviour for an adult.
5. *Normality is not the same as Mental Health*: Normality and mental health are related concepts, but they are not the same thing. Mental health refers to a state of emotional, psychological, and social well-being, while normality refers to a set of criteria used to determine what is typical or expected behaviour, thoughts, or emotions.
6. *Stigma and Discrimination Can Arise from a Narrow Definition of Normality*. If the concept of normality is used to define and label individuals who deviate from societal norms, it can lead to stigma and discrimination against those individuals. Therefore, it is important to approach the concept of normality with cultural sensitivity and understanding.
7. *Normality is Influenced by Historical Context*: What is considered normal or abnormal behaviour, thoughts, or emotions can change over time due to cultural and historical shifts. For example, homosexuality was once considered a mental disorder but is now recognized as a normal and healthy variation of human sexuality.
8. *Normality is Influenced by Power Dynamics*: The concept of normality can be influenced by power dynamics, such as the dominant group's norms and values imposing themselves on marginalized or minority groups. For example, the cultural norms of dominant groups may be used to pathologize the behaviour of minority groups, leading to discrimination and stigma.
9. *Normality can be Limiting*: An overly narrow definition of normality can be limiting, preventing individuals from expressing themselves fully or living fulfilling lives. Therefore, it is important to recognize and embrace diversity in all its forms, including diversity of behaviour, thoughts, and emotions.
10. *Normality can Change over the Lifespan*: What is considered normal or typical behaviour, thoughts, or emotions can change over the lifespan. For example, it is normal for young children to have imaginary friends,

but it would be abnormal for adults to have them. Similarly, it is normal for older adults to experience memory decline, but it would be abnormal for young adults.

11. *Normality is a Social Construct*: Normality is a socially constructed concept that is shaped by cultural, historical, and political factors. Therefore, it is important to approach the concept of normality with a critical lens and to recognize that it is not a fixed or objective standard.
12. *Normality is Influenced by Context*: The context in which a behaviour, thought, or emotion occurs can influence whether it is considered normal or abnormal. For example, it may be normal for someone to cry at a funeral, but it would be abnormal for someone to cry uncontrollably at a workplace meeting.
13. *Normality can be Influenced by Individual Differences in Temperament*: Individual differences in temperament, such as shyness or impulsivity, can influence what is considered normal or abnormal behaviour. For example, a shy person may be seen as normal in some cultures but abnormal in others.
14. *Normality can be Influenced by Mental Health Stigma*: Mental health stigma can influence what is considered normal or abnormal behaviour. For example, a person with depression may be seen as weak or lazy, even though depression is a common and treatable mental illness.
15. *Normality can be Influenced by Diagnostic Criteria*: The diagnostic criteria used to diagnose mental illnesses can influence what is considered normal or abnormal behaviour. For example, the diagnostic criteria for autism spectrum disorder have changed over time, which has led to changes in how it is diagnosed and how individuals with autism are perceived by society.
16. *Normality can be Subjective*: Normality can be a subjective concept that is influenced by individual perceptions, biases, and values. For example, what one person considers normal behaviour may be seen as abnormal by someone else.
17. *Normality is not Synonymous with Conformity*: Normality should not be equated with conformity or the absence of individuality. Rather, it should be seen as a set of criteria used to determine what is typical or expected behaviour, thoughts, or emotions, while recognizing and valuing diversity in all its forms.

The concept of normality in mental health is complex, multifaceted, and is influenced by various factors such as cultural and historical context, individual differences, and diagnostic criteria. It is often defined by statistical norms, but it is important to approach this concept with cultural sensitivity and understanding, recognizing the diversity of human experiences and the fluidity of societal norms over time. Moreover, it is crucial to avoid equating normality with conformity or the absence of individuality, and to value and embrace diversity in all its forms. The concept of normality can be useful in identifying when someone is experiencing significant distress or impairment, but it should not be used to stigmatize or discriminate against individuals who deviate from societal norms or who have mental health conditions. Ultimately, the concept of normality in mental health should be approached with a holistic perspective that takes into account individual experiences, cultural contexts, and the diversity of human behaviour, thoughts, and emotions.

Concept of Abnormality

The term 'Abnormality' comes from the Latin word 'Abnormalis', which means 'deviating from the normal or usual.' The concept of abnormality has been used in various ways throughout history. In ancient times, abnormality was often attributed to supernatural causes, such as possession by evil spirits or punishment from the gods. During the 19th and early 20th centuries, abnormality was often viewed as a sign of moral weakness or degeneracy, and individuals with mental health conditions were often institutionalized or treated as outcasts. However, the concept of abnormality has evolved over time, and mental health professionals now recognize that mental health conditions are complex and multifaceted, and that they can have biological, psychological, and social causes. The use of the term abnormality in mental health is now more nuanced and is generally used to describe behaviours or thoughts that significantly deviate from what is considered typical or expected within a given cultural or societal context, and that can cause significant distress or impairment to the individual experiencing them.

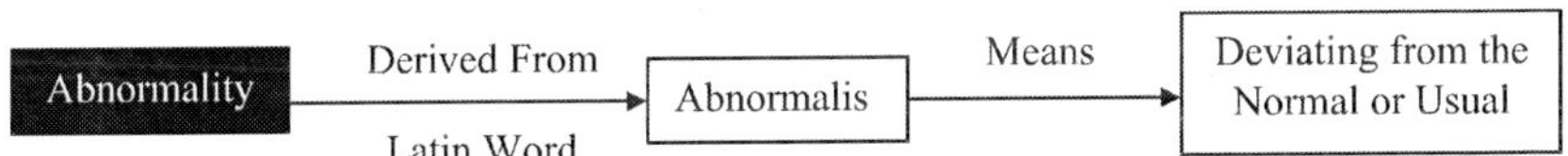

Figure 3.5: *Etymological Meaning of Abnormality*

The concept of abnormality in mental health refers to behaviours, thoughts, or emotions that deviate from what is considered typical or expected within a given society or cultural context. Abnormality can manifest in various ways, ranging from mild deviations from societal norms to severe mental health conditions that significantly impair an individual's functioning. Here are some key points to consider when discussing abnormality in mental health:

1. *Dysfunction*: Abnormality can also be identified by behaviours or thoughts that interfere with an individual's ability to function in their daily life.
2. *Distress*: Abnormality can cause negative emotions or experiences that an individual may experience due to their behaviour or thoughts.
3. *Deviation from Cultural or Societal Norms*: Abnormality can be identified by behaviours or thoughts that are considered unacceptable or inappropriate within a given culture or society.
4. *Role of Cultural and Historical Context*: The concept of abnormality can be influenced by cultural and historical context, as what is considered abnormal in one society or time period may be considered normal in another.

5. *Importance of Empathy and Understanding*: It is important to approach the concept of abnormality with empathy and understanding, recognizing that individuals with mental health conditions are complex and multifaceted, and that they deserve compassion and support.
6. *Potential for Stigmatization and Discrimination*: The use of the term "abnormality" can stigmatize and discriminate against individuals who deviate from societal norms or who have mental health conditions. Therefore, it is important to approach the concept of abnormality with caution and sensitivity.
7. *Importance of Individual Differences*: Abnormality can be influenced by individual differences in personality, temperament, and life experiences. Therefore, it is important to consider individual differences when assessing abnormality.
8. *Role of Power Dynamics*: The concept of abnormality can be influenced by power dynamics within society, such as racism, sexism etc. Therefore, it is important to approach the concept of abnormality with an understanding of the ways in which power and privilege can impact mental health and well-being.
9. *Potential for Misdiagnosis*: The concept of abnormality can be complex and nuanced, and mental health conditions can often be misdiagnosed or misunderstood. Therefore, it is important for mental health professionals to approach the assessment of abnormality with caution and thoroughness.
10. *Importance of Social Support*: Individuals with mental health conditions may benefit from social support, including therapy, medication, and support groups. Therefore, it is important to provide resources and support for individuals with mental health conditions.
11. *Potential for Recovery*: With proper treatment and support, individuals with mental health conditions can often recover and lead fulfilling lives. Therefore, it is important to approach the concept of abnormality with an understanding of the potential for recovery and resilience.
12. *Importance of Considering Co-morbidity*: Mental health conditions often co-occur with other conditions, such as substance abuse or medical conditions. Therefore, it is important to consider co-morbidity when assessing abnormality.
13. *Potential for Resilience and Coping*: Individuals with mental health conditions may develop coping strategies and resilience over time, which can help them manage their symptoms and improve their quality of life.
14. *Impact of Stigma*: The concept of abnormality can be stigmatizing for individuals with mental health conditions, which can lead to discrimination, social exclusion, and other negative outcomes. Therefore, it is important to approach the concept of abnormality with an awareness of the potential for stigma and to work to reduce stigma and discrimination.
15. *Potential for Positive Attributes*: Individuals with mental health conditions may have unique perspectives, strengths, and abilities that should be

recognized and celebrated. Therefore, it is important to approach the concept of abnormality with an appreciation for the diversity of human experiences and strengths.

16. *The Importance of Cultural Competence*: Mental health professionals should have an understanding of cultural differences and the ways in which culture can impact mental health and well-being. Therefore, it is important for mental health professionals to approach the assessment of abnormality with cultural competence and an awareness of the potential for cultural biases and misunderstandings.

Overall, the concept of abnormality in mental health is complex and multifaceted, and should be approached with empathy, cultural competence, and an appreciation for the diversity of human experiences and strengths. By taking a nuanced and holistic approach to the assessment of abnormality, mental health professionals can help individuals with mental health conditions receive the care and support they need to thrive.

Classification of Abnormal Behaviour

Abnormal behaviour is a broad term used to describe behaviour that deviates from what is considered normal or typical within a particular culture or society. However, abnormal behaviour is not necessarily negative or harmful; it simply refers to behaviour that is outside of what is expected or considered typical. There are different ways to classify abnormal behaviour. One common classification system is the DSM-5 (Diagnostic and Statistical Manual of Mental Disorders, Fifth Edition) used by mental health professionals. It categorizes abnormal behaviour into various mental disorders based on specific criteria and symptoms. Some examples of mental disorders include anxiety disorders, mood disorders, personality disorders, and psychotic disorders. Another classification system is the ICD-11 (International Classification of Diseases, Eleventh Revision) used by the World Health Organization. It categorizes abnormal behaviour into various mental and behavioural disorders based on similar criteria to the DSM-5. Maher and Maher (1985) gave four basic categories of abnormal behaviour:Behaviour that is harmful to the self or that is harmful to others without serving the interests of self;Poor reality contact; Emotional reactions inappropriate to the person's situation; Erratic behaviour— which refers to sudden shifts in behaviour shown. Additionally, abnormal behaviour can also be classified based on the causes or underlying factors. For example, abnormal behaviour can be caused by genetics, environmental factors, brain chemistry, traumatic experiences, or a combination of these factors. It's worth noting that the classification of abnormal behaviour is not a perfect science and there is often overlap and disagreement between different classification systems. However, these systems provide a helpful framework for understanding and treating abnormal behaviour in individuals.

Classification of Abnormal Behaviour by Page (1976): Page (1976) classified abnormal behaviour into four major categories: Psychoneuroses,

Psychoses, Mental Retardation, and Anti-social Personalities. Let's discuss each of these categories in more detail:

1. ***Psychoneuroses***: Psychoneurotic disorders are characterized by emotional distress and anxiety, which can manifest in a range of symptoms, such as obsessive-compulsive behaviour, phobias, panic attacks, and depression. These disorders do not typically involve a loss of touch with reality, and people with psychoneurotic disorders can often function reasonably well in their daily lives. Examples of psychoneuroses include:
   - Generalized Anxiety Disorder (GAD)
   - Panic Disorder
   - Obsessive-Compulsive Disorder (OCD)
   - Post-Traumatic Stress Disorder (PTSD)
   - Phobias (such as agoraphobia, social phobia, specific phobia).
2. ***Psychoses***: Psychotic disorders involve a break from reality and a loss of touch with what is considered normal. Symptoms can include delusions, hallucinations, disordered thinking, and abnormal behaviours. People with psychotic disorders may have difficulty functioning in their daily lives and may require hospitalization or other forms of intensive treatment. Examples of psychoses include:
   - Schizophrenia
   - Delusional Disorder
   - Brief Psychotic Disorder
   - Schizoaffective Disorder
   - Substance-Induced Psychotic Disorder.
3. ***Mental Retardation***: Mental retardation (now called intellectual disability) refers to a range of intellectual disabilities, which can affect a person's cognitive functioning, learning abilities, and social skills. These disorders can vary in severity, with some people experiencing only mild cognitive impairments, while others may require significant support to function in society. Examples of intellectual disabilities include:
   - Down Syndrome
   - Fragile X Syndrome
   - Fetal Alcohol Syndrome
   - Rett Syndrome
   - Prader-Willi Syndrome.
4. ***Anti-social Personalities***: Anti-social Personality Disorder (ASPD) is an example of an anti-social disorder. People with ASPD have a disregard for the rights of others and may engage in criminal behaviour. For example, someone with ASPD may engage in theft, vandalism, or physical violence without feeling remorse or empathy for their victims. Other examples of anti-social behaviour include:
   - Conduct Disorder
   - Narcissistic Personality Disorder

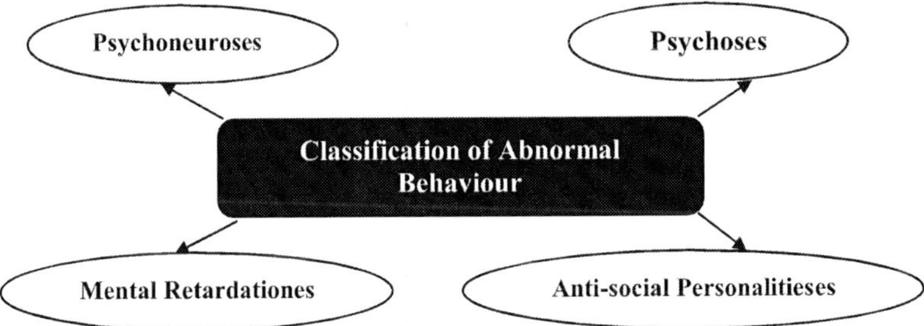

Figure 3.6: *Classification of Abnormal Behaviour by Page (1976)*

- Borderline Personality Disorder
- Histrionic Personality Disorder
- Psychopathy.

It's important to note that these categories are not mutually exclusive, and many people may experience symptoms that fall into multiple categories. Additionally, there is often overlap between these categories and other classification systems used to describe abnormal behaviour. Nonetheless, Page's classification provides a useful framework for understanding and treating abnormal behaviour in individuals.

Role of Parents in Preventing Mental Illness

Parents play a critical role in preventing mental illness in their children. Mental health issues are prevalent in our society, and parents can take proactive steps to help their children maintain good mental health. Here are some points that discuss the role of parents in preventing mental illness:

1. *Nurturing Positive Relationships*: Parents can create a nurturing and supportive environment at home, where their children feel comfortable expressing themselves. This can help reduce stress and anxiety in children and promote positive mental health.
2. *Encouraging Healthy Habits*: Parents can encourage their children to adopt healthy habits, such as regular exercise, healthy eating, and sufficient sleep. These habits can improve overall physical and mental well-being and reduce the risk of developing mental health issues.
3. *Building Resilience*: Resilience is the ability to cope with stress and adversity. Parents can help their children build resilience by encouraging them to face challenges, learn from mistakes, and develop problem-solving skills.
4. *Monitoring for Warning Signs*: Parents should be aware of the warning signs of mental health issues, such as changes in behaviour, mood, or sleep patterns. They should seek professional help if they suspect their child is struggling with mental health issues.
5. *Providing Emotional Support*: Parents can provide emotional support by listening to their children, validating their feelings, and offering comfort

and reassurance. This can help children develop a sense of security and self-worth, which can contribute to positive mental health.

6. *Reducing Stress*: Parents can reduce stress in their children's lives by creating a structured and predictable routine, setting realistic expectations, and providing a safe and secure environment. This can help reduce anxiety and promote positive mental health.
7. *Being a Positive Role Model*: Parents can set a positive example for their children by managing their own stress, practising self-care, and seeking help when needed. By modeling healthy behaviours and attitudes, parents can help their children develop positive coping strategies and build resilience.
8. *Fostering a Sense of Belonging*: Children who feel connected to their family, school, and community are less likely to experience mental health issues. Parents can help their children develop a sense of belonging by encouraging them to participate in social activities, volunteering, and pursuing hobbies.
9. *Addressing Trauma*: Trauma can have a lasting impact on a child's mental health. Parents can help prevent mental health issues by addressing trauma in a supportive and sensitive manner. This may involve seeking professional help, creating a safe and supportive environment, and validating the child's experiences.
10. *Building Coping Skills*: Coping skills are essential for managing stress and adversity. Parents can help their children develop coping skills by teaching them problem-solving techniques, relaxation techniques, and mindfulness practices.
11. *Encouraging Open Communication*: Open communication between parents and children can help prevent mental health issues by allowing children to express their feelings and concerns. Parents can encourage open communication by listening without judgement, validating their children's feelings, and responding in a supportive and caring manner.
12. *Educating Themselves*: Parents can prevent mental illness in their children by educating themselves about mental health issues, including the signs, symptoms, and treatments. This can help them recognize when their child may need professional help and how to access resources and support.
13. *Encouraging Help-seeking Behaviour*: Parents can help prevent mental health issues in their children by encouraging them to seek help when needed. This can involve teaching children about mental health, reducing stigma around seeking help, and connecting them with mental health professionals when necessary.
14. *Creating a Supportive School Environment*: Schools play a crucial role in promoting children's mental health. Parents can advocate for a supportive school environment that prioritizes mental health, such as offering mental health services, anti-bullying programmes, and social-emotional learning curricula.
15. *Prioritizing Family Time*: Spending quality time as a family can help prevent mental health issues by promoting a sense of connection, security,

and support. Parents can prioritize family time by scheduling regular family activities, such as game nights, movie nights, or outdoor activities.

16. *Providing Opportunities for Play and Creativity*: Play and creativity are essential for children's mental health and well-being. Parents can provide opportunities for play and creativity, such as arts and crafts, music lessons, or sports activities, to promote positive mental health.

Parents can prevent mental illness in their children by educating themselves, encouraging help-seeking behaviour, creating a supportive school environment, prioritizing family time, providing opportunities for play and creativity, and taking other proactive steps to promote positive mental health. By working together, parents and children can build resilience, prevent mental health issues, and thrive.

Role of Teachers in Preventing Mental Illness

Mental illness is a growing concern among children and adolescents, with 1 in 6 young people experiencing a mental health disorder worldwide. The consequences of untreated mental illness can be severe, including poor academic performance, social isolation, and even suicide. In this context, the role of teachers in preventing mental illness among their students is crucial. Teachers spend a significant amount of time with their students and are often the first to notice signs of mental health problems. They can create a positive and supportive classroom environment, provide education on mental health, and refer students to appropriate services. Teachers can play a critical role in the prevention of mental illness among their students. Here are some points to consider:

1. *Early Identification*: Teachers can identify early signs of mental health problems in their students, such as changes in behaviour, mood, or academic performance. Early identification can lead to early intervention, which can prevent the development of more serious mental health issues.
2. *Creating a Supportive Environment*: Teachers can create a positive and supportive classroom environment that promotes emotional well-being. This includes fostering a sense of belonging, providing emotional support, and promoting healthy habits such as regular physical activity.
3. *Providing Education on Mental Health*: Teachers can educate their students about mental health and mental illness, reducing the stigma surrounding these issues and promoting help-seeking behaviours.
4. *Referring Students to Appropriate Services*: Teachers can refer students to appropriate mental health services, such as school counselors, psychologists, or community mental health providers. This can help ensure that students receive the support they need to manage their mental health.
5. *Collaboration with Parents and Healthcare Providers*: Teachers can work collaboratively with parents and healthcare providers to ensure that students receive comprehensive mental health care.

6. *Encouraging Open Communication*: Teachers can encourage open communication with their students, creating a safe space for them to express their thoughts and feelings. This can help students feel heard and understood, reducing their risk of developing mental health problems.
7. *Modeling Healthy Behaviours*: Teachers can model healthy behaviours, such as self-care and stress management techniques, for their students. This can help students learn healthy coping mechanisms and reduce their risk of developing mental health problems.
8. *Addressing Bullying and Other Forms of Violence*: Teachers can address bullying and other forms of violence in the classroom, promoting a safe and supportive environment that fosters emotional well-being.
9. *Providing Academic Support*: Teachers can provide academic support to their students, such as tutoring or extra help, reducing their stress levels and preventing academic-related mental health problems.
10. *Engaging Parents and Families*: Teachers can engage parents and families in the promotion of mental health and well-being, creating a collaborative and supportive approach that promotes healthy development.
11. *Identifying and Addressing Sources of Stress*: Teachers can identify sources of stress in the classroom and help students manage them effectively. This might include teaching relaxation techniques, providing study strategies, or adjusting coursework to better meet students' needs.
12. *Providing Positive Reinforcement*: Teachers can provide positive reinforcement for their students' successes and accomplishments, boosting their self-esteem and overall well-being.
13. *Encouraging Physical Activity*: Teachers can encourage physical activity, which has been shown to reduce stress, anxiety, and depression. This might include incorporating movement breaks into the school day or promoting extracurricular physical activities.
14. *Incorporating Mindfulness Practices*: Teachers can incorporate mindfulness practices into their classroom, such as meditation or deep breathing exercises. This can help students develop greater emotional awareness and self-regulation skills.
15. *Building Strong Relationships with Students*: Teachers can build strong relationships with their students, creating a sense of connection and support that promotes emotional well-being.

Teachers can prevent mental illness among their students by identifying and addressing sources of stress, providing positive reinforcement, encouraging physical activity, incorporating mindfulness practices, and building strong relationships. By taking a holistic and proactive approach to mental health promotion, teachers can help their students develop the resilience and coping skills needed to thrive both in school and in life.

4

Adjustment

Meaning of Adjustment

The term 'Adjustment' has its roots in the Latin word 'Adiustare' which means 'To Put Right' or 'To Make Straight'. The term was later adapted into French as 'Ajuster' which means 'To Fit' or 'To Adjust'.

Adjustment refers to the process of modifying or changing something to fit a particular situation or requirement. It can be applied to various areas of life, such as personal, professional, or academic, and can be done intentionally or unintentionally. Adjustment can involve making small changes to improve the way something functions or adapting to new circumstances, such as changes in the environment, people, or technology. It is often required when something doesn't work as planned or when new information becomes available.

In psychology, adjustment refers to the process of adapting to new circumstances, managing stressors, and coping with life's challenges. It involves a range of cognitive and behavioural strategies that individuals use to manage the demands of their environment and maintain a sense of well-being.

Adjustment is a critical aspect of mental health, as individuals who struggle to adjust to new situations or cope with stressors may experience emotional distress, anxiety, and depression. Successful adjustment requires individuals to develop effective coping mechanisms, problem-solving skills, and social support networks.

Psychologists use a variety of theories to understand the process of adjustment, including cognitive-behavioural, humanistic, and social learning theories. These theories emphasize the importance of individuals' thoughts, emotions, and behaviours in the adjustment process.

Cognitive-behavioural theorysuggests that individuals' beliefs and attitudes about themselves and their environment play a crucial role in how

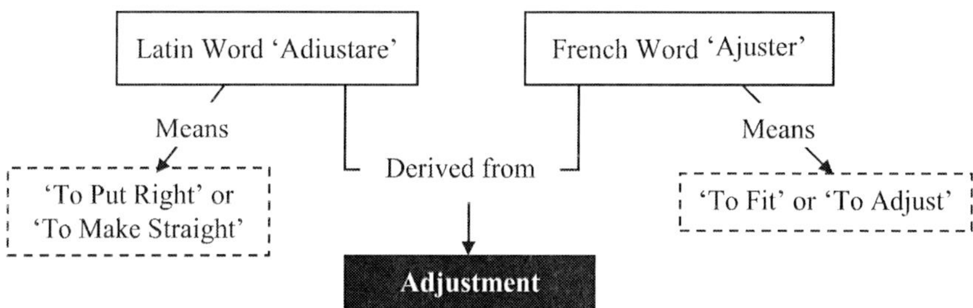

Figure 4.1: *Etymological Meaning of Adjustment*

they cope with stressors. It emphasizes the importance of identifying and challenging negative thoughts and developing more positive and adaptive thinking patterns.

Humanistic theoriesfocus on the individual's capacity for growth, self-awareness, and self-actualization. These theories emphasize the importance of self-reflection, personal growth, and the development of a positive self-concept.

Social learning theory suggests that individuals learn adaptive coping mechanisms through observation and modeling of others. It highlights the importance of social support networks, role models, and exposure to positive coping strategies in promoting successful adjustment.

Definitions of Adjustment

Adjustment can be defined in various ways depending on the context and the field of study. Generally, adjustment refers to the process of modifying or adapting something to fit a particular situation or requirement. In psychology, adjustment refers to the process of adapting to new situations, managing stressors, and coping with life's challenges.

In general usage, adjustment refers to the process of making small changes to improve the way something functions or adapting to new circumstances.

In finance, adjustment refers to the process of modifying the price or value of an asset to reflect new information or changing market conditions.

In physics, adjustment refers to the process of altering the position, speed, or direction of a moving object to achieve a desired outcome.

In biology, adjustment refers to the process of adaptation, where an organism modifies its behaviour or physiology to better suit its environment.

In psychology, adjustment refers to the process of coping with life's challenges and adapting to new situations. It involves a range of cognitive and behavioural strategies that individuals use to manage the demands of their environment and maintain a sense of well-being.

There are several popular psychologists who have provided definitions of adjustment in the context of psychology. Here are some examples:

Sigmund Freud: Freud defined adjustment as the ability to adapt to reality without causing undue stress or anxiety. He believed that individuals who could not adjust effectively would develop maladaptive coping mechanisms that could lead to mental health problems.

Carl Rogers: Rogers defined adjustment as the process of achieving congruence between an individual's self-concept and their experiences. He believed that individuals who were able to adjust effectively would be more self-aware, confident, and resilient.

Gordon Allport: Allport defined adjustment as the process of achieving a balance between an individual's personal goals and the demands of the environment. He believed that individuals who could adjust effectively would be able to achieve a sense of personal fulfillment and satisfaction.

Abraham Maslow: Maslow defined adjustment as the process of self-actualization, where individuals strive to achieve their full potential and become the best version of themselves. He believed that individuals who could adjust effectively would be able to experience a sense of meaning and purpose in their lives.

Albert Bandura: Bandura defined adjustment as the process of social learning, where individuals observe and model the behaviour of others to develop effective coping strategies. He believed that individuals who could adjust effectively would be able to develop a repertoire of effective coping strategies that they could use to manage stressors and achieve their goals.

There are several popular quotes that relate to the concept of adjustment. Here are some examples:

> *"It is not the strongest of the species that survives, or the most intelligent, but the one most responsive to change."*
>
> — Charles Darwin

This quote emphasizes the importance of adaptation and adjustment in the face of changing circumstances. It suggests that those who are most able to adjust to new situations will be the most successful in the long run.

> *"The only way to make sense out of change is to plunge into it, move with it, and join the dance."*
>
> — Alan Watts

This quote emphasizes the importance of embracing change and adapting to new circumstances. It suggests that those who are able to adjust to change and "join the dance" will be able to make the most of life's opportunities.

> *"Life is 10% what happens to us and 90% how we react to it."*
>
> — Charles R. Swindoll

This quote highlights the importance of adjusting our attitudes and reactions to life's challenges. It suggests that we have the power to control our response to external events and that our ability to adjust effectively will determine our overall success and happiness.

> *"The art of life lies in a constant readjustment to our surroundings."*
>
> —Kakuzo Okakura

This quote emphasizes the importance of flexibility and adaptability in life. It suggests that the key to success and happiness is not to cling to fixed ideas or expectations, but to be open to change and to constantly adjust our approach to fit our surroundings.

Overall, these definitions suggest that adjustment is a complex and multifaceted process that involves adapting to new situations, managing stressors, and achieving personal fulfillment and satisfaction. Different psychologists have emphasized different aspects of adjustment, but they all agree that it is a critical aspect of mental health and well-being. They suggest that adjustment is a critical aspect of success and happiness in life. They highlight the importance of adapting to change, embracing new opportunities, and adjusting our attitudes and behaviours to fit our circumstances.

Concept of Adjustment

Adjustment refers to the process of adapting to new situations or changes in our environment, circumstances, or relationships. It involves making changes in our behaviour, attitudes, emotions, or thoughts to cope with new challenges or opportunities.

Adjustment can occur in various domains of life, such as work, family, social life, and personal development. For example, adjusting to a new job may involve learning new skills, building new relationships with colleagues, and adapting to a different work culture. Adjusting to a new relationship may involve adapting to a partner's personality, communication style, and needs.

Adjustment is a dynamic process that requires flexibility, resilience, and a willingness to learn and grow. People who are able to adjust effectively are often more successful, satisfied, and fulfilled in their lives. They are better able to cope with stress, handle uncertainty, and navigate change.

However, adjustment can also be challenging and stressful, especially when the changes are unexpected or unwanted. It may involve letting go of old habits, beliefs, or relationships, which can be difficult and emotional. Moreover, some people may have a harder time adjusting than others, depending on their personality traits, life experiences, and support networks.

Here are some key points to consider when discussing the concept of adjustment:

1. *Adjustment is a process*: It involves adapting to new situations, rather than simply accepting them. This process may take time and effort, and may involve trial and error as we figure out the best ways to cope with new challenges.
2. *Adjustment can occur in many areas of life*: We may need to adjust to changes in our work, relationships, health, living situations, or personal goals. Each of these areas may require different skills or strategies for effective adjustment.
3. *Adjustment requires flexibility*: We need to be willing to try new things and let go of old ways of thinking or behaving. This may involve challenging our beliefs or assumptions, or being open to feedback from others.
4. *Adjustment requires resilience*: We need to be able to cope with stress and setbacks along the way. This may involve developing coping skills, seeking support from others, or practising self-care.
5. *Adjustment can be difficult*: We may experience anxiety, frustration, or other negative emotions when faced with new challenges. It is important to acknowledge these feelings and seek help if needed.

6. *Adjustment can lead to personal growth*: When we successfully adjust to new situations, we may develop new skills, perspectives, or relationships that enhance our lives. We may also develop greater confidence and resilience for future challenges.
7. *Adjustment is an ongoing process*: Life is full of changes, and we may need to adjust multiple times throughout our lives. Each new challenge presents an opportunity for growth and learning.
8. *Adjustment can be proactive or reactive*: Sometimes we choose to make changes in our lives in order to pursue new opportunities or improve our circumstances. Other times, we are forced to adjust due to unexpected events or circumstances beyond our control.
9. *Adjustment can have both positive and negative outcomes*: While successful adjustment can lead to personal growth and well-being, unsuccessful adjustment can lead to negative outcomes such as stress, anxiety, and depression. It is important to seek support if we are struggling with adjustment.
10. *Adjustment involves a balance between adaptation and authenticity*: While it is important to adapt to new situations and circumstances, we also need to remain true to our values, beliefs, and identity. This can be challenging when we are faced with new or conflicting expectations.
11. *Adjustment is influenced by individual and environmental factors*: Our ability to adjust may be influenced by factors such as our personality traits, past experiences, social support networks, and access to resources. The nature of the situation or change we are facing may also play a role.
12. *Adjustment can involve different strategies*: There are many strategies we can use to adjust to new situations, such as seeking social support, learning new skills, practising mindfulness, or seeking professional help. The most effective strategies may vary depending on the situation and individual.
13. *Adjustment involves a balance between stability and change*: While adjustment requires adapting to new situations and circumstances, it is also important to maintain a sense of stability and continuity in our lives. This can involve identifying and maintaining core values or relationships, even as other aspects of our lives change.
14. *Adjustment can involve learning from past experiences*: Previous experiences of adjustment, whether successful or unsuccessful, can provide valuable insights and skills that can be applied to future challenges.
15. *Adjustment can be influenced by cultural or societal norms*: The expectations and values of our cultural or societal context can impact our ability to adjust to new situations or changes. For example, some cultures may place a greater emphasis on social harmony and conformity, while others may prioritize individualism and autonomy.

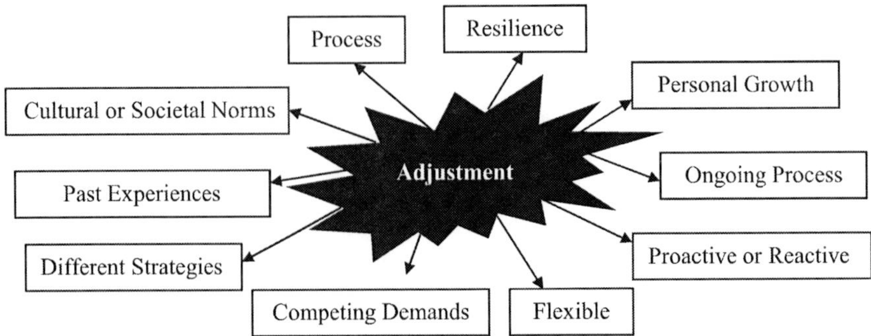

Figure 4.2: *Concept of Adjustment*

16. *Adjustment can involve managing competing demands*: When faced with multiple or conflicting demands, such as work and family responsibilities, adjustment may involve finding ways to balance these demands or prioritize certain areas of our lives.
17. *Adjustment can involve accepting or letting go of things that are beyond our control*: When faced with circumstances that we cannot change, such as a chronic illness or a natural disaster, adjustment may involve accepting these circumstances and finding ways to cope and adapt within them.
18. *Adjustment can be influenced by personal growth and development*: As we grow and develop as individuals, our ability to adjust to new situations and challenges may improve. For example, we may develop greater self-awareness, emotional regulation skills, or interpersonal communication skills that can enhance our ability to adjust.
19. *Adjustment can involve seeking help or support*: When facing difficult or unexpected changes, seeking help or support from friends, family, or professionals can be an important part of the adjustment process. This may involve seeking therapy, joining a support group, or simply talking to a trusted friend or family member.

Overall, adjustment is a complex and dynamic process that requires us to adapt to new situations and circumstances while maintaining a sense of stability and continuity. By developing the skills and strategies to effectively adjust to life's changes and challenges, we can enhance our well-being, personal growth, and resilience.

Nature of Adjustment

Adjustment refers to the ability of an individual to cope with the demands and challenges of their environment in a way that enables them to lead a satisfying and fulfilling life. The process of adjustment involves a range of cognitive, emotional, and behavioural strategies that allow an individual to adapt to changing circumstances and overcome obstacles. Here's a table summarizing the key points about the nature of adjustment:

Nature of Adjustment	*Description*
Dimensions	Adjustment involves multiple dimensions of functioning, including emotional, cognitive, social, and behavioural domains.
Process	Adjustment is a dynamic and ongoing process that involves continual adaptation to new situations and changing circumstances.
Strategies	Effective adjustment requires individuals to engage in a range of cognitive and emotional strategies, such as problem-solving, emotion regulation, and positive thinking.
Individual Factors	The process of adjustment is influenced by a range of individual factors, including personality traits, cognitive abilities, coping skills, and social support.
Environmental Factors	The environment in which individuals live also plays a significant role in the process of adjustment, including social support, economic resources, and cultural norms.
Cultural Factors	Cultural factors play an important role in the process of adjustment, as individuals from different cultures may have different beliefs, values, and coping strategies.
Importance for Well-Being	Effective adjustment is critical for maintaining optimal psychological and physical well-being.
Challenges	The process of adjustment can be challenging and stressful, particularly when individuals are faced with significant life changes or traumatic events.
Lifespan	Adjustment is a lifelong process that continues throughout an individual's lifespan, as they face new challenges and transitions.

Adjustment involves multiple factors and domains of functioning. It requires individuals to balance their autonomy with their need for social connection and support, and to develop a range of coping strategies to adapt to changing circumstances throughout their lifespan. Effective adjustment is critical for maintaining optimal psychological and physical well-being, and for leading a fulfilling and satisfying life.

Need for Adjustment

Adjustment is an important aspect of human life that enables individuals to cope with changes and challenges in their environment. It involves adapting to new situations, managing emotions, building resilience, and maintaining healthy relationships. Whether it is a personal or professional setting, the ability to adjust to new circumstances is critical to success and well-being. The concept of adjustment can be applied to various aspects of life. Here are some points to discuss the need for adjustment:

1. *Changes in Life Circumstances*: Life is unpredictable, and it is essential to adapt to changes in our circumstances. These changes could be related to

personal life, such as a new job, marriage, or the birth of a child. It could also be external factors, such as a pandemic or a significant economic crisis.

2. *Adapting to New Situations*: In many cases, adjusting to a new situation may require learning new skills, developing new habits, or changing our perspective. For example, moving to a new city may require learning the local language or adapting to a new culture.
3. *Managing Emotions*: Adjustment also involves managing emotions. When faced with a difficult situation, it is natural to feel anxiety, fear, or anger. However, it is essential to manage these emotions and find ways to cope effectively.
4. *Building Resilience*: Adjustment is a vital component of building resilience. Resilience is the ability to bounce back from adversity and overcome challenges. By learning how to adjust to new situations, we can become more resilient and better equipped to handle life's ups and downs.
5. *Maintaining Relationships*: Relationships require constant adjustment. As individuals grow and change, so do their needs and expectations. It is essential to adapt to these changes to maintain healthy relationships.
6. *Overcoming Resistance to Change*: Resistance to change is a common phenomenon that can hinder personal growth and development. By embracing the need for adjustment, individuals can overcome resistance to change and be open to new possibilities.
7. *Improving Mental Health*: Failure to adjust to new situations can lead to stress, anxiety, and other mental health issues. By learning how to adjust to new circumstances, individuals can improve their mental well-being and reduce the negative impact of stress.
8. *Enhancing Problem-solving Skills*: Adjusting to new situations involves problem-solving skills. Individuals who can adapt to new circumstances tend to be better problem solvers, which can be beneficial in personal and professional settings.
9. *Achieving Personal Goals*: Adjusting to new situations can help individuals achieve personal goals. By adapting to new circumstances, individuals can overcome obstacles and achieve success in various areas of their lives.
10. *Increasing Self-awareness*: Adjusting to new situations requires self-awareness. By reflecting on their thoughts, emotions, and behaviours, individuals can gain a better understanding of themselves and their environment. This increased self-awareness can lead to personal growth and development.
11. *Increasing Flexibility*: Adjusting to new situations requires flexibility. Individuals who can adjust to new circumstances tend to be more flexible and adaptable, which can be beneficial in personal and professional settings.
12. *Fostering Creativity*: The ability to adjust to new situations can foster creativity. By embracing new ideas and perspectives, individuals can develop innovative solutions to problems.

13. *Enhancing Communication Skills*: Adjusting to new situations requires effective communication skills. By communicating effectively with others, individuals can build better relationships and achieve success in various areas of their lives.
14. *Promoting Growth Mindset*: The need for adjustment can promote a growth mindset. Individuals who embrace the need for adjustment tend to have a growth mindset, which is the belief that skills and abilities can be developed through dedication and hard work.
15. *Navigating Uncertainty*: In today's world, uncertainty is prevalent, and the ability to adjust to new situations is critical to navigating uncertainty. By adapting to new circumstances, individuals can develop the resilience and flexibility needed to navigate uncertainty successfully.

The need for adjustment is multifaceted, and it can have a significant impact on personal and professional growth. By embracing the need for adjustment, individuals can foster creativity, enhance communication skills, promote a growth mindset, and navigate uncertainty successfully. Through effective adaptation, individuals can achieve personal and professional success while maintaining healthy relationships and a positive outlook on life.

Criteria of Good Adjustment

Good adjustment refers to the ability of an individual to cope effectively with the challenges and demands of their environment, including social, emotional, and academic demands. Good adjustment is essential for mental and physical health, social functioning, and overall well-being. Here are some criteria of good adjustment:

1. *Effective Problem-solving Skills*: Individuals who are well-adjusted are able to solve problems effectively. They can identify the problem, come up with possible solutions, and choose the best option. They are also able to evaluate the outcome and modify their approach if necessary.
2. *Positive Self-esteem*: Good adjustment requires a positive self-image and confidence in one's abilities. Individuals with good adjustment have a strong sense of self-worth and feel capable of handling challenges.
3. *Positive Relationships*: Good adjustment also involves positive relationships with others. Individuals who are well-adjusted are able to form and maintain healthy relationships with family, friends, and coworkers. They are also able to communicate effectively, resolve conflicts, and support others.
4. *Adaptability*: The ability to adapt to new situations and changes is crucial for good adjustment. Individuals who are well-adjusted are flexible and can adjust their behaviour, thoughts, and emotions to fit the demands of different situations.
5. *Emotional Regulation*: Good adjustment also involves the ability to manage and regulate emotions effectively. Individuals who are well-adjusted

are able to identify and express their emotions appropriately, as well as regulate their emotions in response to different situations.

6. *Resilience*: Resilience is the ability to bounce back from adversity and overcome challenges. Individuals who are well-adjusted are resilient and can cope effectively with stress and setbacks.
7. *Autonomy*: Individuals who are well-adjusted have a sense of independence and control over their lives. They are able to make decisions and take responsibility for their actions, while also seeking support and guidance when needed.
8. *Open-mindedness*: Good adjustment involves being open-minded and receptive to new ideas and perspectives. Individuals who are well-adjusted are willing to consider different viewpoints and are not resistant to change.
9. *Goal-directed Behaviour*: Individuals who are well-adjusted have clear goals and are motivated to achieve them. They are able to prioritize tasks, manage their time effectively, and work towards their goals with focus and determination.
10. *Pro-social Behaviour*: Good adjustment also involves being caring and compassionate towards others. Individuals who are well-adjusted engage in pro-social behaviours, such as volunteering, helping others, and showing empathy and kindness.
11. *Sense of Purpose*: Individuals who are well-adjusted have a sense of purpose and meaning in their lives. They have a clear sense of direction and are motivated by a larger goal or mission.
12. *Positive Coping Strategies*: Good adjustment also involves using positive coping strategies to manage stress and adversity. Individuals who are well-adjusted engage in activities that promote relaxation and self-care, such as exercise, meditation, or spending time with loved ones.
13. *Self-awareness*: Individuals who are well-adjusted have a high level of self-awareness. They are able to recognize their strengths and weaknesses, understand their emotions and motivations, and reflect on their experiences.
14. *Effective Communication*: Good adjustment also involves effective communication skills. Individuals who are well-adjusted are able to express themselves clearly and listen actively to others. They are able to communicate their needs and desires while also being respectful of others' perspectives.
15. *Sense of Humour*: Good adjustment involves having a sense of humour and the ability to find joy and laughter in life. Individuals who are well-adjusted are able to see the lighter side of situations and find ways to make others smile.
16. *Cultural Competence*: In a diverse world, good adjustment involves being culturally competent and respectful of different cultures, beliefs, and values. Individuals who are well-adjusted are able to interact effectively with people from different backgrounds and adapt to new cultural environments.

17. *Time Management*: Good adjustment also involves effective time management skills. Individuals who are well-adjusted are able to balance their responsibilities and priorities effectively, while also maintaining a healthy work-life balance.
18. *Self-care*: Individuals who are well-adjusted engage in self-care activities that promote physical, emotional, and mental well-being. They prioritize their own health and well-being and take steps to reduce stress and promote relaxation.

Overall, good adjustment requires a combination of personal and interpersonal skills, including self-awareness, effective communication, time management, and self-care. By cultivating these skills, individuals can develop a sense of resilience and adaptability that enables them to thrive in a variety of situations and environments.

Defence Mechanism

Meaning of Defence Mechanism

Defence mechanisms refer to psychological strategies or behaviours that individuals use unconsciously to protect themselves from unpleasant or threatening thoughts, emotions, or situations. These mechanisms can operate at an unconscious level, so people are often unaware of their use.

Defence mechanisms can be adaptive or maladaptive. Adaptive defence mechanisms help individuals deal with stress and maintain their psychological well-being. Examples of adaptive defence mechanisms include humour, sublimation, and altruism.

On the other hand, maladaptive defence mechanisms can cause problems in the long term. They may prevent individuals from dealing effectively with reality and lead to negative consequences such as anxiety, depression, and relationship problems. Examples of maladaptive defence mechanisms include denial, repression, and projection.

Definitions of Defence Mechanism

Defence mechanisms are psychological processes that operate unconsciously, and their function is to protect individuals from anxiety and other unpleasant emotions. These mechanisms are commonly used by individuals to reduce stress, tension, and conflict, and they allow the individual to cope with their problems and difficulties. Psychologists have put forth different definitions of defence mechanisms over time, and here are some of them:

Sigmund Freud was the first psychologist to introduce the concept of defence mechanisms. According to him, defence mechanisms are unconscious mental processes that protect individuals from anxiety and other unpleasant emotions. These mechanisms involve denying or distorting reality to protect the individual from anxiety and distress.

Anna Freud, Sigmund Freud's daughter, further developed the concept of defence mechanisms. According to her, defence mechanisms are unconscious mental processes that operate automatically to protect individuals from anxiety and other unpleasant emotions. She believed that defence mechanisms were a normal part of human development and that they played a critical role in personality development.

George Vaillant, an American psychiatrist, defined defence mechanisms as unconscious processes that protect individuals from anxiety and other unpleasant emotions by distorting reality. He believed that defence mechanisms were essential for maintaining psychological health and that they helped individuals to adapt to changing circumstances.

Karen Horney, a German psychoanalyst, defined defence mechanisms as strategies used by individuals to protect themselves from anxiety and other unpleasant emotions. She believed that defence mechanisms were shaped by early childhood experiences and that individuals used them to cope with feelings of helplessness and vulnerability.

Otto Kernberg, an American psychoanalyst, defined defence mechanisms as unconscious mental processes that help individuals to cope with conflict and stress. According to him, defence mechanisms involve a range of behaviours, from denial and repression to more pathological behaviours such as splitting and projection.

Defence mechanisms are an essential part of human psychology that help individuals to cope with stress, anxiety, and other unpleasant emotions. Different psychologists have defined defence mechanisms in different ways, but they all agree that these mechanisms operate unconsciously and play a critical role in personality development and psychological well-being.

Different Methods of Defence Mechanism

Defence mechanisms are psychological strategies that are used by people unconsciously to protect themselves from anxiety or emotional pain. These mechanisms are developed as a way to cope with difficult or uncomfortable situations, and they serve to protect the individual's ego. There are several different methods of defence mechanisms, and each one operates in a slightly different way.

1. *Denial*: This defence mechanism involves a person refusing to accept the reality of a situation or event. Denial can be a way to avoid dealing with a difficult situation or accepting responsibility for one's actions.
   Example: a person who is struggling with alcohol addiction may deny that they have a problem and insist that they can stop drinking whenever they want.
2. *Repression*: Repression involves pushing unwanted thoughts, memories, or feelings out of conscious awareness. This defence mechanism can be a way to protect oneself from painful or traumatic experiences.
   Example: a person who has experienced sexual abuse may repress memories of the abuse in order to avoid the associated emotional pain.

3. *Projection*: Projection involves attributing one's own unacceptable thoughts or feelings to someone else. This defence mechanism can be a way to avoid accepting responsibility for one's own thoughts or actions.
   Example: a person who is dishonest may accuse others of being untrustworthy.
4. *Rationalization*: Rationalization involves justifying one's behaviour or actions with seemingly logical reasons. This defence mechanism can be a way to avoid acknowledging one's own mistakes or faults.
   Example: a person who cheats on their partner may rationalize their behaviour by saying that their partner was neglectful or emotionally distant.
5. *Displacement*: Displacement involves redirecting one's emotions or impulses onto a less threatening target. This defence mechanism can be a way to avoid confronting the source of one's emotions or impulses.
   Example: a person who is angry with their boss may take out their frustration on a family member or friend.
6. *Regression*: Regression involves reverting to childlike behaviourin order to cope with stress or anxiety. This defence mechanism can be a way to seek comfort or support from others.
   Example: a person who is under a lot of stress at work may start sucking their thumb or engaging in other childish behaviours.
7. *Sublimation*: Sublimation involves channeling unacceptable impulses or behaviours into socially acceptable activities. This defence mechanism can be a way to express one's emotions or impulses in a productive way.
   Example: a person who has a history of violence may channel their aggression into competitive sports or other physically demanding activities.
8. *Intellectualization*: Intellectualization involves analyzing a situation or event in an overly rational or detached manner in order to avoid confronting the associated emotional pain. This defence mechanism can be a way to maintain a sense of control over a difficult situation.
   Example: a person who has just been diagnosed with cancer may focus solely on the medical details and statistics rather than acknowledging the emotional impact of the diagnosis.
9. *Fantasy*: Fantasy involves creating an imaginary world or scenario in order to escape from reality. This defence mechanism can be a way to cope with a difficult situation or to fulfill unmet emotional needs.
   Example: a person who is unhappy in their relationship may daydream about a perfect, idealized partner.
10. *Compensation*: Compensation involves overachieving in one area in order to make up for perceived deficiencies in another area. This defence mechanism can be a way to boost self-esteem or compensate for feelings of inadequacy.
    Example: a person who is not very athletic may become an overachiever in academics or career.

11. *Suppression*: Suppression involves consciously choosing to push unwanted thoughts, emotions, or memories out of one's awareness. This defence mechanism can be a temporary way to cope with a difficult situation, but it can also lead to repressed emotions and unresolved issues.
    Example: a person who is about to give a presentation may consciously suppress feelings of anxiety in order to focus on the task at hand.
12. *Undoing*: Undoing involves attempting to make up for a perceived mistake or wrongdoing through symbolic actions or gestures. This defence mechanism can be a way to alleviate guilt or anxiety.
    Example: a person who is feeling guilty about not spending enough time with their children may buy them expensive gifts as a way to "make up" for their perceived neglect.
13. *Humour*: Humour involves using laughter or jokes to diffuse a difficult or uncomfortable situation. This defence mechanism can be a way to cope with stress or to avoid confronting uncomfortable emotions.
    Example: a person who is nervous about a job interview may use humour to make light of the situation and ease their anxiety.
14. *Idealization*: Idealization involves attributing exaggerated positive qualities to oneself or to another person. This defence mechanism can be a way to boost self-esteem or to avoid acknowledging flaws or faults.
    Example: a person who is attracted to a romantic partner may idealize them as perfect, ignoring any negative qualities or behaviours.
15. *Passive Aggression*: Passive aggression involves expressing aggression or anger in an indirect or passive way. This defence mechanism can be a way to avoid direct confrontation or to maintain a sense of control over a difficult situation.
    Example: a person who is angry with their roommate for leaving a mess in the kitchen may leave a passive-aggressive note instead of confronting them directly.
16. *Intellectual Aggression*: Intellectual aggression involves using intellectual arguments or criticisms to attack or undermine another person's self-esteem or beliefs. This defence mechanism can be a way to avoid acknowledging one's own emotional vulnerabilities or insecurities.
    Example: a person who is feeling insecure about their intelligence may criticize others for being ignorant or uninformed.
17. *Acting Out*: Acting out involves expressing one's emotions or impulses through behaviour rather than words or thoughts. This defence mechanism can be a way to cope with stress or to seek attention or validation.
    Example: a child who is feeling neglected may act in order to get their parents' attention.

It's important to remember that defence mechanisms are not necessarily conscious or deliberate, and that they can serve a protective function in helping individuals cope with difficult situations or emotions. However, if defence mechanisms become entrenched or maladaptive, they can interfere with emotional growth and interpersonal relationships. Seeking the support of a mental health professional can help individuals identify and work through their defence mechanisms in a healthy and productive way.

Role of Family, Teachers, Friends and School in Effective Adjustment

The ability to adjust to new situations is a fundamental life skill that helps individuals to cope with changes and challenges. Effective adjustment requires the development of emotional resilience, problem-solving skills, and social competence. While individuals are ultimately responsible for their own adjustment, the social context in which they develop plays an important role in shaping their ability to adapt to new situations. Family, teachers, friends, and school are some of the most significant social factors that contribute to an individual's ability to adjust effectively.

Role of Family in Effective Adjustment

The concept of effective adjustment refers to an individual's ability to adapt to different situations and environments while maintaining a stable and healthy mental state. It is a crucial aspect of an individual's overall well-being and success in life. While there are several factors that contribute to effective adjustment, the role of family is critical. The family is the primary source of socialization, emotional support, and guidance for individuals, and it plays a significant role in their ability to adjust effectively to different situations. The family plays a critical role in an individual's effective adjustment. Here are some points to discuss this role:

1. *Emotional Support*: A family provides emotional support to an individual, which is essential for their adjustment. When someone is going through a difficult time, having a supportive family can help them cope with the situation and make them feel less alone.
2. *Sense of Belonging*: The family provides a sense of belonging to an individual, which is necessary for their social and emotional development. It also helps them develop a strong sense of identity, which is essential for their adjustment in different social settings.
3. *Socialization*: The family is the primary agent of socialization, where individuals learn social norms, values, and beliefs. Effective socialization helps individuals adjust to different social settings and make appropriate decisions in different situations.
4. *Financial Support*: The family provides financial support to individuals, which is essential for their adjustment. Financial stability helps individuals lead a comfortable life and adjust to different life situations.
5. *Education and Career Guidance*: The family plays a crucial role in an individual's education and career guidance. Providing guidance and support to an individual in these areas can help them make better decisions, achieve their goals, and adjust effectively to different professional environments.

6. *Conflict Resolution*: Conflicts are a part of any relationship, and the family is no exception. However, effective conflict resolution strategies can help individuals adjust to different situations, manage stress, and build stronger relationships.
7. *Role Modeling*: The family is an essential source of role modeling for individuals. Family members often model behaviours and attitudes that influence an individual's behaviour and attitude towards different situations. Positive role modeling can help individuals develop adaptive coping mechanisms, problem-solving skills, and resilience, which are essential for effective adjustment.
8. *Social Support*: Family members provide social support to individuals, which can help them cope with stress, anxiety, and other mental health issues. Social support can be in the form of practical assistance, emotional support, or just being there for someone to talk to. Having a supportive family can make a significant difference in an individual's ability to adjust effectively to different situations.
9. *Cultural and Religious Identity*: The family is often the primary source of cultural and religious identity for individuals. Cultural and religious identity can play a significant role in an individual's sense of self and their ability to adjust effectively to different cultural and social settings.
10. *Attachment*: Attachment is the emotional bond that develops between individuals, and the family is the primary source of attachment for most individuals. Attachment provides a sense of security, safety, and comfort, which is essential for an individual's overall well-being and their ability to adjust effectively to different situations.
11. *Communication*: Effective communication within a family is essential for an individual's ability to adjust effectively to different situations. Clear communication can help individuals express their needs, feelings, and opinions, and it can also help resolve conflicts and build stronger relationships.

The family's role in an individual's effective adjustment is multifaceted, and it includes emotional support, socialization, financial support, education and career guidance, conflict resolution, role modeling, social support, cultural and religious identity, attachment, and communication. Therefore, maintaining strong family ties and nurturing relationships is crucial for an individual's overall well-being and their ability to adjust effectively to different situations.

Role of Teachers in Effective Adjustment of Their Students

Effective adjustment is essential for an individual's success and well-being. As agents of socialization, teachers play a crucial role in their students' effective adjustment. In addition to providing academic instruction, teachers have the opportunity to support their students' social, emotional, and psychological development. Teachers can create a positive learning environment, provide academic and emotional support, encourage self-reflection and self-awareness, and promote resilience. By fulfilling these roles, teachers can help their students adjust effectively to different social and academic settings, develop the skills and knowledge necessary for success, and achieve their goals. In this essay, we will explore the critical role of teachers in their students' effective adjustment and strategies that teachers can use to support their students' adjustment. Teachers play a critical role in an individual's effective adjustment. Here are some points to discuss this role:

1. *Creating a Positive Learning Environment*: A positive learning environment is essential for an individual's effective adjustment. Teachers can create a positive learning environment by encouraging positive interactions between students, providing constructive feedback, and promoting a growth mindset.
2. *Academic Support*: Teachers provide academic support to their students, which is essential for their adjustment. By providing clear instructions, feedback, and guidance, teachers help students develop the skills and knowledge necessary for academic success.
3. *Socialization*: Teachers are a primary agent of socialization, where students learn social norms, values, and beliefs. Teachers can help students adjust to different social settings and promote positive social interactions.
4. *Emotional Support*: Teachers can provide emotional support to their students, which is crucial for their adjustment. Teachers can create a safe space for students to express their emotions, provide encouragement and support, and refer students to appropriate resources if necessary.
5. *Encouraging Self-reflection and Self-awareness*: Teachers can encourage their students to engage in self-reflection and self-awareness, which is essential for effective adjustment. By encouraging students to reflect on their strengths and weaknesses, set goals, and monitor their progress, teachers can help students develop a strong sense of self and make appropriate decisions in different situations.
6. *Providing Guidance and Mentorship*: Teachers can provide guidance and mentorship to their students, which is essential for their adjustment. By providing guidance on academic and personal matters, teachers can help students navigate challenges, make informed decisions, and achieve their goals.
7. *Promoting Resilience*: Teachers can promote resilience in their students by teaching them coping mechanisms and problem-solving skills. By helping students develop resilience, teachers can prepare them to adjust effectively to different situations and overcome challenges.
8. *Providing a Sense of Belonging*: Teachers can create a sense of belonging in their classroom by fostering a positive and inclusive classroom culture. They can facilitate meaningful interactions among students, promote

empathy, and encourage mutual respect, which can help students feel connected to their classmates and school community.

9. *Supporting Students with Special Needs*: Teachers play a critical role in supporting students with special needs, such as those with disabilities or learning differences. They can adapt instruction, provide accommodations, and offer emotional support to ensure that these students have equal access to education and feel included in the classroom.
10. *Encouraging Cultural Sensitivity*: Teachers can promote cultural sensitivity and awareness by creating opportunities for students to learn about different cultures and perspectives. By incorporating diverse perspectives and experiences into their teaching, teachers can help students develop empathy and understanding towards others, which can facilitate effective adjustment in multicultural settings.
11. *Encouraging Self-advocacy*: Teachers can encourage their students to become advocates for themselves by developing their communication and self-advocacy skills. By teaching students how to express their needs and seek help, when necessary, teachers can empower them to take control of their education and personal development.
12. *Monitoring and Addressing Behavioural Issues*: Teachers can play a critical role in identifying and addressing behavioural issues that can impact their students' adjustment. By recognizing and addressing these issues promptly, teachers can help prevent negative consequences, such as poor academic performance, low self-esteem, and social isolation.
13. *Providing Mentorship and Role Modeling*: Teachers can serve as positive role models and mentors to their students, providing guidance and support beyond the classroom. By modeling positive behaviours and attitudes, teachers can help students develop healthy habits, coping strategies, and problem-solving skills that can facilitate effective adjustment in various contexts.

Teachers play a multifaceted role in supporting their students' effective adjustment. By creating a positive learning environment, providing academic and emotional support, encouraging self-reflection and self-awareness, promoting resilience, fostering a sense of belonging, supporting students with special needs, encouraging cultural sensitivity, encouraging self-advocacy, monitoring and addressing behavioural issues, and providing mentorship and role modeling, teachers can help their students adjust effectively to different social and academic settings.

Role of Friends in Effective Adjustment

Effective adjustment is crucial for an individual's personal and social development. Friends play a significant role in this process, especially during adolescence and young adulthood, where individuals seek to establish their identity and navigate social relationships. Friends can provide emotional support, offer guidance and advice, facilitate social connections, and promote healthy behaviours and attitudes. Here are some points to discuss this role:

1. *Emotional Support*: Friends can provide emotional support during times of stress, anxiety, or disappointment. They can listen, offer empathy and validation, and provide practical assistance when needed. This support can promote resilience and help individuals cope with the challenges of life.
2. *Guidance and Advice*: Friends can offer guidance and advice on a range of issues, from academic and career choices to personal relationships and decision-making. They can provide different perspectives and help individuals weigh their options, make informed choices, and pursue their goals.
3. *Social Connections*: Friends can facilitate social connections by introducing individuals to new people, inviting them to social events, and providing opportunities for socialization. These connections can expand an individual's social network and help them feel more connected to their community.
4. *Healthy Behaviours and Attitudes*: Friends can influence an individual's behaviours and attitudes, both positively and negatively. Positive friendships can promote healthy behaviours such as regular exercise, healthy eating, and avoidance of risky behaviours. They can also promote positive attitudes, such as optimism, gratitude, and a sense of purpose.
5. *Challenges of Friendship*: Despite the benefits of friendship, maintaining healthy relationships can be challenging. Friends may have different expectations, values, and interests that can create tension and conflict. They may also experience changes in their lives, such as moving away, that can strain the friendship.
6. *Factors that Influence Friendship Quality*: Several factors can influence the quality of friendships, including shared interests, communication, trust, reciprocity, and conflict resolution skills. The quality of friendships can also be influenced by external factors such as cultural norms and social support networks.
7. *Strategies for Building and Maintaining Healthy Friendships*: To build and maintain healthy friendships, individuals can practiseactive listening, express empathy and understanding, communicate openly and honestly, set boundaries, and seek support when needed. They can also engage in activities that promote shared interests, participate in community events, and prioritize quality time with friends.
8. *Peer Acceptance*: During adolescence and young adulthood, peer acceptance and belongingness are critical for effective adjustment. Friends can provide a sense of acceptance and belongingness that can improve an individual's self-esteem, self-worth, and social identity.
9. *Coping Skills*: Friends can provide coping skills and problem-solving strategies that can help individuals deal with stress and adversity. They can model healthy coping behaviours, offer constructive feedback, and provide emotional support during difficult times.

10. *Diversity and Inclusion*: Friends can expose individuals to diverse perspectives, experiences, and cultures, which can broaden their horizons and promote tolerance and inclusion. Positive friendships can also challenge negative stereotypes and biases and promote social justice and equity.
11. *Romantic Relationships*: Romantic relationships are an essential aspect of social development and adjustment. Friends can provide guidance and support during the pursuit of romantic relationships, offer feedback and advice on relationship issues, and provide emotional support during breakups or conflicts.
12. *Personal Growth*: Positive friendships can foster personal growth and development by providing opportunities for self-discovery, self-expression, and personal exploration. Friends can encourage individuals to pursue their passions, take risks, and embrace their strengths and weaknesses.

The role of friends in effective adjustment is multifaceted and complex. By providing emotional support, guidance and advice, social connections, healthy behaviours and attitudes, peer acceptance, coping skills, diversity and inclusion, and support during romantic relationships, friendships can contribute significantly to personal and social development. To build and maintain healthy friendships, individuals can practice effective communication, empathy, and understanding, engage in activities that promote shared interests and socialization, and seek support when needed.

Role of School in Effective Adjustment

Adjustment is a process that all individuals go through to cope with changes, challenges, and transitions in their lives. Effective adjustment is crucial for success in various areas of life, such as academics, relationships, and career. The school environment plays a significant role in facilitating effective adjustment in students. The school provides a structured environment that promotes socialization, emotional regulation, and academic success. School plays a crucial role in facilitating effective adjustment in students. Here are some ways in which school can promote positive adjustment:

1. *Providing a Structured Environment*: Schools provide a structured environment that helps students learn essential skills such as time management, organization, and socialization. These skills are critical for effective adjustment to school and beyond.
2. *Developing Social Skills*: School offers an excellent opportunity for students to interact and socialize with their peers. Students learn social skills, such as communication, empathy, and teamwork, through group work, extracurricular activities, and sports.
3. *Encouraging Emotional Regulation*: Schools also help students develop emotional regulation skills. Teachers and school counselors can teach students strategies to manage stress, anxiety, and other negative emotions.

4. *Fostering Positive Relationships*: Positive relationships with teachers and peers can promote positive adjustment. Teachers who create supportive and nurturing classroom environments can help students feel safe and secure in their learning environments.
5. *Promoting Academic Success*: School success can also contribute to positive adjustment. Students who are successful in school may have higher self-esteem, stronger academic skills, and better problem-solving abilities, which can all help them navigate challenges and transitions more effectively.
6. *Encouraging Independence*: Schools can also help students develop independence by promoting self-reliance and autonomy. This can include giving students opportunities to make decisions, take responsibility for their actions, and develop their problem-solving skills.
7. *Providing Supportive Resources*: Schools can provide students with supportive resources, such as counseling services, academic support, and extracurricular activities, to help them cope with challenges and build resilience.
8. *Fostering a Sense of Community*: Schools can also foster a sense of community and belonging among students. This can help students feel connected to their school and peers, which can improve their overall well-being and academic performance.
9. *Addressing Diversity and Inclusion*: Schools can also promote effective adjustment by addressing diversity and inclusion. By acknowledging and celebrating differences among students, schools can create a more accepting and inclusive environment that supports positive adjustment for all students.
10. *Offering Opportunities for Exploration*: Schools can provide opportunities for students to explore their interests and passions through elective courses, clubs, and extracurricular activities. This can help students develop a sense of identity and purpose, which can contribute to positive adjustment.
11. *Promoting Physical and Mental Health*: Schools can also promote physical and mental health by offering physical education classes, healthy meal options, and mental health support services. This can help students feel physically and mentally well, which can improve their overall well-being and academic performance.
12. *Providing Clear Expectations*: Schools can provide clear expectations for behaviour and academic performance. This can help students understand what is expected of them and feel more confident in their ability to meet those expectations, which can contribute to positive adjustment.
13. *Encouraging Parent Involvement*: Schools can also encourage parent involvement in students' education. This can include parent-teacher conferences, volunteering opportunities, and communication with parents about students' progress. When parents are involved in their child's education, it can help support positive adjustment.

14. *Responding to Student Needs*: Schools can respond to students' individual needs by providing accommodations for students with disabilities, offering additional support for struggling students, and recognizing students' strengths and talents. This can help students feel valued and supported, which can contribute to positive adjustment.

Schools can promote effective adjustment in students by offering opportunities for exploration, promoting physical and mental health, providing clear expectations, encouraging parent involvement, and responding to student needs. By providing a supportive environment that promotes growth and development, schools can help students navigate the challenges of growing up and prepare them for success in various areas of life.

Relationship between Mental Hygiene and Adjustment

Mental hygiene and adjustment are two critical components of overall mental health and well-being. Mental hygiene refers to the practice of maintaining a healthy and balanced mental state, while adjustment involves an individual's ability to cope with and adapt to various situations and circumstances in life. Both mental hygiene and adjustment are interdependent, and neglecting either area can lead to negative outcomes in both areas. Good mental hygiene practices can enhance an individual's ability to adjust and cope with challenging situations, leading to greater resilience and emotional stability. Similarly, good adjustment skills can contribute to better mental health and well-being, as well as improved social and occupational functioning. Let's discuss the relationship between mental hygiene and adjustment in more detail:

Subject	*Mental Hygiene*	*Adjustment*
Definition	Mental hygiene refers to the practice of maintaining a healthy and balanced mental state.	Adjustment refers to the ability of an individual to cope with and adapt to various situations and circumstances in life.
Importance	Mental hygiene helps individuals to maintain a positive outlook on life, reduce stress, and improve overall well-being.	Adjustment helps individuals to feel more confident, self-assured, and in control of their lives.
Examples	Examples of mental hygiene practices include meditation, exercise, seeking professional help, and practising good sleep hygiene.	Examples of adjustment skills include developing coping skills, problem-solving skills, and social skills to navigate challenges effectively.
Relationship	Good mental hygiene practices can enhance an individual's ability to adjust and cope with challenging situations, leading to greater resilience and emotional stability.	Good adjustment skills can contribute to better mental health and well-being, as well as improved social and occupational functioning.

Subject	*Mental Hygiene*	*Adjustment*
Consequences of Poor Practice	Poor mental hygiene can lead to the development of mental health disorders such as anxiety, depression, and substance abuse.	Poor adjustment can lead to difficulties in relationships, work, and other areas of life.
Interdependence	Mental hygiene and adjustment are closely related, with good mental hygiene practices contributing to better adjustment and overall well-being.	Individuals who have good adjustment skills are more likely to maintain good mental hygiene.
Activities	Activities that promote good mental hygiene include self-reflection, mindfulness, seeking social support, and practising self-care.	Activities that promote good adjustment include problem-solving, seeking help when needed, practising effective communication, and developing healthy coping mechanisms.

The relationship between mental hygiene and adjustment is crucial for overall mental health and well-being. Good mental hygiene practices can help individuals maintain a positive outlook on life, reduce stress, and improve overall well-being, while good adjustment skills can help individuals feel more confident, self-assured, and in control of their lives. The interdependence between mental hygiene and adjustment highlights the importance of prioritizing both areas to promote overall mental health and well-being. Neglecting either area can lead to negative outcomes in both areas, such as the development of mental health disorders, difficulties in relationships, work, and other areas of life. Therefore, it is essential to encourage and promote good mental hygiene practices and adjustment skills to support individuals' overall mental health and well-being.

5

Maladjustment

Meaning of Maladjustment

The word 'Maladjustment' is derived from two Latin words, 'Malus' meaning 'Bad'or 'Ill' and 'Adiustare'meaning 'To Put Right' or 'To Make Straight'. So, the term 'Maladjustment' literally means 'Badly Adjusted' or 'Poorly Regulated'.

The term was first used in psychology in the early 20thcentury to describe individuals who had difficulty adapting to social and environmental demands. Since then, it has become a widely used term in the field of psychology and is commonly used to describe the inability to cope with stress and adjust to changes in one's environment.

Maladjustment refers to an inability to adapt or cope with changes or challenges in one's environment, which can lead to difficulties in personal and social functioning. It is a condition where an individual's behaviour, thoughts, and emotions are out of sync with their environment, leading to problems in daily life.

Maladjustment can manifest in various ways, such as social withdrawal, aggression, anxiety, depression, substance abuse, or academic underachievement. It can be caused by various factors, including biological, psychological, social, and environmental factors, such as trauma, family conflict, cultural dissonance, or physical or mental illness.

Maladjustment is often seen in individuals who are unable to cope with stress and may have difficulty in forming and maintaining relationships with

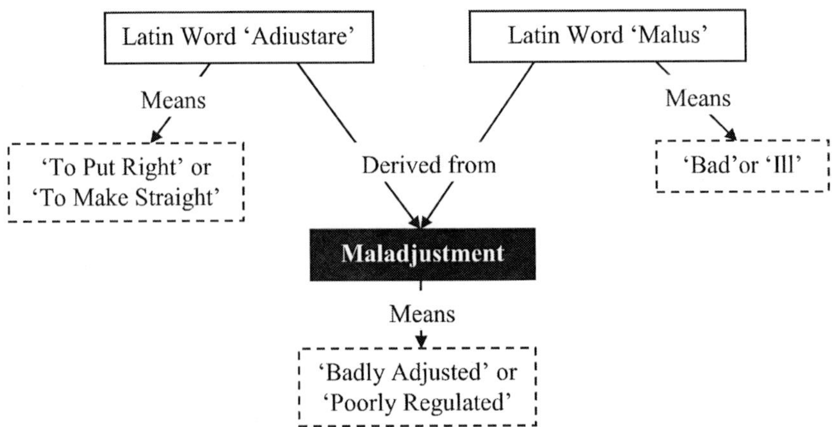

Figure 5.1: *Etymological Meaning of Maladjustment*

others. It can lead to feelings of isolation and low self-esteem, which can further exacerbate the problem. Maladjustment can be treated through various therapeutic interventions, including counseling, cognitive-behavioural therapy, and medication.

Causes of Maladjustment

Maladjustment refers to a state of psychological or emotional imbalance, where an individual experiences difficulty in coping with various aspects of life, such as relationships, work, or social situations. It can be caused by a variety of factors, including internal and external influences. Here are some causes of maladjustment:

1. *Early Life Experiences*: Adverse experiences during childhood, such as trauma, neglect, abuse, or inconsistent parenting, can significantly impact a person's ability to develop healthy coping mechanisms. These experiences may lead to feelings of insecurity, low self-esteem, and difficulty forming trusting relationships, resulting in maladjustment later in life.
2. *Genetic and Biological Factors*: Some individuals may be predisposed to maladjustment due to genetic or biological factors. Certain mental health conditions, such as anxiety disorders, depression, or personality disorders, can have a biological basis and contribute to difficulties in adapting to life's challenges.
3. *Environmental Factors*: The environment in which a person grows up and lives plays a crucial role in their adjustment. Factors such as poverty, violence, discrimination, unstable family dynamics, or living in a high-stress environment can all contribute to maladjustment. Limited access to educational opportunities or supportive social networks can also hinder an individual's ability to adapt effectively.
4. *Major Life Transitions*: Significant life changes, such as divorce, relocation, loss of a loved one, or career changes, can disrupt an individual's sense of stability and lead to maladjustment. These transitions often require individuals to adapt to new circumstances, and if they lack the necessary coping skills or support, they may struggle to adjust successfully.
5. *Social and Cultural Factors*: Social and cultural factors can influence an individual's sense of belonging and acceptance within their community or society. Discrimination, prejudice, marginalization, or cultural clashes can create stress and emotional strain, contributing to maladjustment. Lack of social support or a sense of isolation can also impact an individual's ability to adjust to their social environment.
6. *Personal Factors*: Individual characteristics, such as personality traits, temperament, or cognitive patterns, can influence maladjustment. For example, individuals with perfectionistic tendencies may struggle with high levels of stress and anxiety, making it challenging for them to adapt to changes or setbacks.

7. *Lack of Coping Skills*: Insufficient or ineffective coping mechanisms can contribute to maladjustment. If individuals lack problem-solving skills, emotional regulation techniques, or the ability to seek support, they may struggle to navigate difficult situations and experience maladaptive responses.
8. *Chronic Stress*: Prolonged exposure to high levels of stress, whether due to work, personal relationships, financial difficulties, or other factors, can significantly impact a person's mental and emotional well-being. Chronic stress can lead to feelings of overwhelm, burnout, and difficulty in adapting to new circumstances, resulting in maladjustment.
9. *Substance Abuse*: Substance abuse, including alcohol and drug addiction, can contribute to maladjustment. Substance abuse often masks underlying emotional or psychological issues and can impair an individual's ability to function effectively in various areas of life, including work, relationships, and self-care.
10. *Unrealistic Expectations*: Placing excessively high or unrealistic expectations on oneself or constantly comparing oneself to others can create a sense of inadequacy and frustration. This self-imposed pressure can lead to maladjustment as individuals struggle to meet these unattainable standards and experience disappointment or a loss of self-esteem.
11. *Lack of Boundaries*: Difficulties in establishing and maintaining healthy personal boundaries can contribute to maladjustment. This can manifest as either overly rigid boundaries, leading to isolation and difficulty forming connections, or porous boundaries, resulting in being overwhelmed by others' demands and losing one's sense of self.
12. *Traumatic Events*: Exposure to traumatic events, such as accidents, natural disasters, or witnessing violence, can have a profound impact on an individual's mental well-being. Post-traumatic stress disorder (PTSD) can develop, leading to maladjustment as the person experiences intrusive thoughts, flashbacks, and heightened anxiety that interfere with their daily functioning.
13. *Lack of Social Skills*: Inadequate social skills, such as poor communication, difficulty in expressing emotions, or lacking assertiveness, can hinder an individual's ability to establish and maintain healthy relationships. This social incompetence can contribute to feelings of isolation, loneliness, and maladjustment in social settings.
14. *Cultural or Gender Expectations*: Societal and cultural norms, as well as gender expectations, can impose pressures and limitations on individuals. Trying to conform to rigid societal standards or struggling with gender identity issues can lead to internal conflict, low self-esteem, and difficulties in adapting to social and cultural expectations.
15. *Negative Thought Patterns*: Persistent negative thought patterns, such as self-criticism, catastrophizing, or excessive worry, can contribute to

maladjustment. These cognitive patterns can perpetuate a negative cycle, impair problem-solving abilities, and undermine self-confidence, making it challenging to adapt to life's challenges effectively.

16. *Lack of Emotional Regulation*: Difficulties in managing and regulating emotions can contribute to maladjustment. Individuals who struggle with intense emotions, such as anger, sadness, or anxiety, may find it challenging to navigate interpersonal relationships or cope with everyday stressors, leading to maladaptive behaviours and difficulties in adapting to different situations.
17. *Negative or Dysfunctional Family Dynamics*: Growing up in a family environment characterized by conflict, unhealthy communication patterns, neglect, or dysfunctional relationships can impact an individual's ability to form healthy attachments and develop effective coping strategies. These negative family dynamics can contribute to maladjustment, as individuals may carry these patterns into their adult lives.
18. *Academic or Occupational Challenges*: Difficulties in academic or occupational settings, such as academic underachievement, constant job dissatisfaction, or unemployment, can contribute to maladjustment. These challenges may lead to feelings of inadequacy, lowered self-esteem, and a lack of fulfillment, making it difficult to adapt and thrive in these areas.
19. *Lack of Autonomy or Control*: Feeling a lack of control or autonomy over one's own life can contribute to maladjustment. This can occur in situations where individuals feel trapped in unfulfilling jobs, relationships, or living conditions, or when they perceive a lack of agency in making decisions that affect their lives. This loss of control can lead to a sense of helplessness and maladjustment.
20. *Medical or Physical Conditions*: Chronic physical illnesses, disabilities, or debilitating medical conditions can significantly impact an individual's quality of life and contribute to maladjustment. The physical limitations, pain, or emotional distress associated with these conditions can challenge a person's ability to adapt to their circumstances and engage in activities they once enjoyed.
21. *Lack of Self-identity or Purpose*: A lack of self-identity or a sense of purpose in life can contribute to maladjustment. When individuals struggle to define their values, interests, or long-term goals, they may experience feelings of emptiness, confusion, or a lack of direction, which can hinder their ability to adapt to various aspects of life.
22. *Cultural or Societal Changes*: Rapid cultural or societal changes can lead to maladjustment, particularly when individuals struggle to adapt to new norms, values, or social expectations. Societal shifts, technological advancements, or changes in social structures can create a sense of disconnection or disorientation, resulting in maladjustment.

It's essential to recognize that these causes of maladjustment are not exhaustive, and individual experiences can be influenced by a combination of factors. Addressing maladjustment often requires a comprehensive assessment of the individual's unique circumstances and tailoring appropriate interventions to support their emotional well-being and adaptive functioning.

Different Forms of Maladjustment

Maladjustment is a psychological state that signifies an individual's inability to effectively adapt to and function within their social, marital, or occupational spheres. It encompasses a range of challenges that hinder one's ability to establish fulfilling relationships, maintain a harmonious marriage, or thrive in a work environment. It can manifest in different forms, such as social maladjustment, marital maladjustment, and occupational maladjustment. Let's discuss each of these forms and their elaboration:

1. **Social Maladjustment:** Social maladjustment refers to an individual's inability to adapt and function effectively in social situations or within a community. Here are some key points and elaborations:
   a) *Difficulty in forming relationships*: Socially maladjusted individuals may struggle to establish and maintain healthy relationships with others. They may face challenges in understanding social cues, norms, and appropriate behaviour, leading to isolation and feelings of loneliness.
   b) *Poor social skills*: These individuals may lack essential social skills, such as effective communication, active listening, and empathy. As a result, they may have difficulty engaging in conversations, resolving conflicts, or participating in group activities.
   c) *Social anxiety*: Social maladjustment can also be associated with social anxiety, which is characterized by intense fear or discomfort in social situations. This anxiety can hinder individuals from participating in social gatherings or public events, leading to avoidance behaviours.
   d) *Alienation and rejection*: Socially maladjusted individuals may feel alienated and rejected by their peers or society due to their difficulties in conforming to social expectations. This can further contribute to low self-esteem and a sense of marginalization.
   e) *Social withdrawal*: Socially maladjusted individuals may exhibit withdrawal behaviours, avoiding social interactions and isolating themselves from others. They may prefer to spend excessive time alone and have difficulty initiating or sustaining social connections.
   f) *Bullying or victimization*: Social maladjustment can make individuals more susceptible to bullying or victimization by others. Their difficulty in fitting in or understanding social dynamics may make them targets for mistreatment, further exacerbating their sense of social maladjustment.

g) *Lack of assertiveness*: Socially maladjusted individuals may struggle with assertiveness, finding it challenging to express their needs, opinions, or boundaries. This can lead to feelings of powerlessness and an increased vulnerability to manipulation or mistreatment by others.

h) *Social rejection*: Due to their difficulties in social interactions, socially maladjusted individuals may experience repeated rejection from peers or social groups. This rejection can have a profound impact on their self-esteem and overall psychological well-being.

i) *Inability to navigate social norms*: Socially maladjusted individuals may struggle to understand and adhere to the unwritten rules and norms of social behaviour. This can result in unintentional social faux pas or inappropriate behaviour, leading to further difficulties in social interactions.

j) *Peer pressure and conformity:* Social maladjustment can make individuals more susceptible to peer pressure and a strong desire to conform to social expectations. They may engage in activities or behaviours that they are not comfortable with, solely to fit in or gain acceptance from their peers.

k) *Social media addiction and isolation*: In today's digital age, social maladjustment can also manifest through excessive reliance on social media platforms. Individuals may become addicted to virtual interactions, leading to a decrease in face-to-face social connections and a sense of isolation.

2. **Marital Maladjustment:** Marital maladjustment refers to difficulties and conflicts within a marriage or intimate relationship. Here are some key points and elaborations:

a) *Poor communication*: A lack of effective communication is often a significant factor in marital maladjustment. Couples may struggle to express their needs, concerns, and emotions, leading to misunderstandings and resentment.

b) *Conflict and unresolved issues*: Marital maladjustment can arise from unresolved conflicts or persistent issues within the relationship. These conflicts may be related to differences in values, expectations, or incompatible lifestyles, and can lead to increased tension and dissatisfaction.

c) *Emotional disconnection*: When emotional intimacy diminishes or is absent, marital maladjustment can occur. This may involve feelings of loneliness, emotional distance, or a lack of support and understanding from one's partner.

d) *Infidelity and trust issues*: Marital maladjustment can result from breaches of trust, such as infidelity or betrayal. These actions can significantly impact the trust and stability of the relationship, leading to ongoing marital difficulties.

e) *Intimacy issues*: Marital maladjustment can involve challenges in establishing and maintaining emotional and physical intimacy within a relationship. This may include difficulties in expressing affection, lack of sexual compatibility, or emotional barriers that hinder deep connection.

f) *Role conflicts*: Conflicting expectations regarding gender roles, division of household chores or responsibilities within the marriage can contribute to marital maladjustment. Differences in values, beliefs, or cultural backgrounds may also contribute to these conflicts.

g) *Substance abuse and addiction*: Marital maladjustment can be linked to substance abuse and addiction. Individuals may turn to substance use as a way to cope with the stress and dissatisfaction within the relationship, further exacerbating the marital difficulties.

h) *Domestic violence*: In extreme cases of marital maladjustment, there may be instances of domestic violence or abuse. This can involve physical, emotional, or sexual abuse, and it is crucial for individuals experiencing such situations to seek help and support.

i) *Financial disagreements*: Marital maladjustment can arise from conflicts related to finances and differing financial goals or priorities. Disagreements regarding spending habits, budgeting, or financial responsibilities can strain the relationship and lead to ongoing marital difficulties.

j) *Cultural or religious differences*: Marriages involving individuals from different cultural or religious backgrounds may experience maladjustment due to conflicts arising from contrasting beliefs, values, and traditions. These differences can create challenges in understanding and accommodating each other's cultural or religious practices.

k) *Parenting conflicts*: Marital maladjustment can intensify when couples have divergent parenting styles or conflicting approaches to disciplining their children. Disagreements regarding parenting decisions and responsibilities can lead to tension and strained marital dynamics.

3. **Occupational Maladjustment:** Occupational maladjustment refers to a mismatch between an individual's abilities, interests, and values and the demands and expectations of their work environment. Here are some key points and elaborations:

   a) *Job dissatisfaction*: Individuals who experience occupational maladjustment may feel dissatisfied and unfulfilled in their work. This dissatisfaction can stem from factors such as a lack of interest, unchallenging tasks, limited growth opportunities, or poor work-life balance.

   b) *Lack of motivation and engagement*: When individuals are occupationally maladjusted, they may struggle to find motivation and engage fully in their work. This can lead to decreased productivity, poor performance, and a negative impact on their overall well-being.

c) *Burnout and stress*: Occupational maladjustment can contribute to burnout and chronic stress. When individuals are constantly exposed to job demands that do not align with their abilities or values, they may experience emotional exhaustion, physical symptoms, and a reduced sense of accomplishment.

d) *Career indecision*: Occupational maladjustment can also manifest as a difficulty in making career decisions. Individuals may feel uncertain about their career path, experience frequent job changes, or have difficulty identifying their skills and interests.

e) *Lack of job security*: Occupational maladjustment may involve unstable or insecure employment, such as temporary or precarious work arrangements. The uncertainty regarding job stability can lead to heightened stress and dissatisfaction.

f) *Lack of work-life balance*: Individuals experiencing occupational maladjustment may struggle to balance their work demands with their personal life responsibilities. Long working hours, excessive job demands, or a lack of flexibility can result in increased stress and strain on relationships outside of work.

g) *Skills and competence mismatch*: Occupational maladjustment can arise when there is a significant mismatch between an individual's skills, competencies, and the requirements of their job. This discrepancy can lead to feelings of inadequacy, decreased self-confidence, and difficulty meeting performance expectations.

h) *Occupational hazards and dissatisfaction*: Some forms of maladjustment can be specific to certain occupations. For example, individuals working in high-stress or physically demanding jobs may experience occupational maladjustment due to job-related hazards, burnout, or job dissatisfaction.

i) *Lack of recognition and advancement opportunities*: Occupational maladjustment may occur when individuals feel their efforts and contributions are not acknowledged or rewarded within the workplace. A lack of opportunities for career growth and advancement can result in a sense of stagnation and dissatisfaction.

j) *Unhealthy competition and workplace politics*: Maladjustment in the workplace can stem from a toxic work environment characterized by excessive competition, office politics, and a lack of cooperation among colleagues. Such dynamics can create stress, anxiety, and feelings of alienation.

k) *Ethical conflicts and moral distress*: Some individuals may experience occupational maladjustment due to conflicts between their personal values and the ethical demands of their job. Moral distress can arise when individuals feel compelled to engage in actions that go against their moral compass, leading to inner turmoil and job dissatisfaction.

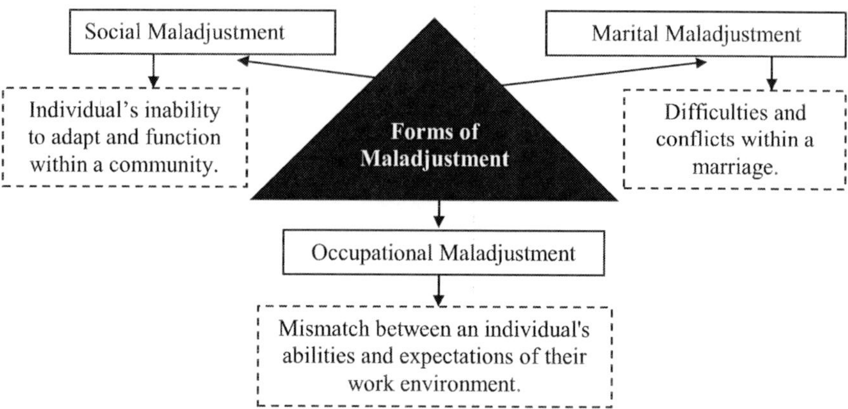

Figure 5.2: *Different Forms of Maladjustment*

It's important to note that these forms of maladjustment are not mutually exclusive and can often overlap. Additionally, seeking professional help, such as therapy or counseling, can provide support and guidance to individuals experiencing maladjustment in any of these areas.

Role of Family, Teachers, Friends and School in Remedial Measures of Maladjustment

In addressing the issue of maladjustment, the involvement of family, teachers, friends, and schools plays a pivotal role in implementing effective remedial measures. Each of these stakeholders brings unique perspectives, resources, and support systems that contribute to the well-being and development of individuals experiencing maladjustment. Through emotional support, guidance, education, and collaboration, they create a comprehensive network that nurtures resilience, promotes social integration, and fosters positive coping strategies. Some key points related to this discussion are given below:

Role of Family in Remedial Measures of Maladjustment

The family plays a crucial role in the remedial measures of maladjustment. Through emotional support, open communication, and the establishment of routines, families create a safe and comforting environment for individuals experiencing maladjustment. They serve as a source of guidance, providing positive role models and setting boundaries that promote stability and predictability. With their love and understanding, families contribute significantly to the well-being and overall adjustment of individuals facing challenges.

1. *Emotional support*: The family plays a crucial role in providing emotional support to an individual experiencing maladjustment. By offering understanding, empathy, and love, family members create a safe and comforting environment that helps the person cope with their challenges.

2. *Open communication*: A healthy family encourages open communication, allowing individuals to express their concerns and emotions freely. Through effective communication, family members can identify the root causes of maladjustment and work together to find appropriate solutions.
3. *Setting routines and structure*: Establishing consistent routines and structure within the family can help individuals develop a sense of stability and predictability. This can be particularly beneficial for someone struggling with maladjustment, as it provides a framework for daily life and reduces uncertainty.
4. *Providing guidance and role models*: Family members can serve as positive role models, offering guidance and support in navigating life's challenges. By demonstrating healthy coping mechanisms, problem-solving skills, and resilience, they can help individuals learn effective ways to overcome maladjustment.
5. *Establishing boundaries and rules*: A family that establishes clear boundaries and rules helps individuals experiencing maladjustment understand expectations and limits. Consistent guidelines promote a sense of security and stability, enabling them to develop self-discipline and adapt to social norms.
6. *Seeking professional help*: Families can actively seek professional help, such as therapy or counseling, for the individual facing maladjustment. Working with trained professionals can provide additional insights, strategies, and interventions to address the underlying causes of maladjustment effectively.
7. *Encouraging healthy lifestyle choices*: Families can promote healthy lifestyle choices, including proper nutrition, regular exercise, and sufficient sleep. These factors have a significant impact on mental well-being and can contribute to reducing maladjustment symptoms.
8. *Modeling effective communication and conflict resolution*: By modeling effective communication and conflict resolution skills, families can teach individuals with maladjustment how to express their needs, resolve conflicts, and build healthy relationships. These skills are crucial for their social and emotional development.
9. *Encouraging self-care practices*: Families can promote self-care practices such as relaxation techniques, mindfulness exercises, and engaging in hobbies or activities that bring joy and relaxation. These practices can help individuals with maladjustment manage stress, enhance self-awareness, and promote overall well-being.
10. *Fostering a positive family environment*: A positive family environment, characterized by love, support, and positive communication, can significantly impact an individual's adjustment. Families can create a nurturing atmosphere where positive interactions and constructive feedback are prioritized, fostering resilience and emotional stability.

Role of Teachers in Remedial Measures of Maladjustment

Teachers play a vital role in addressing maladjustment in students. By identifying signs of maladjustment and offering individualized attention, they can provide targeted support and interventions. Teachers create a supportive classroom environment that fosters inclusivity, respect, and understanding, enabling students to thrive. Through collaboration with other professionals and the implementation of specialized strategies, teachers contribute to the academic, social, and emotional growth of students facing maladjustment.

1. *Identifying signs of maladjustment*: Teachers often spend a significant amount of time with students and can observe their behaviour and academic performance. By recognizing the signs of maladjustment, such as withdrawal, aggression, or decline in academic performance, teachers can intervene early and provide appropriate support.
2. *Individualized attention*: Teachers can provide individualized attention to students experiencing maladjustment, offering them additional guidance and support. This can involve personalized instruction, mentoring, or counseling sessions to address their specific needs and help them catch up with their peers.
3. *Creating a supportive classroom environment*: Teachers play a vital role in creating a positive and supportive classroom environment. By promoting inclusivity, respect, and understanding among students, they can foster a sense of belonging, which can help alleviate feelings of maladjustment.
4. *Collaborating with other professionals*: Teachers can collaborate with school counselors, psychologists, and other professionals to develop comprehensive strategies for addressing maladjustment. By working together, they can create intervention plans, monitor progress, and provide ongoing support to the students.
5. *Providing educational accommodation*: Teachers can collaborate with educational specialists to provide necessary accommodations to students experiencing maladjustment. This might include modified assignments, extra time for exams, or alternative assessment methods to ensure their academic progress and reduce additional stress.
6. *Promoting resilience and self-esteem*: Teachers can facilitate activities that promote resilience, self-esteem, and positive self-image in students with maladjustment. By recognizing their strengths, encouraging their talents, and celebrating their achievements, teachers contribute to building their confidence and overall well-being.
7. *Providing a safe and inclusive learning environment*: Teachers can create a safe and inclusive learning environment where individuals feel accepted and valued. This includes promoting diversity, addressing biases, and fostering a culture of respect and empathy, reducing the risk of maladjustment due to discrimination or exclusion.

8. *Collaborating with parents/guardians*: Teachers can maintain open lines of communication with parents or guardians, sharing observations and concerns related to maladjustment. By working together, they can develop strategies and support plans that are consistent across home and school environments.
9. *Collaboration with mental health professionals*: Teachers can collaborate with mental health professionals such as therapists, counselors, or psychologists to develop personalized strategies and interventions for students with maladjustment. This collaboration ensures a multidisciplinary approach to their well-being and progress.
10. *Promoting self-advocacy skills*: Teachers can empower individuals with maladjustment by promoting self-advocacy skills. By teaching them to communicate their needs, seek help when necessary, and assert themselves in appropriate ways, teachers enable them to take an active role in their own remedial measures.

Role of Friends in Remedial Measures of Maladjustment

Friends hold a significant role in the remedial measures of maladjustment. They provide emotional support, encouragement, and companionship to individuals facing challenges. Friends can be a source of inspiration, promoting healthy coping mechanisms and serving as positive role models. Through their presence, understanding, and shared experiences, friends help individuals develop a sense of belonging, alleviate feelings of isolation, and navigate the complexities of maladjustment.

1. *Social support*: Friends can offer emotional support, understanding, and companionship to individuals facing maladjustment. Having a reliable support network of friends can help alleviate feelings of loneliness, isolation, and low self-esteem, fostering a sense of belonging and acceptance.
2. *Encouragement and motivation*: Friends can provide encouragement and motivation, helping individuals regain confidence and develop a positive outlook. Their words of encouragement and belief in the person's abilities can inspire them to overcome challenges and work towards positive change.
3. *Peer influence*: Positive peer influence can play a significant role in the remedial measures of maladjustment. Friends who exhibit healthy coping mechanisms, problem-solving skills, and resilience can serve as role models, encouraging the individual to adopt similar strategies.
4. *Encouraging healthy coping mechanisms*: Friends can encourage individuals with maladjustment to engage in healthy coping mechanisms, such as physical exercise, creative outlets, or mindfulness practices. Through shared activities and mutual support, friends can help them develop adaptive strategies to manage stress and anxiety.
5. *Providing social integration opportunities*: Friends can actively involve individuals with maladjustment in social activities and group settings. This

inclusion helps them develop social skills, expand their social networks, and feel a sense of belonging, reducing feelings of isolation and alienation.

6. *Encouraging involvement in extracurricular activities*: Friends can encourage individuals with maladjustment to participate in extracurricular activities that align with their interests and strengths. Involvement in clubs, sports teams, or artistic pursuits can provide a sense of purpose, boost self-esteem, and foster social connections.
7. *Practising active listening and empathy*: Friends can practise active listening and empathy when interacting with individuals experiencing maladjustment. By being non-judgemental, supportive, and understanding, they create a safe space for the person to share their thoughts and feelings, which can be therapeutic.
8. *Building a support network*: Friends can assist individuals with maladjustment in building a support network beyond themselves. They can introduce them to supportive individuals, groups, or communities that share similar experiences, providing additional avenues for understanding, guidance, and acceptance.
9. *Promoting healthy social activities*: Friends can engage individuals with maladjustment in healthy social activities that promote personal growth and positive interactions. This may involve participating in volunteer work, engaging in hobbies together, or exploring new shared interests, fostering a sense of purpose and connection.

Role of School in Remedial Measures of Maladjustment

Schools play a crucial role in addressing maladjustment and providing remedial measures. With access to support services such as counselors and psychologists, schools offer individualized assistance and interventions. They create a supportive learning environment that promotes social interaction, skill development, and inclusivity. Through prevention programmes, collaboration with external resources, and the promotion of resilience and self-esteem, schools contribute to the overall well-being and success of students facing maladjustment.

1. *Access to support services*: Schools often have dedicated support services such as counselors, psychologists, and social workers who can provide individualized assistance to students experiencing maladjustment. These professionals can offer counseling, therapy, or other interventions to address the specific needs of the individual.
2. *Individualized education plans*: Schools can develop individualized education plans (IEPs) for students with maladjustment, outlining tailored strategies to support their academic and social development. These plans can include accommodations, modifications, and specialized instruction to address their unique challenges.
3. *Peer interaction and social skills development*: School provides an environment for students to interact with peers and develop essential

social skills. Through group activities, teamwork, and structured social interactions, schools can help individuals improve their social competence, reducing maladjustment-related difficulties.

4. *Prevention and awareness programmes*: Schools can implement prevention and awareness programmes focused on mental health, emotional well-being, and promoting positive coping mechanisms. These initiatives can create a culture of understanding, reduce stigma, and encourage early identification and intervention for maladjustment issues.
5. *Bullying prevention and intervention*: Schools can implement anti-bullying programmes and policies to create a safe and supportive environment. By addressing and preventing bullying, they help protect individuals from potential triggers of maladjustment, promoting their mental well-being and social integration.
6. *Collaboration with external resources*: Schools can collaborate with external resources, such as community organizations or mental health professionals, to enhance the remedial measures for maladjustment. These partnerships expand the support network available to individuals and ensure a comprehensive approach to their well-being.
7. *Empowering students through life skills education*: Schools can integrate life skills education into their curriculum, teaching students essential skills such as problem-solving, communication, and emotional regulation. These skills equip individuals with the tools needed to navigate challenges, manage emotions, and develop healthier coping strategies.
8. *Providing specialized interventions*: Schools can offer specialized interventions tailored to the needs of individuals with maladjustment. These may include individual or group therapy sessions, social skills training, or behaviour management programmes designed to address specific maladjustment issues.
9. *Encouraging peer mentoring and support networks*: Schools can facilitate peer mentoring programmes or support networks where students with maladjustment can connect with their peers for guidance, encouragement, and understanding. Peer support can foster a sense of belonging and reduce feelings of isolation.
10. *Promoting a strengths-based approach*: Schools can adopt a strengths-based approach to education, focusing on individuals' strengths and abilities rather than solely on their challenges. By highlighting their talents and positive attributes, schools can boost self-confidence and empower students to overcome maladjustment.
11. *Implementing positive behaviour support systems*: Schools can implement positive behaviour support systems that focus on reinforcing positive behaviour and providing appropriate consequences for negative behaviour. These systems can help individuals with maladjustment develop self-regulation skills and make positive choices.

12. *Providing access to resources*: Schools can ensure that individuals with maladjustment have access to relevant resources, such as books, educational materials, or online platforms that address their specific challenges. This access to information and support can enhance their understanding, coping skills, and overall well-being.
13. *Celebrating progress and achievements*: Schools can celebrate the progress and achievements of individuals with maladjustment, acknowledging their efforts and growth. This recognition can boost their self-esteem, motivation, and sense of accomplishment, reinforcing positive changes and encouraging further development.

The collaborative efforts of family, teachers, friends, and schools are vital in providing remedial measures for individuals facing maladjustment. The involvement of these stakeholders contributes to the emotional well-being, social integration, and overall development of individuals. By offering support, understanding, and tailored interventions, they create an empowering environment that helps individuals overcome challenges, build resilience, and thrive. Together, they form a strong network that plays a crucial role in addressing maladjustment and promoting the holistic well-being of those affected.

Role of Education in Remedial Measures of Maladjustment

The role of education in remedial measures of maladjustment is crucial, as it plays a significant role in identifying, addressing, and mitigating various forms of maladjustment in individuals. Maladjustment refers to the inability of an individual to cope with the demands and challenges of their environment, leading to emotional, social, or behavioural problems. Education can serve as a powerful tool to support individuals in overcoming maladjustment through various means. Let's discuss some key points and their elaboration:

1. *Awareness and Identification*: Education helps in creating awareness and identifying signs of maladjustment in individuals. Teachers, school counselors, and educational institutions are well-positioned to observe and recognize the behavioural, emotional, or academic struggles that may indicate maladjustment. By raising awareness, education enables early intervention, which is crucial for effective remedial measures.
2. *Individualized Support*: Education provides a platform for individualized support, allowing educators to address the unique needs of students experiencing maladjustment. Teachers can employ differentiated instructional strategies, modify learning environments, and offer personalized guidance to help students overcome their difficulties. Individualized attention and support can help in minimizing the negative impact of maladjustment on academic performance and overall well-being.
3. *Skill Development*: Education focuses on skill development, including social, emotional, and behavioural skills. These skills are essential in helping individuals cope with challenges and adapt to their surroundings.

By incorporating programmes that promote emotional intelligence, conflict resolution, self-regulation, and effective communication, education equips individuals with the tools necessary to manage and overcome maladjustment.

4. *Counseling and Mental Health Services*: Education systems often include counseling and mental health services as part of their support structure. Trained professionals, such as school counselors or psychologists, can work with individuals experiencing maladjustment to address underlying issues, provide guidance, and offer therapeutic interventions. By integrating these services within educational institutions, access to support becomes more convenient, reducing barriers to seeking help.
5. *Social Integration and Peer Support*: Education provides opportunities for social integration and peer support, which are critical factors in addressing maladjustment. Interactions with peers, participation in group activities, and collaborative learning environments foster social skills, empathy, and a sense of belonging. Positive relationships and peer support systems can greatly contribute to an individual's resilience and help them navigate challenges associated with maladjustment.
6. *Holistic Development*: Education aims to foster holistic development, focusing on not just academic achievement but also the overall well-being of individuals. By promoting a balanced approach to education that includes physical education, arts, and extracurricular activities, educational institutions contribute to the comprehensive growth of students. This holistic approach supports the development of self-esteem, confidence, and a positive self-identity, reducing the likelihood of maladjustment.
7. *Prevention and Early Intervention*: Education plays a significant role in prevention and early intervention strategies for maladjustment. By implementing proactive measures, such as creating supportive school environments, teaching social and emotional skills, and fostering a culture of acceptance and inclusion, educational institutions can reduce the occurrence and severity of maladjustment. Early identification and intervention can prevent maladjustment from escalating into more significant challenges later in life.
8. *Inclusive Education*: Education promotes inclusive practices that accommodate the diverse needs of students, including those experiencing maladjustment. Inclusive education ensures that individuals with different abilities, backgrounds, and learning styles receive appropriate support and accommodations. By embracing inclusive practices, educational institutions create an environment that fosters acceptance, empathy, and understanding, helping individuals experiencing maladjustment feel valued and included.
9. *Parent and Family Involvement*: Education involves parents and families in the remedial process of maladjustment. Collaboration between educators and families is crucial for understanding the individual's needs and creating a consistent support system. By providing information,

guidance, and involving parents in decision-making processes, education strengthens the partnership between home and school, maximizing the effectiveness of remedial measures.

10. *Career Guidance and Vocational Training*: Education encompasses career guidance and vocational training, which play a significant role in addressing maladjustment. Helping individuals explore their interests, talents, and strengths allows them to align their educational and career paths with their personal goals and aspirations. By providing guidance and training in areas of interest, education contributes to the development of a sense of purpose and direction, reducing maladjustment related to academic or career dissatisfaction.
11. *Life Skills Education*: Education focuses on equipping individuals with essential life skills that are instrumental in dealing with maladjustment. Life skills education encompasses financial literacy, problem-solving, time management, decision-making, and critical thinking skills. By developing these competencies, education empowers individuals to navigate challenges, make informed choices, and cope effectively with stressors, thereby minimizing the impact of maladjustment.
12. *Collaborative Approach*: Education encourages a collaborative approach involving various stakeholders, such as teachers, counselors, administrators, and community organizations, in addressing maladjustment. By working together, sharing expertise and resources, and establishing partnerships, a comprehensive support network can be created to address the multifaceted needs of individuals experiencing maladjustment. This collaborative approach enhances the effectiveness and sustainability of remedial measures.
13. *Positive Discipline and Conflict Resolution*: Education promotes positive discipline strategies and conflict resolution techniques as part of addressing maladjustment. By emphasizing non-violent communication, problem-solving, and empathy, education cultivates a positive and respectful school culture. Teaching individuals how to manage conflicts constructively and regulate their behaviour fosters emotional well-being and reduces maladaptive responses to challenges.
14. *Continuous Professional Development*: Education emphasizes continuous professional development for educators and other professionals working with individuals experiencing maladjustment. Ongoing training and professional learning opportunities ensure that educators stay updated with evidence-based practices, interventions, and strategies to support individuals effectively. By enhancing their knowledge and skills, educators are better equipped to address the evolving needs of students with maladjustment.
15. *Multi-Tiered Systems of Support (MTSS)*: Education incorporates the use of Multi-Tiered Systems of Support (MTSS) to address maladjustment. MTSS is a framework that provides a continuum of support services

tailored to meet the diverse needs of students. It typically includes three tiers: universal (whole-class instruction), targeted (small group interventions), and intensive (individualized interventions). By employing MTSS, education ensures that individuals experiencing maladjustment receive appropriate interventions at the level of support they require.

16. *Trauma-informed Approaches*: Education adopts trauma-informed approaches to support individuals who have experienced trauma and may exhibit maladjustment as a result. Trauma-informed practices prioritize safety, trust, and emotional well-being, taking into account the impact of trauma on individuals' behaviour and learning. By creating trauma-sensitive environments and providing specialized support, education helps individuals process and heal from trauma, reducing maladjustment symptoms.
17. *Cultural Competence*: Education emphasizes cultural competence, recognizing and respecting the diversity of students' backgrounds and experiences. Cultural competence enables educators to understand and address the unique challenges faced by individuals from different cultural, ethnic, and socio-economic backgrounds. By incorporating culturally responsive practices, education promotes a sense of belonging and validates individuals' identities, reducing the risk of maladjustment associated with cultural dissonance or discrimination.
18. *Technology Integration*: Education leverages technology as a tool for remedial measures of maladjustment. Educational technology platforms, digital resources, and assistive technologies can be utilized to support individuals' learning and well-being. Technology can provide personalized learning experiences, facilitate communication, and offer therapeutic interventions. By harnessing the potential of technology, education enhances accessibility and tailors support to meet the specific needs of individuals experiencing maladjustment.
19. *Research and Evidence-based Practices*: Education emphasizes the use of research and evidence-based practices in addressing maladjustment. By staying informed about the latest research findings and evidence-based interventions, educators can make informed decisions about the most effective approaches for supporting individuals. Education encourages the integration of research and evidence into policies, curricula, and professional development to ensure the highest quality of remedial measures.
20. *Long-term Support and Follow-up*: Education recognizes the importance of long-term support and follow-up for individuals who have experienced maladjustment. Remedial measures should not be limited to short-term interventions but should extend beyond, providing sustained support and monitoring individuals' progress over time. By implementing comprehensive follow-up systems, education ensures that individuals continue to receive the necessary support and intervention, minimizing the risk of relapse or recurrence of maladjustment.

21. *Community Partnerships*: Education establishes partnerships with community organizations, mental health professionals, and social service agencies to provide holistic support to individuals experiencing maladjustment. Collaboration with external resources expands the range of services available, such as therapy, counseling, mentorship programs, and extracurricular activities. By working together, education and community partners create a network of support that addresses the diverse needs of individuals and enhances the effectiveness of remedial measures.
22. *Peer Mediation and Support Programmes*: Education promotes peer mediation and support programmes to address maladjustment. Peer mediation involves trained students who help resolve conflicts and facilitate communication between their peers. Peer support programmes create a safe space for individuals to connect with and receive support from their peers who have undergone similar experiences. These programmes encourage empathy, build social skills, and reduce feelings of isolation, contributing to the remediation of maladjustment.
23. *Individualized Education Plans (IEPs)*: Education develops Individualized Education Plans (IEPs) for students with specific learning needs, including those related to maladjustment. IEPs outline personalized goals, accommodations, and support strategies to meet the unique needs of individuals. By tailoring educational plans to address maladjustment-related challenges, education ensures that students receive targeted interventions and support to overcome their difficulties and succeed academically and socially.
24. *Strength-based Approaches*: Education adopts strength-based approaches to focus on individuals' strengths, talents, and positive attributes rather than solely on their challenges and deficits. By recognizing and harnessing the strengths of individuals experiencing maladjustment, education promotes self-confidence, resilience, and a positive self-concept. Strength-based approaches empower individuals to build upon their assets and overcome maladjustment, fostering a sense of empowerment and motivation.
25. *Teacher Training and Professional Development*: Education invests in teacher training and professional development programmes to enhance educators' knowledge and skills in addressing maladjustment. Training focuses on recognizing the signs of maladjustment, implementing effective interventions, promoting positive classroom management, and fostering a supportive learning environment. By equipping teachers with the necessary tools and strategies, education ensures that educators are well-prepared to meet the needs of individuals experiencing maladjustment.
26. *School-based Prevention Programmes*: Education incorporates school-based prevention programmes that aim to address risk factors associated with maladjustment. These programmes may focus on substance abuse prevention, anti-bullying initiatives, mental health

awareness, and promoting healthy coping mechanisms. By addressing risk factors early on and fostering a positive school climate, education aims to prevent the development of maladjustment and promote overall well-being.

27. *Continuous Monitoring and Evaluation*: Education emphasizes continuous monitoring and evaluation of the effectiveness of remedial measures for maladjustment. Regular assessment and data analysis help identify areas of improvement, refine interventions, and ensure that individuals are receiving the appropriate support. By collecting and analyzing data, education can make evidence-based decisions to enhance the remediation process and achieve better outcomes for individuals experiencing maladjustment.

In summary, education serves as a vital catalyst in remedial measures for maladjustment. Through awareness, individualized support, skill development, counseling services, social integration, holistic development, and prevention strategies, education empowers individuals to overcome maladjustment, fostering their well-being and enabling them to thrive in their personal and academic lives.

Contribution of Freud to Understand Maladjustment

Sigmund Freud, the renowned Austrian neurologist and founder of psychoanalysis, made significant contributions to our understanding of maladjustment and psychological disorders. His theories revolutionized the field of psychology and continue to influence it to this day. Here are several key points elaborating Freud's contributions to understanding maladjustment:

Unconscious Mind: Freud proposed that the human mind is composed of three parts: the conscious mind, the preconscious mind, and the unconscious mind. According to Freud, many psychological conflicts and maladjustments stem from unconscious processes and repressed memories. He believed that unresolved conflicts from childhood could manifest in maladaptive behaviours and emotional difficulties later in life.

Psychosexual Development: Freud's theory of psychosexual development suggests that children pass through distinct stages, each characterized by a focus on different erogenous zones. Unresolved conflicts or fixations at any of these stages can lead to maladjustment. For example, oral fixations, such as excessive smoking or overeating, might result from unresolved conflicts during the oral stage.

Defence Mechanisms: Freud introduced the concept of defence mechanisms, which are unconscious strategies the mind employs to cope with anxiety and protect the individual from psychological distress. Defence mechanisms, such as repression, denial, projection, and displacement, can contribute to maladjustment by distorting reality or preventing the conscious recognition of underlying issues.

Psychoanalysis: Freud developed the therapeutic technique of psychoanalysis to explore and resolve unconscious conflicts. Through free association, dream analysis, and the interpretation of slips of the tongue, Freud aimed to bring repressed memories and unresolved conflicts into conscious awareness, allowing patients to work through and resolve them.

Role of Childhood Experiences: Freud emphasized the significance of early childhood experiences in shaping an individual's personality and psychological well-being. Traumatic or adverse experiences during childhood, such as abuse or neglect, can contribute to maladjustment later in life. Freud's theories underscored the importance of addressing these early experiences to promote healing and adjustment.

Id, Ego, and Superego: Freud proposed that the psyche is composed of three components: the id, the ego, and the superego. The id represents instinctual drives and desires, the superego represents the internalized moral standards and societal norms, and the ego mediates between the two. Imbalances between these components can lead to maladaptive behaviours and psychological distress.

Transference and Counter Transference: Freud recognized the phenomenon of transference, where patients develop strong emotions and reactions towards their therapists, often based on unresolved feelings from past relationships. This transference dynamic can offer insights into unconscious conflicts and unresolved issues contributing to maladjustment. Similarly, counter transference refers to the therapist's emotional reactions to the patient, which can impact the therapeutic relationship and uncover their own unresolved conflicts.

The Oedipus Complex: Freud proposed that during the phallic stage of psychosexual development, children experience unconscious sexual desires for the opposite-sex parent and view the same-sex parent as a rival. This conflict, known as the Oedipus complex in boys (and the Electra complex in girls), can result in feelings of guilt, anxiety, and maladjustment if not resolved successfully.

Repression and Unconscious Processes: Freud highlighted the role of repression in the formation of maladaptive behaviours and psychological disorders. Repression involves pushing distressing thoughts, memories, or desires into the unconscious mind, where they continue to influence behaviour. Unresolved repressed material can contribute to maladjustment by creating internal conflicts and affecting daily functioning.

Dreams as a Path to Unconscious: Freud considered dreams as the "royal road to the unconscious." He believed that analyzing dreams could reveal hidden desires, fears, and conflicts. By interpreting dream symbolism and latent content, Freud sought to uncover unconscious processes and shed light on maladjustment rooted in unresolved issues.

Sexual and Aggressive Drives: Freud's theory emphasized the role of sexual and aggressive drives in human behaviour and maladjustment. He argued that repressed or unresolved sexual and aggressive impulses could manifest in various psychological symptoms and disturbances. Understanding and addressing these underlying drives became crucial in his approach to therapy.

Case Studies and Observational Research: Freud's work was heavily influenced by his clinical observations and case studies. Through in-depth exploration of individual cases, such as the famous case of Anna O., Freud developed theories and therapeutic techniques to understand and treat maladjustment. These case studies provided valuable insights into the complex nature of psychological disorders.

Influence on Psychodynamic Approach: Freud's theories laid the groundwork for psychodynamic approaches to therapy and understanding maladjustment. Psychodynamic therapy continues to incorporate many of Freud's concepts, such as the exploration of unconscious processes, the importance of early experiences, and the significance of the therapeutic relationship in uncovering and resolving maladaptive patterns.

Legacy and Impact: Freud's contributions to understanding maladjustment extended beyond his own lifetime. His theories influenced subsequent psychological theories and therapeutic approaches, such as Carl Jung's analytical psychology and object relations theory. Freud's emphasis on the unconscious mind and the exploration of underlying conflicts paved the way for advancements in psychoanalysis and psychotherapy.

It is important to note that while Freud's theories and techniques have made significant contributions to our understanding of maladjustment, they are not without criticism. Over the years, various psychologists and researchers have offered alternative perspectives and challenged specific aspects of Freudian theory. Nonetheless, Freud's ideas remain highly influential in the field of psychology and have played a vital role in shaping our understanding of maladjustment and psychological well-being.

Contributions of Neo-Freudians to Understand Maladjustment

The Neo-Freudians made significant contributions to our understanding of maladjustment by building upon and revising Sigmund Freud's psychoanalytic theories. While they shared some core concepts with Freud, such as the importance of the unconscious mind and the impact of early childhood experiences, they also introduced new ideas and perspectives. Here are the key contributions of Neo-Freudians to understanding maladjustment:

Emphasis on Social and Cultural Factors: Neo-Freudians, such as Alfred Adler, Karen Horney, and Erich Fromm, expanded Freud's focus beyond individual instincts and drives to consider the role of social and cultural factors in shaping maladjustment. They highlighted the significance of social relationships, cultural influences, and societal expectations in determining psychological well-being. For example, Adler proposed that feelings of inferiority and the pursuit of superiority are strongly influenced by an individual's social context.

Importance of Interpersonal Relationships: Neo-Freudians recognized the significance of interpersonal relationships, particularly in early childhood, in the development of maladaptive behaviours and psychological disorders. They emphasized the impact of attachment patterns, family dynamics, and the quality of relationships on an individual's emotional and psychological well-being. For instance, Horney's concept of "Basic Anxiety" highlighted the role of early interpersonal relationships in the formation of maladaptive coping mechanisms.

Focus on Conscious Experience and Self-identity: While Freud emphasized the unconscious mind, Neo-Freudians placed greater emphasis on conscious experience and the development of self-identity. They explored the ways in which an individual's perception of oneself and others contributes to maladjustment. Fromm, for instance, emphasized the importance of developing an authentic sense of self, as well as the impact of societal pressures on an individual's ability to do so.

Revision of Freudian Sexual Theories: Neo-Freudians challenged some of Freud's sexual theories and their exclusive focus on sexual drives as the primary motivators of human behaviour. They recognized the significance of factors like power, social influence, and the desire for intimacy in shaping maladaptive behaviours. Horney, for example, emphasized the role of basic anxiety and the need for security in influencing an individual's behaviour and relationships.

Expansion of the Concept of Defence Mechanisms: Neo-Freudians expanded the understanding of defence mechanisms beyond Freud's original conceptualization. They identified new defence mechanisms and explored their role in maladjustment. For instance, Anna Freud, Sigmund Freud's daughter, contributed to the understanding of defence mechanisms in children, highlighting the importance of mechanisms such as regression, displacement, and identification.

Integration of Eastern and Western Philosophical Traditions: Some Neo-Freudians, such as Erich Fromm and D.W. Winnicott, drew on Eastern and Western philosophical traditions to enhance our understanding of maladjustment. They incorporated concepts from Buddhism, Taoism, and existential philosophy to explore themes of self-identity, alienation, and the search for meaning in life.

Exploration of Gender and Feminine Psychology: Neo-Freudians, particularly Karen Horney, made significant contributions to understanding maladjustment in relation to gender. They challenged Freud's primarily male-centered theories and examined the impact of societal expectations and gender roles on psychological well-being. Horney's work on feminine psychology emphasized the effects of societal pressures on women's self-esteem, relationships, and overall adjustment.

Emphasis on the Unconscious Mind and Symbolism: Neo-Freudians continued to emphasize the importance of the unconscious mind in understanding maladjustment but expanded the exploration of symbolism and interpretation. Carl Jung, a prominent Neo-Freudian, developed the concept of the collective unconscious, which includes universal symbols and archetypes that influence human behaviour. This expanded understanding of the unconscious mind offered new insights into the roots of maladaptive thoughts, emotions, and behaviours.

Psychodynamic Perspectives on Developmental Stages: Neo-Freudians expanded upon Freud's theory of psychosexual development by examining the psychosocial stages across the lifespan. Erik Erikson, a Neo-Freudian theorist, proposed a comprehensive model of psychosocial development that encompassed various stages and the challenges individuals face at each stage. This perspective shed light on the potential sources of maladjustment and psychopathology that arise from unresolved conflicts at different developmental periods.

Integration of Psychology and Sociology: Some Neo-Freudians sought to bridge the gap between psychology and sociology, recognizing the influence of social structures on individual well-being. Fromm, for instance, explored the impact of social structures, such as economic systems and cultural norms, on psychological adjustment. By integrating these disciplines, Neo-Freudians offered a more holistic understanding of maladjustment that incorporated both individual and societal factors.

Exploration of Neurosis and Healthy Personality Development: Neo-Freudians delved into the nature of neurosis and the process of achieving healthy personality development. They explored the factors that contribute to neurotic tendencies, such as unresolved conflicts and maladaptive defence mechanisms, and proposed methods for promoting personal growth and psychological well-being. This emphasis on healthy personality development provided a framework for understanding and treating maladjustment.

Application of Psychoanalytic Concepts in Therapy: Neo-Freudians expanded the application of psychoanalytic concepts in therapeutic settings. They developed and refined psychoanalytic therapy techniques, such as psychodynamic psychotherapy, to help individuals gain insight into their unconscious conflicts, defence mechanisms, and maladaptive patterns of behaviour. These therapeutic approaches aimed to facilitate the resolution of conflicts and promote psychological adjustment.

Emphasis on the Role of Anxiety: Neo-Freudians placed significant emphasis on the role of anxiety in maladjustment. They explored different types of anxiety, such as neurotic anxiety and existential anxiety, and how it manifests in various psychological disorders. By understanding the sources and dynamics of anxiety, Neo-Freudians provided insights into the underlying mechanisms of maladaptive behaviours and coping strategies.

Exploration of Object Relations: Neo-Freudians, particularly Melanie Klein and D.W. Winnicott, focused on object relations theory, which examines the impact of early relationships and the internalized representations of others on maladjustment. They highlighted the significance of the infant-mother relationship and how disruptions or unresolved conflicts in these early relationships can contribute to later difficulties in forming healthy relationships and adaptive behaviours.

Integration of Humanistic and Existential Perspectives: Some Neo-Freudians integrated humanistic and existential perspectives into their understanding of maladjustment. They explored concepts such as personal growth, self-actualization, and the search for meaning in life. By incorporating these perspectives, Neo-Freudians offered a broader understanding of maladjustment that acknowledged the importance of individual agency, personal values, and the quest for a fulfilling existence.

Examination of Cultural and Racial Identity: Neo-Freudians, such as Franz Fanon and Erik Erikson, examined the impact of cultural and racial identity on maladjustment. They highlighted how societal prejudices, discrimination, and the internalization of cultural norms can contribute to psychological distress and identity conflicts. Their work shed light on the unique challenges faced by individuals from different cultural backgrounds and the importance of cultural identity in psychological well-being.

Integration of Cognitive and Behavioural Approaches: Neo-Freudians integrated cognitive and behavioural approaches into their understanding of maladjustment. They recognized the role of cognition, beliefs, and learned behaviours in shaping psychological disorders and maladaptive patterns. By combining these perspectives, Neo-Freudians enriched the understanding of the cognitive and behavioural aspects of maladjustment, paving the way for cognitive-behavioural therapies that emerged in later years.

Exploration of Creative Expression and Symbolic Communication: Some Neo-Freudians, such as D.W. Winnicott, emphasized the role of creative expression and symbolic communication in understanding maladjustment. They recognized the significance of art, play, and symbolic gestures as means of expressing unconscious thoughts, emotions, and conflicts. By exploring these non-verbal forms of communication, Neo-Freudians provided insights into the deeper layers of maladjustment and facilitated therapeutic interventions through creative mediums.

Examination of the Impact of Trauma and Early Adversity: Neo-Freudians extended the understanding of maladjustment by examining the impact of trauma and early adversity on psychological well-being. They explored the long-lasting effects of childhood trauma, abuse, and neglect on the development of maladaptive behaviours, attachment issues, and personality disorders. Their research highlighted the importance of trauma-informed approaches and interventions to address maladjustment resulting from early adverse experiences.

The contributions of Neo-Freudians to understanding maladjustment were diverse, encompassing a range of perspectives and incorporating concepts from various psychological and philosophical frameworks. Their work expanded the understanding of maladjustment, provided therapeutic insights, and paved the way for subsequent advancements in psychological theory and practice.

6

Mental Disorder

Concept of Mental Disorder

The meaning of mental disorder refers to a condition or set of conditions that significantly impact an individual's thoughts, emotions, behaviour, and overall mental well-being. It represents a deviation from the expected patterns of psychological functioning and can cause distress and impairment in various aspects of a person's life. Mental disorders are characterized by disturbances in thinking, perception, mood, behaviour, or a combination of these factors. These disturbances often lead to significant distress or impairment in social, occupational, or other important areas of functioning. Mental disorders can affect people of all ages, genders, races, and socio-economic backgrounds. It is important to recognize that mental disorders are not simply personal weaknesses or character flaws. They are medical conditions that arise from a complex interaction of genetic, biological, psychological, and environmental factors. These factors can influence the brain's structure and function, impacting how individuals perceive, think, and respond to the world around them. The experience of a mental disorder can vary widely among individuals. Symptoms can range from mild to severe and may fluctuate over time. Common symptoms include persistent sadness, anxiety, changes in sleep or appetite, difficulty concentrating, hallucinations, irrational thoughts or fears, and impaired social interactions. The field of mental health acknowledges that mental disorders can have a significant impact on an individual's quality of life. Therefore, seeking appropriate diagnosis and treatment is crucial. Treatment for mental disorders often involves a combination of approaches, including psychotherapy, medication, and lifestyle modifications. The goal is to alleviate symptoms, enhance functioning, and improve overall well-being. It is important to foster a supportive and understanding environment for individuals with mental disorders. Reducing stigma, promoting awareness, and providing access to mental health services are essential for creating a society that supports the well-being of all individuals, regardless of their mental health status. Overall,

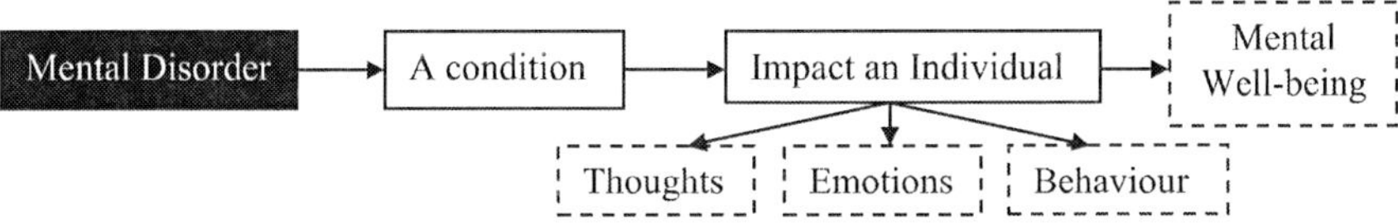

Figure 6.1: *Mental Disorder*

the meaning of mental disorder encompasses a wide range of conditions that affect an individual's mental well-being, emphasizing the need for accurate diagnosis, effective treatment, and societal support to help individuals lead fulfilling and productive lives.

Some definitions of mental disorder are mentioned below:

Diagnostic and Statistical Manual of Mental Disorders (DSM-5): The DSM-5, published by the American Psychiatric Association, defines mental disorder as "A syndrome characterized by clinically significant disturbance in an individual's cognition, emotion regulation, or behaviour that reflects a dysfunction in the psychological, biological, or developmental processes underlying mental functioning."

World Health Organization (WHO): The WHO defines mental disorders as "Health conditions characterized by alterations in thinking, mood, or behaviour associated with significant distress and impaired functioning."

National Institute of Mental Health (NIMH): The NIMH defines mental disorders as "Health conditions that are characterized by changes in thinking, mood, or behaviour (or a combination thereof) associated with distress and/or impaired functioning."

American Psychiatric Association (APA): The APA defines mental disorder as "A syndrome characterized by clinically significant disturbance in an individual's cognition, emotion regulation, or behaviour that reflects a dysfunction in the psychological, biological, or developmental processes underlying mental functioning. Mental disorders are usually associated with significant distress or disability in social, occupational, or other important activities."

National Alliance on Mental Illness (NAMI): NAMI defines mental disorder as "A medical condition that disrupts a person's thinking, feeling, mood, ability to relate to others, and daily functioning. Mental disorders are not the result of personal weakness, lack of character, or poor upbringing."

Substance Abuse and Mental Health Services Administration (SAMHSA): SAMHSA defines mental disorder as "A health condition that changes a person's thinking, feeling, behaviour, or all three, and that causes the person distress and difficulty in functioning."

British Psychological Society (BPS): The BPS defines mental disorder as "A psychological or behavioural pattern that occurs in an individual and is associated with distress (e.g., a painful symptom) or disability (i.e., impairment in one or more important areas of functioning) or with a significantly increased risk of suffering death, pain, disability, or an important loss of freedom."

These definitions highlight the disruption and impairment caused by mental disorders, their impact on various areas of functioning, and the recognition that mental disorders are not indicative of personal weakness or lack of character. They emphasize the distress, disability, or increased risk associated with mental disorders and highlights the need for support, treatment, and understanding.

Classifications of Mental Disorder

The classification of mental disorders is also known as psychiatric nosology or psychiatric taxonomy. It represents a key aspect of psychiatry and other mental health professions and is an important issue for people who may be diagnosed. There are currently two widely established systems for classifying mental disorders:

- Chapter V of the tenth International Classification of Diseases (ICD-10) produced by the World Health Organization (WHO);
- The Diagnostic and Statistical Manual of Mental Disorders (DSM-IV&DSM-V) produced by the American Psychiatric Association (APA).

The International Classification of Diseases, 10th Revision (ICD-10), is a widely used classification system developed by the World Health Organization (WHO) for various health conditions, including mental disorders. Here are some classifications of mental disorders according to the ICD-10:

F0-F09: Organic, Including Symptomatic, Mental Disorders:

- F00-F03: Dementia, including Alzheimer's disease.
- F04: Organic amnesic syndrome and other organic memory disorders.
- F05: Delirium, not induced by alcohol and other psychoactive substances.

F10-F19: Mental and Behavioural Disorders due to Psychoactive Substance Use:

- F10: Mental and behavioural disorders due to alcohol use.
- F11: Mental and behavioural disorders due to opioids use.
- F12: Mental and behavioural disorders due to cannabinoids use.

F20-F29: Schizophrenia, Schizotypal and Delusional Disorders:

- F20: Schizophrenia.
- F21: Schizotypal disorder.
- F22: Persistent delusional disorders.

F30-F39: Mood [Affective] Disorders:

- F30: Manic episode and bipolar affective disorder.
- F31: Bipolar affective disorder.
- F32: Depressive episode and depressive disorders.

F40-F48: Neurotic, Stress-related, and Somatoform Disorders:

- F40: Phobic anxiety disorders.
- F41: Other anxiety disorders.
- F42: Obsessive-compulsive disorder (OCD).

F50-F59: Behavioural Syndromes Associated with Physiological Disturbances and Physical Factors:

- F50: Eating disorders.
- F51: Non-organic sleep disorders.
- F52: Sexual dysfunction not caused by organic disorder or disease.

F60-F69: Disorders of Adult Personality and Behaviour:

- F60: Specific personality disorders.
- F61: Mixed and other personality disorders.
- F63: Impulse disorders, not elsewhere classified.

F80-F89: Pervasive and Specific Developmental Disorders:

- F81: Specific developmental disorders of scholastic skills.
- F84: Pervasive developmental disorders.

F90-F98: Behavioural and Emotional Disorders with Onset Usually Occurring in Childhood and Adolescence:

- F90: Hyperkinetic disorders (ADHD).
- F91: Conduct disorders.
- F94: Disorders of social functioning with onset specific to childhood and adolescence.

F99: Unspecified Mental Disorder:

- F99 represents mental disorders that do not fit into any specific category or those with unclear diagnoses.

Within each group there are more specific subcategories. The WHO has revised ICD-10 to produce the latest version of the ICD; ICD-11 adopted by the 72nd World Health Assembly in 2019 and came into effect on 1 January 2022. It's important to note that the ICD-10 classification system provides a comprehensive framework for diagnosing mental disorders but may differ slightly from the DSM-IV (Diagnostic and Statistical Manual of Mental Disorders) classification system.

The DSM-IV is the predecessor to the current DSM-V. The DSM-IV was originally published in 1994 and listed more than 250 mental disorders. It was produced by the American Psychiatric Association and it characterizes mental disorder as «a clinically significant behavioural or psychological syndrome or pattern that occurs in an individual,...is associated with present distress...or disability...or with a significantly increased risk of suffering" but that "...no definition adequately specifies precise boundaries for the concept of 'mental disorder'...different situations call for different definitions" (APA, 1994 and 2000). The DSM also states that "there is no assumption that each category of mental disorder is a completely discrete entity with absolute boundaries dividing it from other mental disorders or no mental disorders."

The DSM-IV-TR (Text Revision, 2000) included a multi-axial system that allowed for a comprehensive assessment of mental disorders. The system consisted of five axes on which disorders could be assessed. Here are the five axes of the DSM-IV-TR:

Axis I: Clinical Disorders: This axis included major mental disorders and clinical conditions that cause significant distress or impairment. It encompassed disorders such as mood disorders, anxiety disorders, psychotic disorders, and substance use disorders.

Axis II: Personality Disorders and Intellectual Disabilities: Axis II focused on personality disorders, which are enduring patterns of thoughts, emotions, and behaviours that significantly deviate from cultural expectations. It also included intellectual disabilities (previously referred to as mental retardation).

Axis III: General Medical Conditions: Axis III involved the assessment of any relevant general medical conditions that might be influencing the individual's mental health. This included physical illnesses or conditions that could have an impact on the person's psychological well-being.

Axis IV: Psychosocial and Environmental Problems: Axis IV addressed psychosocial and environmental factors that could affect aperson's functioning and contribute to the development or exacerbation of mental disorders. This included stressors such as interpersonal conflicts, financial difficulties, or housing problems.

Axis V: Global Assessment of Functioning (GAF): Axis V provided an overall assessment of the individual's psychological, social, and occupational functioning on a continuum. The Global Assessment of Functioning (GAF) scale ranged from 0 to 100, with higher scores indicating better functioning.

It's important to note that with the release of the DSM-V, the multi-axial system was eliminated, and the diagnostic criteria were reorganized into a more streamlined format. The DSM-V uses a non-axial approach, focusing on specific diagnostic criteria for each disorder. The DSM has undergone several revisions over the years, with the most recent version being the DSM-V, released in 2013. The DSM-V is widely used by psychiatrists, psychologists, clinicians, researchers, and other mental health professionals worldwide. It serves as a comprehensive guide that outlines diagnostic criteria, symptom descriptions, and other relevant information for various mental disorders.

The DSM-V categorizes mental disorders into different groups, each representing a distinct set of conditions with shared characteristics. These groups encompass a wide range of disorders, reflecting the diverse nature of mental health challenges individuals may experience. Let's explore each of these groups:

1. *Neurodevelopmental Disorders*: Neurodevelopmental disorders typically manifest early in childhood and are characterized by impairments in cognitive, social, and motor development. Examples include Attention-Deficit/Hyperactivity Disorder (ADHD), Autism Spectrum Disorder, and Specific Learning Disorder.

2. *Schizophrenia Spectrum and Other Psychotic Disorders*: This group includes disorders marked by disruptions in thinking, perception, and behaviour. Schizophrenia, Schizoaffective Disorder, and Delusional Disorder are examples within this category.
3. *Bipolar and Related Disorders*: Bipolar and related disorders involve significant fluctuations in mood, ranging from episodes of elevated mood (mania) to periods of depression. Bipolar I Disorder, Bipolar II Disorder, and Cyclothymic Disorder fall under this group.
4. *Depressive Disorders*: Depressive disorders are characterized by persistent feelings of sadness, loss of interest, and impaired functioning. Major Depressive Disorder and Persistent Depressive Disorder (Dysthymia) are prominent examples.
5. *Anxiety Disorders*: Anxiety disorders involve excessive and persistent worry or fear that significantly impacts daily life. Generalized Anxiety Disorder, Panic Disorder, and Social Anxiety Disorder are representative conditions.
6. *Obsessive-Compulsive and Related Disorders*: This group comprises disorders characterized by intrusive thoughts (obsessions) and repetitive behaviours (compulsions). Obsessive-Compulsive Disorder (OCD), Body Dysmorphic Disorder, and Hoarding Disorder fall into this category.
7. *Trauma and Stressor-related Disorders*: Trauma and stressor-related disorders result from exposure to traumatic or stressful events. Posttraumatic Stress Disorder (PTSD), Acute Stress Disorder, and Adjustment Disorders are examples in this group.
8. *Dissociative Disorders*: Dissociative disorders involve disruptions in consciousness, memory, identity, or perception. Dissociative Identity Disorder and Depersonalization/Derealization Disorder are representative conditions.
9. *Somatic Symptom and Related Disorders*: Somatic symptom and related disorders involve physical symptoms that cannot be fully explained by a medical condition. Somatic Symptom Disorder, Illness Anxiety Disorder, and Conversion Disorder are included in this group.
10. *Feeding and Eating Disorders*: Feeding and eating disorders are characterized by disturbances in eating patterns, body image, and weight. Anorexia Nervosa, Bulimia Nervosa, and Binge-eating disorder are examples.
11. *Elimination Disorders*: Elimination disorders refer to conditions involving difficulties with controlling urination or bowel movements, typically observed in children. Enuresis (Bedwetting) and Encopresis (Soiling) are included in this group.
12. *Sleep-wake Disorders*: Sleep-wake disorders encompass conditions related to disruptions in sleep patterns and quality. Insomnia Disorder, Narcolepsy, and Restless Legs Syndrome are representative examples.
13. *Sexual Dysfunctions*: Sexual dysfunctions involve difficulties in experiencing sexual desire, arousal, or satisfaction. Examples include erectile disorder, female orgasmic disorder, and premature ejaculation.

14. *Gender Dysphoria*: Gender dysphoria is the distress caused by the incongruence between a person's assigned gender at birth and their gender identity. It is not a mental disorder but reflects the discomfort resulting from this incongruence. Supportive interventions aim to alleviate distress and align physical appearance with gender identity.
15. *Disruptive, Impulse-control, and Conduct Disorders*: Disruptive, impulse-control, and conduct disorders involve problems with self-control, defiance, and antisocial behaviour. Oppositional Defiant Disorder, Conduct Disorder, and Intermittent Explosive Disorder fall under this category.
16. *Substance-related and Addictive Disorders*: Substance-related and addictive disorders are characterized by dependence on substances or engaging in addictive behaviours. Alcohol Use Disorder, Opioid Use Disorder, and Gambling Disorder are examples.
17. *Neurocognitive Disorders*: Neurocognitive disorders result from cognitive decline or impairment, often associated with neurological conditions or aging. Alzheimer's Disease, Mild Cognitive Impairment, and Vascular Neurocognitive Disorder are included in this group.
18. *Personality Disorders*: Personality disorders involve enduring patterns of thinking, feeling, and behaving that significantly deviate from societal norms and cause distress. Borderline Personality Disorder, Antisocial Personality Disorder, and Narcissistic Personality Disorder fall within this category.
19. *Paraphilic Disorders:* Paraphilic disorders include intense sexual urges or behaviours that involve non-consenting individuals or non-typical preferences. Exhibitionistic Disorder, Voyeuristic Disorder, and Pedophilic Disorder are examples.
20. *Other Mental Disorders*: This category encompasses mental disorders that do not fit into specific groups but are still significant and require clinical attention. Examples include Body Dysmorphic Disorder, Factitious Disorder, and Adjustment Disorder.

It's important to note that this discussion provides a brief overview of the main categories in the DSM-V. Each category contains numerous specific disorders with unique diagnostic criteria and considerations. Mental health professionals utilize the DSM-V as a valuable resource to guide their assessment, diagnosis, and treatment planning to provide effective support to individuals experiencing mental health challenges.

Depression

Depression is a common mental disorder characterized by persistent feelings of sadness, loss of interest or pleasure in activities, and a range of physical and psychological symptoms.

It affects people of all ages, genders, and backgrounds, and can significantly impact their daily lives, relationships, and overall well-being. In this response,

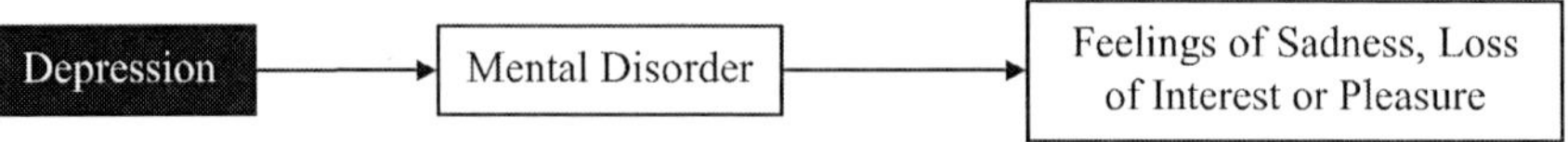

Figure 6.2: *Depression*

we will explore the concept, identification characteristics, causes, and treatment options for depression. Depression is more than just experiencing occasional feelings of sadness or temporary emotional lows. It is a clinical condition that involves a prolonged and intense state of sadness, despair, and hopelessness. It often affects multiple aspects of a person's life, including their emotions, thoughts, behaviours, and physical health. Depression can be categorized into various subtypes, such as major depressive disorder (MDD), persistent depressive disorder (PDD), and seasonal affective disorder (SAD), among others.

Major Depressive Disorder (MDD): MDD, also known as clinical depression, is the most well-known and prevalent form of depression. It is characterized by experiencing a depressive episode that lasts for at least two weeks and includes a combination of symptoms such as low mood, loss of interest or pleasure, changes in appetite and weight, sleep disturbances, fatigue, difficulty concentrating, feelings of worthlessness or guilt, and recurrent thoughts of death or suicide. MDD significantly affects a person's ability to function in daily life.

Persistent Depressive Disorder (PDD): PDD, previously referred to as dysthymia, is a chronic form of depression where individuals experience a depressed mood for most days over a period of at least two years. While the symptoms of PDD may not be as severe as those of MDD, they can still interfere with daily life and lead to functional impairment. PDD is characterized by a persistent feeling of sadness or low mood, along with other symptoms such as changes in appetite, sleep problems, low energy, poor self-esteem, difficulty making decisions, and feelings of hopelessness.

Seasonal Affective Disorder (SAD): SAD is a subtype of depression that typically occurs in a seasonal pattern. It is most commonly associated with the onset of symptoms during the fall and winter months when daylight hours are reduced. People with SAD may experience symptoms such as low mood, lack of energy, increased sleep, carbohydrate cravings, weight gain, and social withdrawal during these seasons. The symptoms tend to improve in the spring and summer months.

These different forms of depression share some common symptoms but also have distinct features that help differentiate them. It's important to note that a proper diagnosis can only be made by a qualified mental health professional based on a comprehensive evaluation of an individual's symptoms, history, and other relevant factors. Treatment options, including therapy and medication, can vary depending on the specific type of depression and the individual's needs.

Identification Characteristics of Depression

Depression is a mental health disorder that is characterized by persistent feelings of sadness, hopelessness, and loss of interest or pleasure in activities that were once enjoyable. Here are some common identification characteristics of depression:

1. Feelings of sadness or hopelessness that persist for two weeks or more.
2. Loss of interest or pleasure in activities that were once enjoyable.
3. Significant changes in appetite, weight, or sleep patterns.
4. Fatigue or loss of energy.
5. Difficulty concentrating, making decisions, or remembering things.
6. Feelings of worthlessness or guilt.
7. Thoughts of death or suicide.
8. Restlessness or agitation.
9. Physical symptoms such as headaches, digestive issues, or unexplained pain.
10. Withdrawal from social activities or relationships.
11. Feelings of irritability, anger, or restlessness.
12. Persistent feelings of emptiness or numbness.
13. Physical symptoms such as aches and pains, digestive issues, or changes in menstrual cycles.
14. Loss of libido or interest in sexual activity.
15. Persistent negative thoughts or feelings of pessimism.
16. Difficulty in falling or staying asleep, or sleeping too much.
17. Withdrawal from previously enjoyed activities, hobbies, or social relationships.
18. Difficulty performing daily tasks, such as work or schoolwork.
19. Increased use of alcohol or drugs as a coping mechanism.
20. Feelings of worthlessness or excessive guilt, even in the absence of clear reasons for feeling this way.

It's important to note that depression can manifest differently in different people and may not always be present with all of these symptoms. Additionally, some symptoms of depression can also be associated with other mental health disorders or medical conditions, so it's important to seek an evaluation from a trained mental health professional to obtain an accurate diagnosis and treatment plan.

Causes of Depression

Depression is a complex mental disorder with multiple causes. While the exact mechanisms are not fully understood, several factors contribute to the development of depression. Here are some key causes:

Biological Factors

1. *Genetics*: Research suggests that there is a genetic component to depression. Having a family history of depression increases the risk of developing the disorder.

2. *Brain Chemistry*: Imbalances in neurotransmitters, such as serotonin, norepinephrine, and dopamine, which regulate mood and emotions, are associated with depression.
3. *Hormonal Changes*: Hormonal imbalances, such as those occurring during puberty, pregnancy, postpartum period, and menopause, can influence mood and contribute to depression.

Environmental Factors

1. *Life Events*: Traumatic experiences like the loss of a loved one, divorce, abuse, or financial difficulties can trigger depression. Chronic stress, such as work-related stress or ongoing relationship problems, can also play a role.
2. *Childhood Trauma*: Adverse experiences during childhood, such as physical, emotional, or sexual abuse, neglect, or parental separation, can increase the vulnerability to depression later in life.

Social Factors

Social isolation, loneliness, lack of support, or poor social relationships can contribute to depression. Living in an unsupportive or dysfunctional family environment can also be a risk factor.

Psychological Factors

1. *Negative Thinking Patterns*: Pervasive negative thoughts, self-criticism, low self-esteem, or distorted thinking patterns can contribute to depression.
2. *Personality Traits*: Certain personality traits, such as perfectionism, excessive self-criticism, or high levels of neuroticism, can increase the likelihood of developing depression.
3. *Coping Skills*: Inadequate coping mechanisms or a lack of effective problem-solving skills can make individuals more susceptible to depression.

Medical Conditions and Medications

1. *Chronic Illnesses*: Certain medical conditions, such as chronic pain, cancer, heart disease, diabetes, or neurological disorders, are associated with an increased risk of depression.
2. *Medications*: Some medications, including corticosteroids, anticonvulsants, beta-blockers, and certain hormonal medications, have been linked to depression as a potential side effect.

It is important to note that the causes of depression can vary from person to person, and often, multiple factors interact to contribute to its development. Understanding these causes can help in identifying risk factors, implementing appropriate preventive measures, and developing effective treatment approaches. If you or someone you know is experiencing symptoms of depression, it is important to seek professional help from a mental health provider.

Treatments of Depression

The treatment of depression typically involves a combination of approaches tailored to the individual's needs. Here are some key points about the treatments of depression:

Psychotherapy

1. *Cognitive Behavioural Therapy (CBT)*: CBT helps individuals identify and modify negative thought patterns and behaviours that contribute to depression. It focuses on developing coping skills and strategies to manage symptoms effectively.
2. *Interpersonal Therapy (IPT)*: IPT focuses on improving interpersonal relationships and addressing social difficulties that may contribute to depression. It aims to enhance communication skills, resolve conflicts, and build a stronger support system.
3. *Psychodynamic Therapy*: This type of therapy explores underlying unconscious conflicts and past experiences to gain insight into the root causes of depression and promote healing.

Medication

1. *Antidepressant Medications*: Selective Serotonin Reuptake Inhibitors (SSRIs) and Serotonin-Norepinephrine Reuptake Inhibitors (SNRIs) are commonly prescribed medications for depression. They work by increasing the availability of certain neurotransmitters in the brain. Other classes of antidepressants, such as tricyclic antidepressants (TCAs) and monoamine oxidase inhibitors (MAOIs), may be prescribed in specific cases.
2. *Medication Management*: Regular monitoring and adjustment of medication dosage and type are important to ensure effectiveness and manage potential side effects. This is typically done in collaboration with a psychiatrist or prescribing healthcare professional.

Lifestyle Changes

1. *Regular Exercise*: Engaging in regular physical activity, such as aerobic exercises, has been shown to have a positive impact on mood and can help alleviate symptoms of depression.
2. *Healthy Diet*: A balanced diet rich in fruits, vegetables, whole grains, lean proteins, and omega-3 fatty acids can support overall mental well-being.
3. *Sleep Hygiene*: Establishing a consistent sleep routine, practising good sleep hygiene, and ensuring adequate sleep duration can positively affect mood and energy levels.

Supportive Interventions

1. *Support Groups*: Participating in support groups or group therapy can provide individuals with a sense of belonging, support, and the opportunity to share experiences with others who have faced similar challenges.

2. *Social Support*: Building and maintaining a strong support network of family and friends who can provide emotional support and practical assistance is beneficial for individuals with depression.

Brain Stimulation Therapies

1. *Electroconvulsive Therapy (ECT)*: ECT is a treatment option for severe depression that does not respond to other interventions. It involves the administration of a controlled electrical current to induce a brief seizure, leading to changes in brain chemistry and improvement in depressive symptoms.
2. *Transcranial Magnetic Stimulation (TMS)*: TMS uses magnetic fields to stimulate specific areas of the brain implicated in depression. It is a non-invasive procedure and is generally used when other treatments have been ineffective.

It's important to note that treatment plans for depression should be individualized, and what works for one person may not work for another. A comprehensive assessment by a mental health professional is crucial to determine the most appropriate treatment approach. Often, a combination of therapies, such as psychotherapy and medication, yields the best results. Regular follow-up and ongoing support are also essential for managing and preventing relapses.

Obsessive Compulsive Disorder (OCD)

Obsessive-Compulsive Disorder (OCD) is a mental disorder characterized by recurring, intrusive, and unwanted thoughts, images, or impulses (obsessions) and repetitive, ritualistic behaviours or mental acts (compulsions). People with OCD often feel compelled to perform these rituals to alleviate anxiety or prevent perceived harm. OCD affects individuals of all ages, genders, and backgrounds, and it can have a significant impact on their daily lives.

Identification Characteristics of Obsessive Compulsive Disorder (OCD)

Identification characteristics of Obsessive-Compulsive Disorder (OCD) typically involve the presence of obsessions and compulsions, which can be identified through the following characteristics:

Obsessions

- Recurrent and persistent thoughts, urges, or images those are intrusive and unwanted.
- These thoughts are experienced as intrusive, causing distress or anxiety.
- Attempts are made to ignore or suppress these thoughts, urges, or images.
- The individual recognizes that these obsessions are a product of their own mind and not based on real dangers.

Examples: Fear of germs, dirt, or contamination; Persistent doubt or fear of having forgotten to perform a crucial task, such as locking the door or turning off the stove; A need for everything to be perfectly symmetrical, aligned, or in a specific order; Unwanted, distressing, or taboo thoughts, often related to harm or violence; Persistent difficulty discarding or parting with possessions, regardless of their value etc.

Compulsions

- Repetitive behaviours or mental acts that are aimed at reducing anxiety or preventing a feared event.
- The behaviours or mental acts are not connected realistically to the event they are designed to prevent.
- The compulsions are not pleasurable in them but are performed to relieve anxiety or distress.
- The individual feels driven to perform these compulsions and has difficulty resisting or controlling them.

Examples: Excessive hand washing, avoiding touching certain objects, compulsive cleaning or sanitizing of personal belongings or surroundings; Repeatedly checking locks, appliances, or other items to ensure they are secure or turned off; Rearranging objects repeatedly until they feel "Just Right", aligning items meticulously, or needing to perform tasks in a particular sequence; Engaging in mental rituals, such as mentally repeating phrases or prayers, or mentally counting or reciting specific sequences to neutralize or prevent the feared thoughts or events; Excessive acquisition and accumulation of items, feeling distress or anxiety when attempting to discard items, and living in cluttered or overcrowded living spaces etc.

It is important to note that individuals with OCD may experience a combination of different obsessions and compulsions, and symptoms may overlap or change over time. For example, a person may have contamination fears alongside checking rituals or intrusive thoughts accompanied by cleaning compulsions.

Impact on Daily Life

- Obsessions and compulsions consume a significant amount of time (usually more than one hour per day).
- The individual's daily routine, activities, and relationships are significantly disrupted due to OCD symptoms.
- The distress caused by obsessions and compulsions is not proportional to the realistic risks involved.

Interference and Avoidance

- The individual may avoid situations or triggers that provoke obsessions and compulsions.
- The avoidance behaviour may result in limitations on social, occupational, or academic functioning.

Awareness of Irrationality

- The person recognizes that their obsessions and compulsions are excessive or unreasonable.
- Despite this recognition, they find it challenging to control or resist compulsions.

Distress and Anxiety

- Obsessions and compulsions cause significant distress, anxiety, or discomfort.
- The distress is often alleviated temporarily by performing compulsions, but the anxiety returns.

Impact on Relationships and Well-being

- OCD symptoms can strain relationships, as obsessions and compulsions may be difficult for others to understand.
- The individual may experience a diminished quality of life, depression, or other mental health issues due to the impact of OCD.

It's important to note that OCD symptoms can vary in severity and may differ among individuals. A qualified mental health professional should make a diagnosis based on a thorough evaluation of an individual's symptoms and history.

Causes of Obsessive Compulsive Disorder (OCD)

The causes of Obsessive-Compulsive Disorder (OCD) are not yet fully understood. However, research suggests that a combination of genetic, neurological, environmental, and psychological factors contribute to the development of OCD. Here are some key points regarding the causes of OCD:

Genetic Factors

1. *Family History*: OCD tends to run in families, indicating a genetic predisposition to the disorder.
2. *Inherited Vulnerability*: Certain genetic variations or mutations may increase the likelihood of developing OCD.
3. *Specific Genes*: Researchers have identified potential candidate genes that may be associated with OCD, although more research is needed to fully understand their role.

Neurological Factors

1. *Brain Structure and Function*: Studies using brain imaging techniques have shown differences in the structure and functioning of certain brain areas in individuals with OCD.
2. *Neurotransmitters*: Imbalances in neurotransmitters, particularly serotonin, dopamine, and glutamate, are thought to play a role in OCD. These neurotransmitters are involved in regulating mood, anxiety, and repetitive behaviours.

Environmental Factors

1. *Early Life Experiences*: Traumatic events, such as physical or sexual abuse, can contribute to the development of OCD in some individuals.
2. *Stressful Life Events*: Significant life changes, academic or work-related stress, or major transitions can trigger or exacerbate OCD symptoms.
3. *Infections and Autoimmune Disorders*: Some research suggests that certain infections, such as streptococcal infections, may trigger OCD symptoms in individuals, particularly in children (known as Pediatric Autoimmune Neuropsychiatric Disorders Associated with Streptococcal Infections — PANDAS).

Cognitive and Behavioural Factors

1. *Cognitive Biases*: Certain thinking patterns, such as excessive responsibility, perfectionism, and intolerance of uncertainty, may contribute to the development or maintenance of OCD.
2. *Learned Behaviours*: Engaging in repetitive behaviours or rituals may initially provide temporary relief from anxiety, reinforcing their association with reducing distress and leading to the development of OCD symptoms.

It is important to note that OCD is a complex disorder, and different individuals may have unique combinations of factors contributing to their condition. Additionally, these factors interact in complex ways, making it difficult to pinpoint a single cause. Further research is ongoing to better understand the underlying mechanisms and causes of OCD. It's important to seek professional help from a mental health provider for a comprehensive assessment and diagnosis of OCD, as they can provide appropriate treatment and support based on an individual's specific needs.

Treatments of Obsessive Compulsive Disorder (OCD)

Treatment options for Obsessive-Compulsive Disorder (OCD) typically involve a combination of medication and psychotherapy. The goal of treatment is to reduce the severity of symptoms, improve functioning, and enhance the individual's quality of life. Here are the key treatment approaches for OCD:

Cognitive-Behavioural Therapy (CBT)

1. *Exposure and Response Prevention (ERP)*: ERP is a specific form of CBT widely considered the most effective treatment for OCD. It involves gradually exposing individuals to situations, thoughts, or images that trigger their obsessions while preventing the associated compulsions or rituals.
2. *Cognitive Restructuring*: This component of CBT helps individuals challenge and modify their irrational or distorted thoughts and beliefs related to their obsessions. It aims to develop more realistic and adaptive thinking patterns.

3. *Skills Training*: CBT may also involve teaching individuals coping skills, problem-solving techniques, and stress management strategies to better manage their OCD symptoms.

Medication

1. *Selective Serotonin Reuptake Inhibitors (SSRIs)*: These antidepressant medications are commonly prescribed to treat OCD. SSRIs, such as fluoxetine, sertraline, and fluvoxamine, can help reduce the severity of obsessions and compulsions. It may take several weeks to see the full therapeutic effects.
2. *Other Medications*: In some cases, other types of medications, such as tricyclic antidepressants or antipsychotics, may be prescribed to augment the effects of SSRIs or when SSRIs are ineffective.

Combination Therapy

1. *Medication and CBT*: Combining medication with CBT, particularly ERP, can yield the most significant symptom improvement for many individuals with OCD. Medication can help reduce anxiety, while CBT provides long-term coping skills and addresses underlying cognitive patterns.
2. *Augmentation Strategies*: If an individual does not respond adequately to one medication, the addition of another medication or augmentation strategies may be considered under the guidance of a healthcare professional.

Support and Education

1. *Support Groups*: Joining support groups or therapy groups with individuals experiencing similar challenges can provide a sense of community, understanding, and emotional support.
2. *Psycho-education*: Learning about OCD, its causes, and treatment options can empower individuals and their families to better understand the disorder and actively participate in the treatment process.

Lifestyle Factors

1. *Stress Management*: Implementing stress reduction techniques, such as regular exercise, relaxation exercises, mindfulness, and healthy lifestyle habits, can help manage anxiety and improve overall well-being.
2. *Sleep Hygiene*: Prioritizing good sleep habits, maintaining a regular sleep schedule, and ensuring adequate rest can positively impact OCD symptoms.

It is important for individuals with OCD to work with qualified mental health professionals, such as psychiatrists, psychologists, or licensed therapists, who specialize in treating OCD. Treatment plans should be tailored to the individual's specific needs and may require adjustments over time. Continued support, monitoring, and maintenance strategies are essential for long-term management of OCD.

Bipolar Mood Disorder

Bipolar mood disorder, also known as bipolar disorder or manic-depressive illness, is a mental health condition characterized by recurrent and extreme shifts in mood, energy levels, and activity levels. It is a chronic and often lifelong condition that affects a person's ability to function and impacts various aspects of their life, including relationships, work, and overall well-being.

Bipolar disorder is classified into different types based on the pattern and severity of mood episodes.

- Bipolar I disorder involves the occurrence of manic episodes,
- While bipolar II disorder involves hypomanic episodes and depressive episodes.
- Cyclothymic disorder is a milder form of bipolar disorder characterized by numerous periods of hypomanic and depressive symptoms that do not meet the criteria for full-blown episodes.

The exact cause of bipolar disorder is not known, but it is believed to result from a combination of genetic, biological, and environmental factors. Research suggests that imbalances in neurotransmitters, such as serotonin, dopamine, and norepinephrine, play a role in the development of the disorder.

Bipolar disorder often emerges in late adolescence or early adulthood, but it can occur at any age. It is a chronic condition that requires ongoing management and treatment. With proper care, including medications, psychotherapy, and lifestyle adjustments, individuals with bipolar disorder can lead fulfilling lives and effectively manage their symptoms. Early diagnosis, education, and a strong support system are crucial in helping individuals with bipolar disorder navigate their condition and maintain stability in their mood and daily functioning.

Identification Characteristics of Bipolar Mood Disorder

The identification characteristics of bipolar mood disorder encompass a wide range of symptoms that vary in severity and duration.

- During a manic episode, individuals may exhibit elevated or expansive moods, racing thoughts, impulsive behaviour, and decreased need for sleep.
- Hypomanic episodes share similarities with manic episodes but are less severe and typically do not cause significant impairment in functioning.
- Depressive episodes are characterized by profound sadness, loss of interest or pleasure, changes in appetite and sleep patterns, fatigue, and difficulty concentrating.

Proper identification of bipolar disorder is crucial to initiate appropriate treatment and support. It is important to consult with a mental health professional for an accurate diagnosis, as bipolar disorder can often be mistaken for other mental health conditions or dismissed as normal mood swings. Early recognition and intervention can significantly improve the individual's quality of life and minimize the impact of mood episodes.

In the following sections, we will explore the identification characteristics of bipolar mood disorder in more detail, shedding light on the signs and symptoms that individuals may experience during manic, hypomanic, and depressive episodes.

Manic Episode

1. *Elevated or expansive mood*: Individuals may feel abnormally high or euphoric, often described as feeling "on top of the world" or invincible.
2. *Increased energy and restlessness*: They may have a surplus of energy, engage in multiple activities simultaneously, and have difficulty sitting still.
3. *Decreased need for sleep*: Individuals may require less sleep than usual and still feel highly energized.
4. *Racing thoughts and rapid speech*: Thoughts may race through their mind, making it challenging to focus or concentrate. They may also speak rapidly, jumping between topics.
5. *Grandiose beliefs or inflated self-esteem*: Individuals may have an exaggerated sense of self-importance, believing they possess special abilities or talents.
6. *Impulsive behaviour and risk-taking*: They may engage in reckless behaviours such as excessive spending, risky sexual encounters, substance abuse, or impulsive decision-making.
7. *Irritability or Agitation*: Some individuals may experience irritability or an agitated state during a manic episode.

Hypomanic Episode

1. *Similar symptoms to a manic episode*: Hypomania shares several characteristics with mania but is less severe and does not typically cause significant impairment in functioning.
2. *Shorter duration*: Hypomanic episodes last for at least four days and are shorter in duration compared to manic episodes.

Major Depressive Episode

1. *Persistent feelings of sadness*: Individuals experience a profound and pervasive sense of sadness, emptiness, or hopelessness.
2. *Loss of interest or pleasure*: They may lose interest in activities they once enjoyed, experience a lack of motivation, and have difficulty deriving pleasure from anything.
3. *Changes in appetite and weight*: Significant changes in appetite, resulting in weight loss or weight gain, may occur.
4. *Sleep disturbances*: Individuals may experience insomnia (difficulty falling asleep or staying asleep) or hypersomnia (excessive sleeping).
5. *Fatigue and low energy*: They may feel constantly tired, lacking energy and motivation to engage in daily activities.

6. *Difficulty concentrating and making decisions*: Cognitive difficulties arise, making it challenging to concentrate, remember details, and make even simple decisions.
7. *Feelings of guilt or worthlessness*: Individuals may experience excessive guilt or feel unworthy, even in the absence of reasonable justification.
8. *Recurrent thoughts of death or suicide*: They may have persistent thoughts about death, suicidal ideation, or engage in self-harming behaviours.

It is important to note that the identification characteristics of bipolar mood disorder can vary in severity and duration among individuals. A professional diagnosis by a mental health practitioner is necessary to accurately assess and identify bipolar disorder based on an individual's symptoms and history.

Causes of Bipolar Mood Disorder

The causes of bipolar mood disorder, also known as bipolar disorder, are complex and multifaceted, involving a combination of genetic, biological, and environmental factors. While the exact cause is not fully understood, researchers have identified several key factors that contribute to the development of this mental health condition. Here are the main causes of bipolar disorder:

Genetic Factors

1. *Family History*: Bipolar disorder tends to run in families, suggesting a genetic predisposition. Having a close family member, such as a parent or sibling, with bipolar disorder increases the risk of developing the condition.
2. *Genetic Markers*: Researchers have identified specific genes and gene variations that may be associated with bipolar disorder. However, it is important to note that genetics alone do not determine the development of the disorder, as other factors also play a role.

Neurochemical Imbalances

1. *Brain Chemistry*: Neurotransmitters, which are chemical messengers in the brain, play a crucial role in regulating mood, emotions, and other brain functions. Imbalances in neurotransmitters such as serotonin, dopamine, and norepinephrine have been implicated in bipolar disorder. Disruptions in the intricate interplay between these neurotransmitters can contribute to mood swings and other symptoms associated with the disorder.
2. *Brain Structure and Function*: Abnormalities in Brain Structure: Imaging studies have revealed differences in the brain structure of individuals with bipolar disorder, particularly in areas involved in emotion regulation, decision-making, and impulse control. These structural abnormalities may contribute to the manifestation of bipolar symptoms.
3. *Dysregulation of Neural Circuits*: Disruptions in the functioning of neural circuits, which are networks of interconnected brain regions, have been observed in individuals with bipolar disorder. These circuit dysfunctions can affect mood regulation and lead to mood instability.

Environmental Factors

1. *Stressful Life Events*: Traumatic experiences, significant life changes, relationship difficulties, and high levels of stress can trigger the onset of bipolar episodes in individuals with a genetic vulnerability. Stress management and coping skills are important components of bipolar disorder management.
2. *Substance Abuse*: Substance abuse, including alcohol and illicit drugs, can worsen symptoms and trigger episodes in individuals with bipolar disorder. Substance use can also complicate treatment and increase the severity of the condition.

It's important to note that while these factors contribute to the development of bipolar disorder, they do not guarantee its occurrence. The interplay of genetic and environmental factors is complex, and not all individuals with genetic predisposition or exposure to environmental triggers will develop bipolar disorder. Understanding the causes of bipolar disorder helps guide treatment approaches and interventions. By addressing these factors, such as through medication, therapy, stress reduction techniques, and lifestyle modifications, individuals with bipolar disorder can better manage their symptoms and lead fulfilling lives. It is crucial to consult with a mental health professional for a comprehensive evaluation and personalized treatment plan.

Treatments of Bipolar Mood Disorder

The treatment of bipolar mood disorder aims to stabilize mood, manage symptoms, prevent relapses, and improve overall functioning and quality of life. The treatment approach often involves a combination of medication, psychotherapy, lifestyle adjustments, and ongoing support. Here are the key components of bipolar disorder treatment:

Medications

1. *Mood Stabilizers*: Medications such as lithium, valproate, and carbamazepine are commonly prescribed to help stabilize mood and prevent both manic and depressive episodes. These medications help regulate neurotransmitter activity in the brain.
2. *Atypical Antipsychotics*: Some antipsychotic medications, such as quetiapine, olanzapine, and risperidone, may be used during acute manic or mixed episodes to control symptoms.
3. *Antidepressants*: In some cases, when used with caution and in combination with a mood stabilizer, antidepressant medications may be prescribed to alleviate depressive symptoms. However, they are usually not used alone to avoid triggering manic episodes.

Psychotherapy

1. *Cognitive-Behavioural Therapy (CBT)*: CBT helps individuals identify and modify negative thought patterns and behaviours associated with

bipolar disorder. It focuses on developing coping skills, improving problem-solving abilities, and managing stress.

2. *Interpersonal and Social Rhythm Therapy (IPSRT)*: IPSRT aims to stabilize daily routines and sleep-wake cycles, as disruptions in these rhythms can trigger mood episodes. It also addresses interpersonal relationships and helps individuals develop strategies for maintaining stable social connections.

Lifestyle Management

1. *Regular Routine*: Establishing and maintaining a consistent daily routine can help stabilize mood and prevent triggers. Regular sleep patterns, mealtimes, and structured activities contribute to stability.
2. *Stress Reduction*: Learning stress management techniques, such as relaxation exercises, mindfulness, and stress-reducing activities (e.g., yoga, meditation), can help individuals cope with stressors that may contribute to mood episodes.
3. *Substance Abuse Avoidance*: Avoiding alcohol and recreational drugs is crucial, as substance abuse can worsen symptoms and interfere with the effectiveness of medications.

Support and Self-Care

1. *Education and Self-Management*: Learning about bipolar disorder, its symptoms, and treatment options empowers individuals to actively participate in their own care. Self-monitoring of mood and early recognition of warning signs can help prevent relapses.
2. *Supportive Relationships*: Building a strong support system, including family, friends, and support groups, can provide understanding, encouragement, and assistance during difficult times.
3. *Ongoing Professional Support*: Regular follow-up visits with mental health professionals, including psychiatrists and therapists, are essential to monitor progress, adjust medication dosages if needed, and provide guidance and support.

Hospitalization and Electroconvulsive Therapy (ECT)

1. *Hospitalization*: In severe cases or during acute manic or depressive episodes, hospitalization may be necessary to ensure the safety and well-being of the individual. It allows for intensive treatment, medication adjustments, and protection from harm.
2. *Electroconvulsive Therapy (ECT)*: In rare cases when other treatments have not been effective or if rapid intervention is required, ECT may be considered. ECT involves delivering controlled electric currents to the brain to induce a brief seizure, which can alleviate severe symptoms.

It's important to remember that treatment for bipolar disorder is highly individualized, and finding the most effective treatment combination may require some trial and error. Collaborating closely with healthcare professionals, maintaining open communication, and adhering to the treatment plan are crucial for managing bipolar disorder successfully.

Occupational Disorders

Occupational disorders refer to physical or mental health conditions that arise primarily due to the nature of one's occupation or work environment. These disorders are often caused or aggravated by occupational hazards, prolonged exposure to certain substances, repetitive tasks, work-related stress, or poor ergonomics. Occupational disorders can have a significant impact on an individual's well-being, job performance, and overall quality of life.

Identification Characteristics of Occupational Disorders

The identification characteristics of occupational disorders can vary widely depending on the specific condition and the nature of the occupational exposure. However, here are some common identification characteristics associated with different types of occupational disorders:

1. *Musculoskeletal Disorders*

- *Pain*: Individuals may experience pain in the affected area, such as the hands, wrists, back, neck, or joints.
- *Stiffness*: Reduced flexibility and stiffness in the affected area may be present.
- *Weakness*: Decreased strength or difficulty performing certain tasks due to muscle or joint involvement.
- *Swelling*: Inflammation or swelling may occur in the affected area.
- *Limited Range of Motion*: Reduced ability to move the affected body part fully or comfortably.
- *Numbness or Tingling*: Sensations of numbness, tingling, or "pins and needles" in the affected area.

2. *Respiratory Disorders*

- *Shortness of Breath*: Difficulty breathing or a feeling of breathlessness, especially during or after work.
- *Coughing*: Persistent or chronic cough, often accompanied by phlegm production.
- *Wheezing*: Whistling or high-pitched sounds when breathing.
- *Chest Tightness*: A sensation of pressure or tightness in the chest.
- *Reduced Lung Function*: Decreased ability to exhale forcefully or impaired lung capacity.

3. Mental Health Disorders

- *Stress*: Excessive or prolonged feelings of stress, anxiety, or tension related to work.
- *Fatigue*: Persistent fatigue, even after adequate rest or sleep.

- *Mood Changes*: Fluctuations in mood, such as irritability, sadness, or a sense of hopelessness.
- *Difficulty Concentrating*: Trouble focusing or staying attentive to tasks.
- *Sleep Disturbances*: Insomnia, restless sleep, or excessive sleepiness.
- *Changes in Appetite*: Increased or decreased appetite, leading to weight changes.

4. Occupational Dermatitis

- *Redness*: Skin may appear red or flushed.
- *Itching*: Persistent or intense itching sensation.
- *Rash*: Development of a rash, which may be dry, scaly, or blistered.
- *Blisters*: Formation of small fluid-filled blisters on the skin.
- *Swelling*: The affected area may be swollen or puffy.

5. Noise-Induced Hearing Loss

- *Hearing Loss*: Gradual or sudden loss of hearing, often affecting high-frequency sounds.
- *Tinnitus*: Ringing, buzzing, or other phantom sounds in the ears.
- *Sensitivity to Noise*: Increased sensitivity to loud sounds or discomfort in noisy environments.

6. Occupational Lung Diseases

- *Chronic Cough*: A persistent cough that lasts for an extended period.
- *Difficulty in Breathing*: Shortness of breath or a feeling of breathlessness, especially with exertion.
- *Chest Pain*: Discomfort or pain in the chest area, which may worsen during breathing or coughing.
- *Fatigue*: Unexplained tiredness or lack of energy.
- *Respiratory Infections*: Frequent or recurring respiratory infections, such as bronchitis or pneumonia.

7. Occupational Asthma

- *Wheezing*: Whistling or musical sounds when breathing out.
- *Chest Tightness*: A sensation of pressure or constriction in the chest.
- *Coughing*: Frequent or persistent cough, especially at night or during work.
- *Shortness of Breath*: Difficulty breathing or a feeling of breathlessness, particularly after exposure to occupational triggers.

8. Work-related Stress and Mental Health Disorders

- *Irritability*: Increased sensitivity or impatience, leading to irritability or anger.
- *Cognitive Difficulties*: Trouble with memory, concentration, or decision-making.
- *Social Withdrawal*: Avoidance of social interactions or decreased interest in social activities.

- *Changes in Appetite or Weight*: Significant changes in appetite, resulting in weight gain or loss.
- *Physical Symptoms*: Headaches, gastrointestinal problems, or increased susceptibility to illnesses.

9. Vision Problems

- *Eye Irritation*: Redness, itchiness, or burning sensation in the eyes.
- *Blurred Vision*: Difficulty focusing or seeing clearly.
- *Dry Eyes*: Feeling of dryness or discomfort in the eyes, potentially exacerbated by the work environment.
- *Eye Strain*: Fatigue or discomfort in the eyes, often accompanied by headaches or difficulty with visual tasks.

10. Occupational Cancer

- *Unexplained Weight Loss*: Significant and unintentional weight loss without apparent cause.
- *Fatigue*: Persistent tiredness or lack of energy.
- *Pain or Swelling*: Persistent pain or swelling in a specific area of the body.
- *Changes in Skin*: Appearance of unusual moles, skin discoloration, or new growths.
- *Digestive Issues*: Digestive problems, such as abdominal pain, changes in bowel habits, or blood in the stool.

It's important to note that these symptoms can overlap and may not be exclusive to occupational disorders. Additionally, the severity of symptoms can vary depending on factors such as the duration and intensity of occupational exposure, individual susceptibility, and the presence of other health conditions. Top of FormIt is important to note that the identification of occupational disorders should be carried out by qualified healthcare professionals, such as occupational health physicians or specialists, who have the knowledge and expertise in recognizing and managing these specific conditions.

Causes of Occupational Disorders

The causes of occupational disorders can vary depending on the specific condition and the nature of the work environment. Here are some common causes associated with different types of occupational disorders:

1. *Occupational Hazards*

- *Chemical Exposure*: Exposure to hazardous chemicals, such as solvents, heavy metals, or toxic gases, in certain occupations can contribute to the development of respiratory disorders, skin conditions, or systemic health problems.
- *Physical Agents*: Prolonged exposure to physical agents like vibrations, extreme temperatures, ionizing radiation, or non-ionizing radiation (e.g., ultraviolet rays, electromagnetic fields) can lead to various occupational

disorders, including musculoskeletal disorders, burns, or certain types of cancer.

- *Biological Agents*: Working with infectious agents, such as bacteria, viruses, or fungi, in healthcare settings or research laboratories can increase the risk of developing occupational infections or respiratory disorders.
- *Noise*: Exposure to excessive noise levels without proper hearing protection can lead to noise-induced hearing loss or tinnitus.

2. *Repetitive Tasks and Ergonomics*

- *Repetitive Motion*: Performing repetitive tasks or movements, such as assembly line work, typing, or operating machinery, can strain muscles, tendons, or joints, leading to musculoskeletal disorders like carpal tunnel syndrome or tendinitis.
- *Poor Ergonomics*: Inadequate workstation design, improper body mechanics, uncomfortable seating, or repetitive awkward postures can contribute to musculoskeletal disorders and related injuries.

3. *Work-related Stress*

- *High Work Demands*: Jobs with high workloads, tight deadlines, or excessive responsibilities can lead to chronic stress, which may contribute to mental health disorders such as anxiety, depression, or burnout.
- *Lack of Control*: Feeling a lack of control over one's work environment, decision-making, or job tasks can increase stress levels and impact mental well-being.
- *Job Insecurity*: Uncertainty about job stability, fear of layoffs, or precarious employment conditions can contribute to work-related stress and mental health issues.

4. *Occupational Exposures*

- *Respiratory Irritants*: Exposure to respiratory irritants such as dust, fumes, allergens, or airborne pollutants in industries like construction, manufacturing, or agriculture can cause respiratory disorders, including occupational asthma or chronic obstructive pulmonary disease (COPD).
- *Dermatological Irritants*: Contact with irritants or allergens in the workplace, such as chemicals, cleaning agents, or certain materials, can lead to occupational dermatitis or other skin conditions.
- *Carcinogens*: Prolonged exposure to carcinogens, such as asbestos, silica dust, or certain chemicals, in occupations like mining, construction, or manufacturing, can increase the risk of occupational cancers.

5. *Psychosocial Factors*

- *Work Organization*: Poorly organized work processes, lack of clear roles or responsibilities, or insufficient support and resources can contribute to work-related stress and mental health disorders.

- *Job Demands*: High job demands, including long work hours, shift work, or high psychological demands, can increase the risk of occupational disorders.
- *Work-life Imbalance*: Difficulty in balancing work and personal life responsibilities can impact mental health and contribute to occupational disorders.

6. *Physical Overexertion*

- *Heavy Lifting*: Jobs that involve frequent or excessive lifting of heavy objects can lead to musculoskeletal disorders, such as strains, sprains, or herniated discs.
- *Awkward Postures*: Working in awkward or uncomfortable positions, such as bending, stooping, or reaching, can strain muscles and joints, contributing to musculoskeletal disorders.

7. *Lack of Work-life Balance*

- *Long Work Hours*: Working excessively long hours, including overtime or multiple jobs, can lead to fatigue, increased stress levels, and a higher risk of mental health disorders.
- *Inflexible Schedules*: Jobs with inflexible schedules, including irregular or rotating shifts, can disrupt sleep patterns, negatively impact overall well-being, and contribute to various occupational disorders.

8. *Psychological and Emotional Factors*

- *Workplace Violence or Bullying*: Exposure to workplace violence, harassment, or bullying can have detrimental effects on mental health, leading to anxiety, depression, or post-traumatic stress disorder (PTSD).
- *Emotional Demands*: Jobs that require constant emotional labour, such as customer service roles or healthcare professions, can contribute to emotional exhaustion and mental health disorders.

9. *Lack of Occupational Health and Safety Measures*

- *Inadequate Training*: Insufficient training on proper work techniques, safe handling of hazardous substances or ergonomics can increase the risk of occupational disorders.
- *Lack of Personal Protective Equipment (PPE)*: Failure to provide or utilize appropriate PPE, such as gloves, goggles, or respirators, can lead to exposure-related occupational disorders.

10. *Organizational Factors*

- *Poor Communication*: Ineffective communication channels or lack of feedback between employees and management can contribute to increased stress levels and reduced job satisfaction.
- *Lack of Employee Involvement*: Limited participation in decision-making processes or lack of control over work-related matters can impact job satisfaction and increase stress levels.

11. ***Economic Factors***

- *Job Inadequacy*: Jobs that do not provide fair wages, benefits, or job security can contribute to stress, anxiety, and reduced well-being.
- *Precarious Employment*: Engaging in precarious employment, such as temporary contracts, gig work, or lack of employment protections, can increase the risk of occupational disorders.

It's important to note that some occupational disorders may have multiple causative factors and interactions between different causes. Identifying and addressing these causes is essential for preventing occupational disorders and promoting a healthier work environment. Implementing appropriate control measures, such as engineering controls, personal protective equipment, ergonomic modifications, stress management programmes, and regular workplace assessments, can help mitigate these causes and reduce the risk of occupational disorders.

Treatments of Occupational Disorders

The treatment of occupational disorders depends on the specific condition and its severity. Here are some common treatment approaches for occupational disorders:

1. ***Medical Intervention***

- *Medications*: Depending on the condition, medications may be prescribed to alleviate symptoms or manage underlying causes. For example, pain relievers, anti-inflammatory drugs, or bronchodilators may be prescribed for musculoskeletal disorders, respiratory conditions, or occupational asthma, respectively.
- *Surgery*: In some cases, surgical intervention may be necessary to address structural issues or alleviate symptoms. This can be relevant for conditions like carpal tunnel syndrome, herniated discs, or certain occupational injuries.

2. ***Physical Therapy and Rehabilitation***

- *Exercise and Rehabilitation*: Physical therapy exercises, stretching routines, and specific rehabilitation programmes can help manage and rehabilitate musculoskeletal conditions. These exercises aim to improve flexibility, strength, and range of motion.
- *Manual Therapy*: Techniques such as massage, joint mobilization, or manipulation performed by physical therapists or occupational therapists can help relieve pain and restore function.
- *Assistive Devices*: The use of assistive devices, such as braces, splints, or ergonomic tools, can provide support, promote proper posture, and reduce the risk of further injury.

3. ***Psychological Support and Counseling***

- *Counseling and Therapy*: Psychological support, counseling, and therapy sessions can assist individuals in managing work-related stress, anxiety, depression, or other mental health disorders. Techniques such as cognitive-behavioural therapy (CBT), stress management strategies, or relaxation techniques may be employed.

- *Employee Assistance Programmes (EAPs)*: EAPs are workplace-based programmes that provide confidential counseling and support services to employees dealing with various personal or work-related issues. EAPs can offer assistance in managing work stress, improving coping mechanisms, and accessing appropriate resources.

4. *Environmental Modifications*

- *Ergonomic Adjustments*: Modifying the work environment to improve ergonomics, such as adjusting workstation setup, providing ergonomic furniture, or implementing proper lighting, can help prevent or alleviate musculoskeletal disorders.
- *Engineering Controls*: Implementing engineering controls, such as ventilation systems, soundproofing, or proper equipment design, can minimize exposure to hazardous substances or reduce the risk of respiratory disorders or hearing loss.
- *Personal Protective Equipment (PPE)*: Proper use of PPE, such as gloves, masks, safety goggles, or hearing protection devices, can mitigate exposure to occupational hazards and prevent associated disorders.

5. *Education and Prevention*

- *Training and Education*: Providing workers with comprehensive training and education on occupational hazards, proper work techniques, ergonomics, and the use of PPE can help prevent occupational disorders.
- *Workplace Policies and Procedures*: Implementing workplace policies and procedures that prioritize worker health and safety, including regular breaks, ergonomic assessments, and adherence to occupational health and safety regulations, can create a healthier work environment.
- *Health Promotion Programmes*: Promoting healthy lifestyle practices, stress management, and work-life balance initiatives can contribute to overall well-being and reduce the risk of occupational disorders.

6. *Occupational Rehabilitation Programmes*

- *Work Conditioning Programmes*: These programmes aim to gradually restore physical function and work-related abilities through supervised exercises and simulated work tasks. Work conditioning programmes focus on improving strength, endurance, and functional capacity for returning to work.
- *Work Hardening Programmes*: Work hardening programs involve comprehensive, multidisciplinary interventions that address physical, functional, and psychosocial aspects of occupational disorders. These programmes aim to prepare individuals to return to their pre-injury or modified work tasks through targeted exercises, work simulations, and vocational counseling.

7. *Vocational Rehabilitation*

- *Vocational Assessment and Planning*: Vocational rehabilitation specialists can assess an individual's functional abilities, interests, and transferable skills to develop a tailored plan for returning to work or transitioning to a different occupation.
- *Job Modification or Accommodation*: In some cases, modifying work tasks, job duties, or the work environment may be necessary to accommodate individuals with occupational disorders. This may involve adjustments to work schedules, workstation ergonomics, or the introduction of assistive technologies.

8. *Health and Wellness Programmes*

- *Health Promotion and Lifestyle Modifications*: Encouraging healthy lifestyle habits, such as regular exercise, proper nutrition, stress management, and adequate sleep, can support overall well-being and help manage or prevent occupational disorders.
- *Smoking Cessation Programmes*: For individuals with respiratory disorders, quitting smoking is crucial to prevent further damage and improve lung health.
- *Weight Management*: In cases where excess weight contributes to or exacerbates an occupational disorder, weight management programmes may be recommended to reduce strain on the musculoskeletal system or improve overall health.

9. *Follow-up and Monitoring*

- *Regular Check-ups*: Following the initial treatment phase, periodic check-ups with healthcare professionals can help monitor progress, address any recurring or new symptoms, and provide ongoing support.
- *Surveillance Programmes*: In certain industries or occupations with known occupational hazards, participating in occupational health surveillance programmes can aid in early detection, monitoring, and management of occupational disorders.

10. *Return-to-Work Planning*

- *Gradual Return-to-Work Programmes*: Gradually reintroducing individuals to their work tasks, either through reduced hours, modified duties, or a phased return, can help facilitate a smooth transition back to work while considering their health and recovery needs.
- *Workplace Accommodations*: Collaborating with employers to implement workplace accommodations, such as ergonomic adjustments, flexible work schedules, or task rotations, can support the successful return to work and ongoing management of occupational disorders.

It is important to note that the specific treatment options should be determined by healthcare professionals based on the individual's specific condition, symptoms, and needs. Collaborative efforts between healthcare providers, employers, and employees are essential for effectively managing occupational disorders, implementing preventive measures, and creating a safe and healthy work environment. Top of Form

Truancy

The concept of truancy refers to the intentional and repeated absence or skipping of school by a student without a legitimate or valid reason. It involves the act of not attending classes or being present at school as required by law and educational regulations. Truancy can be seen as a form of educational neglect, as it disrupts a student's regular participation in the educational system and hinders their academic progress and overall development.

Truancy is often characterized by a pattern of unauthorized absences, where students intentionally avoid attending school or specific classes. It goes beyond occasional absences due to illness or other valid reasons. Instead, truancy reflects a persistent behaviour that can have serious consequences for the student, including academic underachievement, decreased educational opportunities, and an increased risk of dropping out of school.

Truancy can manifest in various ways, such as:

- Skipping entire school days without permission or authorization.
- Missing specific classes or periods within the school day.
- Arriving late to school or leaving early without a valid reason or permission.
- Chronic absenteeism, where a student accumulates a significant number of unexcused absences over a period of time.

The concept of truancy extends beyond mere non-attendance. It encompasses the deliberate avoidance of school and the disengagement from the learning process. Truant students often exhibit a lack of interest, motivation, or connection to the educational environment, which can further contribute to their academic struggles.

Identification Characteristics of Truancy

Several identification characteristics can help identify truancy:

1. *Unexcused Absences*: Truant students often have a pattern of unexcused absences from school. These absences are not supported by valid reasons such as illness, family emergencies, or school-sanctioned activities.
2. *Tardiness*: Truancy can also manifest as frequent tardiness. Students may consistently arrive late to school or frequently leave early without proper permission or justification.
3. *Decline in Academic Performance*: Truancy is often associated with a decline in academic performance. Students who regularly skip school or miss classes are likely to fall behind in their coursework, miss important lessons, assignments, and assessments, and struggle to keep up with their peers academically.

4. *Lack of Engagement*: Truant students may display a lack of interest, motivation, or participation in school activities. They may be disengaged in the classroom, exhibit minimal effort in completing assignments, show little enthusiasm for learning, and may not actively participate in extracurricular activities or social interactions.
5. *Behavioural Changes*: Truancy can lead to behavioural changes in students. They may exhibit increased defiance, become more disengaged or disruptive in class, show a lack of respect for authority figures, or develop negative attitudes toward school and learning. Truant students may also be more prone to engage in delinquent or risky behaviours.
6. *Poor Relationships with Peers and Teachers*: Truant students may struggle to develop positive relationships with their peers and teachers. They may feel disconnected from their classmates and may have difficulty forming meaningful friendships. Additionally, truant students may have strained relationships with teachers and other school staff due to their irregular attendance and lack of engagement.
7. *Excuse Patterns*: Truant students often provide recurring or inconsistent excuses for their absences. They may come up with different justifications each time they miss school or fail to provide a reasonable explanation for their absence.
8. *History of Absenteeism*: Truancy is typically not an isolated incident but rather a pattern of absenteeism. Truant students may have a history of accumulating unexcused absences over an extended period, indicating a consistent pattern of skipping school.
9. *Frequent "Doctor's Appointments" or "Family Emergencies"*: Truant students may frequently use excuses like doctor's appointments or family emergencies to justify their absences. However, these excuses may be inconsistent, exaggerated, or unsubstantiated upon investigation.
10. *Inconsistent Parental Communication*: Truant students may have a lack of parental communication regarding their absences. Parents may fail to provide proper documentation or notifications explaining their child's absence or may not respond to school communication attempts.
11. *Excessive Absences on Specific Days*: Truancy can sometimes exhibit a pattern of absences on certain days of the week, such as Mondays or Fridays. This may indicate a deliberate attempt to extend weekends or avoid specific classes or subjects.
12. *Change in Social Circle*: Truant students may associate with peers who exhibit similar truant behaviours or engage in risky activities. They may form new friendships with students who encourage or enable their absenteeism.
13. *Negative Attitudes toward School*: Truant students often express negative attitudes, resentment, or boredom when discussing school. They may make negative comments about teachers, subjects, or the educational system in general.

14. *Lack of Support at Home*: Truant behaviour may be influenced by a lack of support or involvement from parents or guardians. Parents may not prioritize or value education, fail to enforce attendance, or show little interest in their child's academic progress.
15. *Disconnected from School Community*: Truant students may feel disconnected from the school community, such as not participating in extracurricular activities, avoiding social events, or lacking a sense of belonging within the school environment.
16. *Poor Time Management Skills*: Truant students may struggle with time management skills, resulting in frequent tardiness or absences. They may have difficulty in organizing their schedules or may engage in time-wasting activities outside of school.
17. *Deterioration in Physical Appearance*: In some cases, truant students may exhibit a decline in personal hygiene, disheveled appearance, or inappropriate clothing. This may indicate a lack of structure or care associated with regular school attendance.

It's important to note that the presence of these identification characteristics does not automatically confirm truancy. Some characteristics may have alternative explanations or may vary depending on individual circumstances. Therefore, a comprehensive assessment involving collaboration between school staff, parents, and other relevant professionals is crucial to accurately identify truant behaviour and provide appropriate interventions.

Causes of Truancy

Several factors contribute to truancy, such as:

Individual Factors

- *Personal Issues*: Students may experience personal issues such as low self-esteem, mental health problems, learning difficulties, or a lack of interest in academics. These factors can contribute to a disengagement from school and a desire to avoid attending.
- *Lack of Motivation*: Some students may lack intrinsic motivation for education. They may not see the relevance of school to their future goals or struggle to find meaning in the curriculum, leading to a decreased desire to attend.

Family Factors

- *Dysfunctional Family Dynamics*: Truancy can be influenced by dysfunctional family dynamics, including conflicts, neglect, abuse, or a lack of support and supervision. These issues can create an environment that discourages regular school attendance.
- *Parental Attitudes and Priorities*: Parents who do not prioritize education or have negative attitudes toward school may inadvertently contribute to their child's truancy. Lack of parental involvement or indifference towards their child's education can also play a role.

School Factors

- *Unwelcoming School Environment*: Schools that fail to provide a welcoming and supportive environment may contribute to truancy. Factors such as bullying, a lack of positive relationships with teachers and peers, or a sense of alienation can lead students to avoid attending school.
- *Ineffective Teaching Methods*: Students may become disengaged if teaching methods are not engaging or fail to meet their individual needs. When students feel uninterested or struggle to understand the material, they may be more likely to skip classes or avoid school.
- *Lack of Relevance and Meaningful Education*: When students perceive the curriculum as irrelevant to their lives or future aspirations, they may lose interest and motivation to attend school regularly.

Social Factors

- *Peer Pressure*: Negative peer influences and the desire to fit in with a certain group can contribute to truancy. Students may skip school to participate in activities with their peers that are not conducive to regular attendance.
- *Delinquent Behaviours*: Involvement in delinquent activities outside of school can lead to truancy. Students engaged in negative behaviours may see attending school as an obstacle or feel compelled to avoid school due to their extracurricular activities.

Socio-Economic Factors

- *Poverty*: Students from economically disadvantaged backgrounds may face various challenges that contribute to truancy, including lack of resources, unstable living conditions, and the need to work to support their families.
- *Lack of Access to Transportation*: Difficulty accessing reliable transportation to and from school can result in frequent absences, especially for students living in rural areas or areas with limited public transportation options.

Academic Challenges

- *Learning Difficulties*: Students who struggle academically, particularly if their needs are not adequately addressed, may develop negative attitudes towards school and experience a sense of frustration or failure. This can lead to truancy as they attempt to avoid the challenges they face in the classroom.
- *Lack of Individualized Support*: Students with special educational needs or those who require additional academic support may become disengaged if they do not receive the necessary accommodations or interventions. This can contribute to truancy as they feel overwhelmed or unable to keep up with their peers.

Cultural or Language Barriers

- *Language Barriers*: Students who are non-native speakers of the language of instruction may face difficulties understanding the material or communicating with their peers and teachers. This can create feelings of isolation and frustration, potentially leading to truancy.

- *Cultural Disconnection*: Students from diverse cultural backgrounds may experience a disconnection between their own cultural identity and the school environment. This can contribute to a lack of engagement and a desire to avoid attending school.

Health-Related Factors

- *Chronic Illness or Disability*: Students with chronic illnesses or disabilities may face physical or emotional challenges that make regular school attendance difficult. This can result in increased absences or a need for extended medical leave, leading to truancy.
- *Mental Health Issues*: Students experiencing mental health issues, such as anxiety, depression, or social phobia, may find it challenging to attend school regularly. Feelings of distress, social pressure, or the fear of judgement from peers can contribute to truancy.

Lack of Positive Role Models

- *Absence of Positive Influences*: Students who lack positive role models or mentors in their lives may struggle to find motivation and guidance regarding the importance of education. The absence of supportive figures may contribute to a lack of accountability and commitment to attending school.

Systemic and Structural Factors

- *Educational Disparities*: Disparities in educational resources, opportunities, and quality can impact student engagement and contribute to truancy. Students in under-resourced or disadvantaged communities may face additional barriers to regular school attendance.
- *School Policies and Practices*: Certain school policies or disciplinary practices, if perceived as unfair or overly punitive, can lead to student disengagement and truancy. Inflexible attendance policies or a lack of supportive interventions can inadvertently contribute to increased absenteeism.

It is important to recognize that the causes of truancy can be complex and interconnected. Students may experience a combination of these factors, and the extent to which each factor contributes may vary among individuals. Addressing truancy requires a comprehensive approach that addresses the underlying causes while providing support, intervention, and resources to help students overcome barriers to regular school attendance.

Treatments of Truancy

Addressing truancy requires a comprehensive approach involving various stakeholders:

Early Intervention and Monitoring

- *Early Identification*: Establish systems to identify truant behaviour at the earliest stage possible. This includes tracking attendance, monitoring patterns of absences, and identifying students who are at risk of becoming truant.
- *Regular Communication*: Maintain open lines of communication between teachers, school staff, parents, and guardians to promptly address concerns related to absenteeism and intervene when necessary.

Parental Involvement and Support

- *Parent Education*: Provide parents and guardians with information about the importance of regular school attendance and the potential consequences of truancy. Offer workshops, seminars, or individual meetings to educate them on strategies to support their child's attendance.
- *Parent-teacher Collaboration*: Foster strong partnerships between parents and teachers. Regularly communicate with parents to discuss their child's attendance, academic progress, and any challenges they may be facing. Involve parents in developing strategies to improve attendance and engage them in their child's education.

Individualized Support and Interventions

- *Counseling Services*: Offer counseling and support services to truant students. This includes addressing underlying issues such as academic struggles, mental health concerns, family problems, or lack of motivation. Provide a safe and confidential space for students to express their concerns and receive guidance.
- *Individualized Education Plans (IEPs)*: Develop tailored plans for truant students that address their specific needs, learning styles, and goals. Provide additional resources, accommodations, or alternative education options, if necessary, to help them succeed academically and re-engage with their education.

Positive School Environment and Engagement

- *Engaging Teaching Methods*: Implement interactive and student-centered teaching methods that promote active participation, critical thinking, and relevance to students' lives. Foster a positive classroom atmosphere that encourages curiosity, creativity, and collaboration.
- *Extracurricular Activities*: Offer a variety of extracurricular activities, clubs, and sports to engage students in areas of interest outside the traditional classroom setting. These activities can provide a sense of belonging, build social connections, and increase overall engagement in the school community.

Collaboration and Community Engagement

- *Community Partnerships*: Collaborate with community organizations, local agencies, and stakeholders to address truancy comprehensively. Develop partnerships that offer mentoring programmes, after-school activities, and support services to promote regular attendance and provide additional resources for students.

- *Truancy Prevention Programmes*: Implement evidence-based truancy prevention programmes that target both individual and systemic factors contributing to truancy. These programmes can involve mentoring, academic support, life skills training, and parent education to address the root causes of truancy.

Legal Interventions

- *Attendance Enforcement*: In cases of persistent truancy, legal interventions may be necessary to enforce attendance laws and ensure accountability. This can involve court-mandated attendance programmes, fines, or other legal measures designed to motivate and encourage regular school attendance.

Mentorship and Role Models

- *Mentorship Programmes*: Implement mentorship programmes where students are paired with responsible and supportive adult mentors. Mentors can provide guidance, positive role modeling, and encouragement to help truant students develop a sense of purpose and connection with their education.

Attendance Contracts and Incentives

- *Attendance Contracts*: Develop attendance contracts with truant students and their parents or guardians. These contracts outline expectations, rewards for improved attendance, and consequences for continued truancy. They can serve as a commitment to regular school attendance and provide a sense of accountability.
- *Incentive Programmes*: Establish incentive programmes that recognize and reward students for consistent attendance and improvement in their attendance record. Incentives can include certificates, recognition ceremonies, small rewards, or participation in special events.

Alternative Education Options

- *Flexible Learning Formats*: Explore flexible learning formats such as online courses, blended learning, or vocational training programmes. These alternatives can accommodate individual needs, provide personalized learning experiences, and help re-engage truant students who may benefit from non-traditional educational approaches.
- *Alternative Schools*: Consider referral to alternative schools or specialized programmes designed to support students who have struggled with regular attendance. These schools often provide smaller class sizes, tailored support services, and individualized attention to help students overcome barriers to attendance.

Comprehensive Case Management

- *Case Management Teams*: Establish multidisciplinary teams involving school counselors, social workers, psychologists, and other relevant professionals to provide comprehensive support to truant students. These teams can assess the underlying causes of truancy, develop intervention plans, coordinate services, and provide ongoing monitoring and support.

Follow-up and Monitoring

- *Regular Follow-up*: Continuously monitor and follow-up with truant students to ensure they are progressing in their attendance goals and receiving the necessary support. This can involve regular meetings, check-ins, and tracking of attendance data to identify any emerging issues or relapses.
- *Reintegration Support*: Provide reintegration support for students returning to school after a period of truancy. This may include transition programmes, academic catch-up plans, peer support, and additional resources to help students smoothly reintegrate into the school community.

It is important to adopt a multidimensional approach to truancy treatment, addressing the individual needs of students while considering the systemic and environmental factors that contribute to truancy. By combining early intervention, parental involvement, targeted support, engaging educational practices, and community collaboration, schools can help truant students overcome barriers, re-engage with their education, and work towards academic success.

Anxiety

The concept of anxiety refers to a complex and multifaceted emotional state characterized by feelings of fear, worry, unease, or apprehension. It is a natural and normal response to perceived threats or stressful situations. Anxiety can vary in intensity and duration, ranging from mild and temporary to severe and chronic. While occasional anxiety is a part of life, excessive and persistent anxiety can significantly impact an individual's daily functioning and overall well-being.

Anxiety can manifest in different forms, including generalized anxiety disorder (GAD), social anxiety disorder, panic disorder, specific phobias, and post-traumatic stress disorder (PTSD), among others. Each type of anxiety disorder has its own unique set of symptoms and triggers, but they all involve an excessive and uncontrollable sense of fear or worry. The experience of anxiety encompasses both cognitive and physiological aspects. On a cognitive level, individuals with anxiety may have racing or intrusive thoughts, excessive worrying about future events or potential dangers, difficulty in concentrating, and a sense of impending doom. Physiologically, anxiety can manifest as physical symptoms such as rapid heartbeat, sweating, trembling, shortness of breath, muscle tension, gastrointestinal problems, and sleep disturbances.

It's important to note that anxiety is a common mental health condition and seeking professional help is essential for an accurate diagnosis and appropriate treatment plan. With proper support and interventions, individuals with anxiety can learn to manage their symptoms effectively and improve their overall quality of life. Top of Form

Identification Characteristics of Anxiety

Anxiety is a complex emotional state characterized by various identification characteristics. These features help in recognizing and understanding the presence of anxiety. Let's discuss these identification characteristics in points:

1. *Excessive Worry*: One of the primary identification characteristics of anxiety is experiencing excessive and persistent worry. Individuals with anxiety disorders often find it challenging to control their worrying. Their concerns may be unrealistic or disproportionate to the actual situation, and they may anticipate negative outcomes.
2. *Physical Symptoms*: Anxiety can manifest in a range of physical symptoms. These can include increased heart rate, sweating, trembling or shaking, shortness of breath, dizziness, headaches, muscle tension, gastrointestinal issues, and fatigue. These physical symptoms often accompany the emotional distress associated with anxiety.
3. *Restlessness and Irritability*: Anxiety can lead to feelings of restlessness, agitation, and irritability. People with anxiety may have a constant sense of being on edge, finding it difficult to relax or calm down. They may become easily irritated or have difficulty in concentrating on tasks.
4. *Cognitive Disturbances*: Anxiety significantly impacts an individual's thoughts and cognitive processes. Common cognitive disturbances include difficulty in concentrating, racing or intrusive thoughts, catastrophic thinking, excessive worry about the future, and a sense of impending doom. These cognitive patterns can be intrusive and make it challenging to focus on daily activities.
5. *Sleep Disturbances*: Anxiety can disrupt normal sleep patterns, leading to difficulties in falling asleep, staying asleep, or experiencing restless sleep. Individuals with anxiety may have racing thoughts, experience nightmares, or wake up frequently during the night. The resulting sleep deprivation can further exacerbate anxiety symptoms.
6. *Avoidance Behaviour*: Anxiety often triggers a strong desire to avoid situations, places, or activities that are perceived as potential triggers. This avoidance behaviour can range from social situations to specific phobias and can interfere with daily activities, social interactions, and personal growth. Avoidance can provide temporary relief but can reinforce anxiety in the long run.
7. *Impact on Daily Functioning*: Anxiety disorders can significantly impair an individual's ability to function in various areas of life. The constant worry, physical symptoms, and cognitive disturbances can make it

challenging to concentrate, engage in social activities, perform well at work or school, and pursue personal goals and interests.

8. *Emotional Distress*: Anxiety is characterized by intense emotional distress, including feelings of fear, panic, unease, or a sense of impending danger. Individuals with anxiety may feel overwhelmed by their emotions and struggle to regulate them effectively. Emotional distress can affect mood, overall well-being, and relationships.
9. *Intense Fear or Panic Attacks*: Anxiety disorders can involve the occurrence of intense fear or panic attacks. Panic attacks are sudden episodes of overwhelming fear accompanied by physical symptoms such as heart palpitations, chest pain, shortness of breath, trembling, sweating, and a sense of impending doom. These attacks can be unexpected or triggered by specific situations.
10. *Hypervigilance*: Individuals with anxiety may exhibit hypervigilance, a state of heightened alertness and sensitivity to potential threats. They may constantly scan their environment for signs of danger, leading to an increased sense of anxiety and difficulty relaxing.
11. *Perfectionism and Excessive Self-criticism*: Anxiety can be associated with perfectionism and excessive self-criticism. Individuals may have high expectations of themselves, fear making mistakes, and engage in constant self-evaluation. This self-imposed pressure can contribute to anxiety symptoms.
12. *Difficulty in Social Situations*: Social anxiety disorder is characterized by intense fear or anxiety in social situations. Individuals may experience excessive self-consciousness, fear of being judged, or embarrassment. They may avoid social interactions or endure them with significant distress.
13. *Intrusive Thoughts*: Anxiety disorders can involve intrusive thoughts, which are unwanted, distressing, and recurrent thoughts or mental images. These thoughts can be distressing, irrational, or related to a specific fear or concern. The individual may find it challenging to control or dismiss these thoughts.
14. *Sensitivity to Uncertainty*: Individuals with anxiety may have a heightened sensitivity to uncertainty. They may struggle with ambiguity, overanalyze potential outcomes, and seek excessive reassurance to alleviate their anxiety about uncertain situations or future events.
15. *Impact on Relationships*: Anxiety can impact relationships with others. Individuals may have difficulty trusting, expressing themselves, or engaging in social interactions. They may worry excessively about being liked or judged, leading to social withdrawal or strained relationships.
16. *Comorbidity with Other Mental Health Conditions*: Anxiety disorders frequently co-occur with other mental health conditions such as depression, obsessive-compulsive disorder (OCD), and post-traumatic stress disorder (PTSD). The presence of multiple mental health conditions can complicate the identification and treatment of anxiety.

Understanding and recognizing these identification characteristics of anxiety can help individuals, loved ones, and healthcare professionals identify when anxiety may be present. It is important to note that everyone's experience of anxiety may vary, and a comprehensive assessment by a qualified healthcare professional is necessary to determine the presence of an anxiety disorder and develop an appropriate treatment plan.

Causes of Anxiety

Anxiety disorders can have various underlying causes, involving a combination of biological, psychological, and environmental factors. Understanding the causes can provide insights into the development and maintenance of anxiety. Let's discuss the causes of anxiety in points:

1. *Genetic Predisposition*: There is evidence to suggest that genetics plays a role in the development of anxiety disorders. Individuals with a family history of anxiety or other mental health conditions may have an increased risk of developing anxiety themselves. Certain genetic variations or inherited traits may contribute to an individual's vulnerability to anxiety.
2. *Imbalances in Brain Chemistry*: Neurotransmitters, which are chemical messengers in the brain, play a crucial role in regulating mood and anxiety. Imbalances in neurotransmitters such as serotonin, norepinephrine, and gamma-aminobutyric acid (GABA) can contribute to the development of anxiety disorders. Disruptions in the brain's fear circuitry and the body's stress response system may also be involved.
3. *Traumatic Experiences*: Traumatic events, such as physical or emotional abuse, accidents, or witnessing or experiencing violence, can trigger or exacerbate anxiety disorders. The impact of trauma on the brain and the body's stress response can lead to persistent anxiety symptoms and heightened vigilance.
4. *Chronic Stress*: Prolonged exposure to stressful situations, such as work pressure, relationship difficulties, financial problems, or ongoing life challenges, can contribute to the development of anxiety. Chronic stress can dysregulate the body's stress response system, leading to heightened anxiety levels.
5. *Environmental Factors*: Environmental factors, including upbringing, family dynamics, and early life experiences, can influence the development of anxiety. Adverse childhood experiences, inconsistent or insecure attachment, or a lack of supportive environments can contribute to the risk of developing anxiety disorders later in life.
6. *Personality Traits*: Certain personality traits and temperament can predispose individuals to anxiety. Traits such as high levels of neuroticism, perfectionism, low self-esteem, or a tendency towards negative thinking patterns can increase the likelihood of developing anxiety disorders.

7. *Cognitive Factors*: Cognitive factors refer to distorted thinking patterns and beliefs that contribute to anxiety. These may include catastrophic thinking (anticipating the worst outcome), excessive worry about future events, overgeneralization (drawing broad negative conclusions based on limited evidence), and a tendency to focus on perceived threats or dangers.
8. *Substance Abuse*: Substance abuse, including alcohol or drug use, can contribute to the development or exacerbation of anxiety symptoms. Substance abuse can disrupt brain chemistry, increase feelings of anxiety or panic, and impair one's ability to cope with stress.
9. *Medical Conditions*: Certain medical conditions and health issues can contribute to the development of anxiety. Conditions such as thyroid disorders, hormonal imbalances, cardiovascular problems, chronic pain, and respiratory disorders can have an impact on anxiety levels. Additionally, individuals with chronic illnesses or those facing a serious medical diagnosis may experience heightened anxiety.
10. *Substance Withdrawal*: Abruptly stopping or reducing the use of certain substances, including alcohol, benzodiazepines, or illicit drugs, can lead to withdrawal symptoms, including anxiety. The body's reliance on these substances can cause physiological and psychological imbalances, triggering anxiety as a withdrawal symptom.
11. *Co-occurring Mental Health Disorders*: Anxiety often co-occurs with other mental health conditions, such as depression, obsessive-compulsive disorder (OCD), and post-traumatic stress disorder (PTSD). These conditions can interact and influence each other, leading to a higher risk of developing anxiety.
12. *Learned Behaviour*: Anxiety can be learned through experiences and observation. If individuals have witnessed or been repeatedly exposed to anxious behaviour or traumatic events, they may develop anxiety as a learned response to similar situations.
13. *Cultural and Societal Factors*: Cultural and societal factors can contribute to anxiety. Societal pressures, expectations, and norms can create stress and anxiety. Cultural factors, such as collective anxiety or intergenerational transmission of anxiety, can influence the development of anxiety disorders.
14. *Childhood Adversities*: Adverse experiences during childhood, such as neglect, abuse, parental conflict, or loss, can significantly impact emotional development and increase the risk of anxiety disorders later in life. Childhood adversities can affect the development of brain structures and stress response systems, contributing to heightened anxiety.
15. *Personal Life Circumstances*: Significant life changes, such as moving, changing jobs, starting school, or going through a divorce or loss of a loved one, can trigger or exacerbate anxiety. These life events can disrupt routines, create uncertainty, and increase stress levels, leading to the development of anxiety symptoms.

16. *Media and Information Overload*: Exposure to constant media coverage, news of global events, or social media platforms can contribute to anxiety. The influx of information, often focusing on negative events, can fuel anxiety symptoms and heighten feelings of fear and uncertainty.

It is important to note that the causes of anxiety can be complex and multifaceted. Often, multiple factors interact to contribute to an individual's susceptibility to anxiety disorders. Additionally, the specific causes may vary from person to person. Understanding the underlying causes can help inform appropriate treatment approaches and interventions tailored to each individual's needs.

Treatments of Anxiety

Anxiety disorders are highly treatable conditions, and several effective treatment options are available. The goal of treatment is to reduce anxiety symptoms, improve daily functioning, and enhance overall well-being. Let's discuss the treatments of anxiety in points:

1. Psychotherapy

- *Cognitive-Behavioural Therapy (CBT)*: CBT is a widely used and evidence-based therapy for anxiety disorders. It helps individuals identify and challenge negative thought patterns and beliefs associated with anxiety. Through CBT, individuals learn to develop more balanced and realistic thinking, acquire effective coping skills, and gradually confront anxiety-provoking situations through exposure therapy.
- *Acceptance and Commitment Therapy (ACT)*: ACT focuses on acceptance of anxious thoughts and feelings, while encouraging individuals to engage in value-driven behaviours. It helps individuals develop mindfulness skills and cultivate a more accepting and compassionate attitude towards their anxiety.
- *Other Therapies*: Other therapeutic approaches, such as psychodynamic therapy, interpersonal therapy, and mindfulness-based therapies, may also be beneficial in treating anxiety disorders. The choice of therapy depends on individual preferences, the specific anxiety disorder, and the expertise of the therapist.

2. Medications

- *Antidepressants*: Selective Serotonin Reuptake Inhibitors (SSRIs) and Serotonin-Norepinephrine Reuptake Inhibitors (SNRIs) are commonly prescribed medications for anxiety disorders. They work by increasing the availability of certain neurotransmitters in the brain, helping to reduce anxiety symptoms.
- *Benzodiazepines*: Benzodiazepines are fast-acting sedatives that may be prescribed for short-term relief of severe anxiety or panic attacks. However, they are generally used with caution due to their potential for dependence and side effects.

3. Relaxation Techniques and Stress Management

- *Deep Breathing Exercises*: Deep breathing exercises can help activate the body's relaxation response, reducing anxiety symptoms. Techniques such as diaphragmatic breathing and box breathing are commonly practised.
- *Progressive Muscle Relaxation (PMR)*: PMR involves systematically tensing and relaxing different muscle groups to promote relaxation and reduce muscle tension associated with anxiety.
- *Mindfulness and Meditation*: Practising mindfulness and meditation techniques can help individuals cultivate present-moment awareness, reduce rumination, and manage anxiety more effectively.
- *Stress Management*: Learning effective stress management techniques, such as time management, setting boundaries, and prioritizing self-care, can help individuals reduce anxiety triggers and improve overall well-being.

4. Lifestyle Modifications

- *Regular Exercise*: Engaging in regular physical exercise, such as aerobic activities, can have a positive impact on anxiety. Exercise helps reduce stress, improve mood, and promote overall mental and physical well-being.
- *Healthy Sleep Habits*: Establishing a consistent sleep routine, creating a conducive sleep environment, and practising relaxation techniques before bedtime can improve sleep quality and reduce anxiety symptoms.
- *Balanced Diet*: Maintaining a balanced diet that includes whole foods, avoiding excessive caffeine and alcohol intake, and staying hydrated can support overall well-being and help manage anxiety.

5. Support Network

Seeking support from friends, family, or support groups can provide comfort, understanding, and encouragement during times of anxiety. Connecting with others who have similar experiences can offer valuable insights and coping strategies.

6. Self-help Strategies and Resources

- *Self-help Books and Resources*: There are numerous self-help books, online resources, and mobile applications available that provide guidance, information, and exercises to manage anxiety. These resources can be helpful in conjunction with professional treatment or as a supplement to therapy.

7. Group Therapy and Support Groups

- *Group Therapy*: Participating in group therapy sessions with others experiencing similar anxiety challenges can provide a supportive and understanding environment. Group therapy allows individuals to share their experiences, learn from others, and practise new coping skills.
- *Support Groups*: Joining support groups specific to anxiety disorders or mental health can provide a sense of community, validation, and the opportunity to learn from others facing similar challenges.

8. Mind-body Techniques

- *Yoga*: Practising yoga combines physical postures, breathing exercises, and meditation to promote relaxation and reduce anxiety. It can help individuals cultivate mindfulness, improve body awareness, and enhance overall well-being.
- *Tai Chi and Qigong*: These mind-body practices involve gentle movements, deep breathing, and focused attention. They can help reduce anxiety, improve relaxation, and enhance mental clarity.

9. Complementary and Alternative Approaches

- *Herbal Supplements*: Some herbal supplements, such as lavender, chamomile, and passionflower, are believed to have calming properties and may be used as a complementary approach to manage anxiety. It's important to consult with a healthcare professional before starting any herbal supplements.
- *Acupuncture*: Acupuncture involves the insertion of thin needles into specific points on the body. Some research suggests it may help alleviate anxiety symptoms by promoting relaxation and balancing the body's energy flow.
- *Massage Therapy*: Massage therapy can help reduce muscle tension, promote relaxation, and relieve stress, which can contribute to anxiety reduction.

10. Continued Monitoring and Maintenance

- *Regular Check-ins*: Continued monitoring with a mental health professional, even after symptoms improve, can help ensure long-term management of anxiety. Regular check-ins provide an opportunity to address any emerging issues, adjust treatment strategies if necessary, and maintain overall mental well-being.
- *Lifestyle Habits*: Maintaining healthy lifestyle habits, such as regular exercise, balanced nutrition, adequate sleep, and stress management techniques, can support ongoing anxiety management and overall mental health. Top of Form

It's important to remember that treatment for anxiety should be individualized, and what works for one person may not work for another. Collaborating with a healthcare professional or mental health provider is essential to determine the most suitable treatment options and develop a comprehensive plan for managing anxiety effectively.

Personality Disorders

Personality disorders are a group of mental health conditions characterized by enduring patterns of thoughts, feelings, and behaviours that deviate significantly from societal expectations and cause significant distress and impairment in functioning. These patterns are ingrained and inflexible, often leading to difficulties in relationships, work, and daily life.

To better understand the concept of personality disorders, let's discuss a few examples:

Antisocial Personality Disorder (ASPD): ASPD is characterized by a pervasive pattern of disregard for and violation of the rights of others. Individuals with ASPD often exhibit a lack of empathy and remorse, engage in impulsive and irresponsible behaviour, and have a disregard for societal rules and norms. They may manipulate others for personal gain and exhibit a persistent pattern of deceitfulness. For example, a person with ASPD may repeatedly engage in criminal activities, such as theft or fraud, without remorse or regard for the well-being of others.

Narcissistic Personality Disorder (NPD): NPD is characterized by an inflated sense of self-importance, a constant need for admiration, and a lack of empathy for others. Individuals with NPD often have a grandiose view of themselves and believe they are superior to others. They may exploit or manipulate others to maintain their self-esteem and seek constant validation. For example, a person with NPD may constantly demand attention and praise, exaggerate their achievements, and lack empathy for others' needs and emotions.

Borderline Personality Disorder (BPD): BPD is characterized by a pervasive pattern of instability in interpersonal relationships, self-image, and emotions. Individuals with BPD often struggle with intense and unstable relationships, impulsive behaviours, and emotional dysregulation. They may engage in self-harming behaviours and have a fear of abandonment. For example, a person with BPD may have frequent intense arguments with loved ones, engage in impulsive and risky behaviours such as excessive spending or substance abuse, and experience rapid mood swings and feelings of emptiness.

Avoidant Personality Disorder (AvPD): AvPD is characterized by a pervasive pattern of social inhibition, feelings of inadequacy, and hypersensitivity to negative evaluation. Individuals with AvPD often have an intense fear of rejection and avoid social interactions or situations that may trigger feelings of embarrassment or humiliation. They may struggle with forming close relationships and have low self-esteem. For example, a person with AvPD may avoid social gatherings, experience extreme anxiety when speaking in public, and have a constant fear of being judged or criticized by others.

These examples highlight the diverse nature of personality disorders and how they manifest in different ways. It's important to note that individuals may exhibit traits or behaviours associated with personality disorders without meeting the full diagnostic criteria. The diagnosis and understanding of personality disorders should be made by qualified mental health professionals based on a comprehensive assessment and evaluation of an individual's symptoms and experiences.

Identification Characteristics of Personality Disorder

The identification of personality disorders is based on a comprehensive assessment conducted by mental health professionals. Some common characteristics that may indicate the presence of a personality disorder include:

1. *Enduring Pattern*: Personality disorders are characterized by enduring patterns of thoughts, feelings, and behaviours that are consistent and stable over time. These patterns typically emerge in adolescence or early adulthood and persist into adulthood.
2. *Inflexibility and Ingrained Nature*: The patterns associated with personality disorders are inflexible and ingrained, meaning that individuals with personality disorders have difficulty adapting their thoughts, emotions, and behaviours to different situations or contexts. This inflexibility can lead to difficulties in various areas of life, including relationships, work, and personal functioning.
3. *Deviation from Societal Expectations*: The thoughts, feelings, and behaviours exhibited by individuals with personality disorders deviate significantly from societal expectations and norms. They may display patterns of behaviour that are seen as extreme, unusual, or inappropriate in a given cultural or social context.
4. *Impairment in Functioning*: Personality disorders often cause significant impairment in multiple areas of an individual's life. This can include difficulties in maintaining stable and fulfilling relationships, holding down a job or pursuing a career, managing daily responsibilities, and maintaining emotional stability.
5. *Distress and Emotional Impact*: Personality disorders are associated with significant emotional distress and inner turmoil. Individuals with personality disorders may experience chronic feelings of emptiness, low self-esteem, frustration, anxiety, or depression as a result of their maladaptive patterns of thinking and behaving.
6. *Interpersonal Challenges*: Difficulties in interpersonal relationships are common among individuals with personality disorders. They may struggle with establishing and maintaining healthy connections, experiencing conflicts, mistrust, or frequent changes in relationships. These challenges can be attributed to patterns of unstable emotions, fear of abandonment, and difficulty understanding and empathizing with others.
7. *Lack of Insight or Awareness*: Individuals with personality disorders may have limited insight into their own patterns of thoughts, feelings, and behaviours. They may be unaware of the impact of their behaviours on themselves and others, making it challenging for them to recognize the need for help or seek appropriate treatment.
8. *Maladaptive Coping Mechanisms*: Individuals with personality disorders often employ maladaptive coping mechanisms in response to stress or emotional challenges. These coping strategies may include self-destructive

behaviours, such as self-harm or substance abuse, as well as avoidance of difficult situations or emotional numbing.

9. *Impulsivity*: Impulsive behaviours are commonly seen in individuals with personality disorders. They may engage in reckless or risky activities without considering the potential consequences. This impulsivity can manifest in areas such as spending money excessively, engaging in unsafe sexual behaviours, or engaging in impulsive aggression.
10. *Identity Disturbance*: Many personality disorders involve a disturbance in an individual's sense of self or identity. They may have an unstable self-image, an unclear understanding of their values or goals, and difficulty establishing a consistent sense of who they are. This lack of identity stability can contribute to feelings of emptiness and confusion.
11. *Co-occurring Mental Health Disorders*: Personality disorders frequently co-occur with other mental health disorders, such as depression, anxiety disorders, or substance use disorders. The presence of multiple disorders can complicate diagnosis and treatment, and it is essential to assess and address all relevant conditions.
12. *Chronic Nature*: Personality disorders are chronic conditions that tend to persist over time. Although symptoms may fluctuate in intensity, the underlying patterns of thoughts, feelings, and behaviours remain relatively stable. This chronicity highlights the importance of long-term treatment and support for individuals with personality disorders.
13. *Resistance to Change*: Due to the ingrained nature of their patterns, individuals with personality disorders often exhibit resistance to change. They may be reluctant to seek help, dismiss the need for treatment, or struggle with making sustained progress in therapy. This resistance can pose challenges to the therapeutic process.
14. *Impact on Others*: Personality disorders can have a significant impact on the people around the affected individual. Family members, friends, and colleagues may experience emotional distress, conflicts, and difficulties in their relationships with the individual. The disruptive and unpredictable nature of personality disorders can strain interpersonal dynamics and social connections.

It is important to recognize that while these identification characteristics provide a general understanding, each specific personality disorder has its own unique set of diagnostic criteria and nuances. A comprehensive assessment by mental health professionals is necessary to accurately identify and diagnose personality disorders. Top of Form

Causes of Personality Disorder

The causes of personality disorders are complex and multifaceted, involving a combination of genetic, environmental, and psychosocial factors. It's important to note that the exact causes of personality disorders are not fully understood, and different factors may play varying roles in the development of each specific disorder. Here are some key factors that contribute to the development of personality disorders:

1. *Genetic Factors*: There is evidence suggesting a genetic predisposition to certain personality disorders. Family and twin studies have shown a higher prevalence of personality disorders among individuals who have a family history of the disorder. Genetic factors are believed to influence temperament, personality traits, and vulnerabilities to specific disorders.
2. *Environmental Factors*: Adverse childhood experiences and environmental factors contribute significantly to the development of personality disorders. Traumatic experiences such as abuse, neglect, or unstable family environments can have a profound impact on personality development. Chronic stress, early attachment issues, disrupted family dynamics, and inconsistent parenting styles can also contribute to the development of maladaptive patterns of thinking and behaviour.
3. *Neurobiological Factors*: Neurobiological factors, including differences in brain structure, function, and neurotransmitter systems, are thought to contribute to the development of personality disorders. Abnormalities in brain regions involved in emotional regulation, impulse control, and decision-making have been observed in individuals with certain personality disorders.
4. *Early Developmental Issues*: Early developmental issues, such as insecure attachment or disruptions in early emotional bonding with caregivers, can influence personality development. Lack of nurturing, inconsistent parenting, or a lack of emotional attunement during critical developmental stages may contribute to the formation of maladaptive patterns of behaviour and interpersonal difficulties.
5. *Cognitive and Psychological Factors*: Cognitive processes and psychological factors also play a role in the development of personality disorders. Distorted thinking patterns, such as black-and-white thinking, cognitive biases, or irrational beliefs, can contribute to maladaptive behaviours and emotional dysregulation. Negative self-perceptions, low self-esteem, and dysfunctional coping mechanisms can also contribute to the development of personality disorders.
6. *Socio-cultural Factors*: Socio-cultural factors, including cultural norms, societal expectations, and socialization processes, can influence the manifestation of personality disorders. Cultural factors may shape the expression and perception of certain traits or behaviours associated with personality disorders. For example, cultural emphasis on collectivism or individualism may influence the development and expression of specific personality traits.
7. *Childhood Trauma*: Childhood trauma, including physical, sexual, or emotional abuse, as well as neglect, can significantly increase the risk

of developing a personality disorder. Traumatic experiences during childhood can disrupt healthy psychological development and contribute to the development of maladaptive coping mechanisms and difficulties in emotional regulation.

8. *Parental Influences*: The parenting style and behaviours of caregivers can impact the development of personality disorders. Inconsistent, neglectful, or overly controlling parenting practices can contribute to the formation of maladaptive personality traits and patterns. Lack of emotional warmth, overprotection, or harsh disciplinary methods can also play a role.
9. *Learned Behaviour*: Observing and internalizing maladaptive behaviours or coping mechanisms from significant individuals in one's life, such as parents or peers, can influence the development of personality disorders. For example, a person growing up in an environment where aggression is normalized or rewarded may be more prone to exhibiting aggressive or antisocial behaviours.
10. *Interaction of Factors*: It is essential to understand that personality disorders typically arise from a complex interaction of multiple factors. Genetic predispositions, combined with environmental stressors and early life experiences, can interact to increase the risk of developing a personality disorder. No single factor can solely account for the development of personality disorders.
11. *Temperament and Early Personality Traits*: Individual differences in temperament and early personality traits can influence the vulnerability to developing a personality disorder. For example, individuals with high levels of impulsivity, emotional reactivity, or difficulty in self-regulation may be more prone to developing certain types of personality disorders.
12. *Social Isolation and Lack of Support*: Social isolation, a lack of social support, or limited access to healthy relationships and positive role models can contribute to the development of personality disorders. A lack of nurturing and stable relationships during critical developmental stages can hinder the development of healthy interpersonal skills and adaptive coping mechanisms.
13. *Resilience and Protective Factors*: While risk factors contribute to the development of personality disorders, it is important to acknowledge the presence of resilience and protective factors that can mitigate the impact of these risk factors. Supportive relationships, access to mental health resources, effective coping strategies, and opportunities for personal growth and development can serve as protective factors and reduce the likelihood or severity of personality disorders.

It is essential to understand that the causes of personality disorders are complex and multi-factorial. Additionally, each individual's experience is unique, and the specific combination of factors influencing the development of a personality disorder can vary from person to person.

Treatments of Personality Disorder

The treatment of personality disorders typically involves a combination of psychotherapy, medication, and support. It is important to note that treatment plans should be tailored to the individual's specific needs and preferences. Here are some common treatment approaches for personality disorders:

1. ***Psychotherapy:*** Psychotherapy, or talk therapy, is a central component of treatment for personality disorders. Different therapeutic modalities may be utilized, depending on the specific type of personality disorder and the individual's needs. Some common types of therapy include:
   - *Dialectical Behaviour Therapy (DBT)*: DBT is often used for individuals with borderline personality disorder. It focuses on enhancing emotional regulation, developing distress tolerance skills, improving interpersonal effectiveness, and promoting mindfulness.
   - *Cognitive-Behavioural Therapy (CBT)*: CBT helps individuals identify and challenge maladaptive thought patterns, beliefs, and behaviours. It aims to promote healthier thinking patterns and develop effective coping strategies.
   - *Psychodynamic Therapy*: Psychodynamic therapy explores the underlying unconscious conflicts and unresolved issues that contribute to personality disorders. It helps individuals gain insight into their thoughts, emotions, and patterns of behaviour.
2. ***Medication:*** Medication may be prescribed to manage specific symptoms or co-occurring mental health conditions associated with personality disorders. For example:
   - *Antidepressants*: Antidepressants may be prescribed to alleviate symptoms of depression or anxiety that commonly co-occur with personality disorders.
   - *Mood Stabilizers*: Mood stabilizers can help regulate and stabilize mood swings and impulsivity in certain personality disorders.
   - *Antipsychotics*: Antipsychotic medications may be used in cases where individuals with personality disorders experience psychotic symptoms, such as hallucinations or delusions.
3. ***Group Therapy:*** Group therapy provides individuals with an opportunity to interact with others who share similar challenges. It can offer support, validation, and a sense of community. Group therapy settings allow individuals to practise interpersonal skills, learn from others' experiences, and receive feedback in a supportive environment.
4. ***Skills Training:*** Skills training programmes can be beneficial for individuals with personality disorders. These programmes focus on developing specific skills such as emotion regulation, communication, problem-solving, and stress management. These skills enable individuals to cope more effectively with challenges and improve their overall functioning.
5. ***Self-help and Support:*** Engaging in self-help strategies and seeking support can be valuable complements to formal treatment. This can

include self-care practices, such as exercise, relaxation techniques, and healthy lifestyle habits. Joining support groups or online communities can also provide a sense of belonging, understanding, and shared experiences.

6. ***Family Therapy:*** Involving family members in therapy can be beneficial, particularly for individuals with personality disorders that affect family dynamics. Family therapy aims to improve communication, address conflicts, and enhance support systems within the family unit.
7. ***Case Management:*** Case management involves coordinating and accessing various support services, such as housing, vocational training, financial assistance, and healthcare. Case managers can help individuals with personality disorders navigate these systems and ensure they receive appropriate support.
8. ***Integrated Treatment Approach:*** An integrated treatment approach involves combining different therapeutic modalities and interventions tailored to the individual's needs. It may include a combination of individual therapy, group therapy, medication management, skills training, and family involvement. This comprehensive approach recognizes the complexity of personality disorders and addresses various aspects of an individual's life.
9. ***Psycho-education:*** Psycho-education involves providing individuals and their families with information and knowledge about personality disorders. Psycho-education helps individuals understand their diagnosis, symptoms, and treatment options. It empowers individuals to actively participate in their treatment and enhances their ability to manage their condition effectively.
10. ***Crisis Intervention and Safety Planning:*** For individuals with personality disorders who are at risk of self-harm, suicidal ideation, or engaging in impulsive behaviours, crisis intervention and safety planning are essential. Mental health professionals work with individuals to develop strategies for managing crises, identifying warning signs, and implementing safety measures to minimize harm.
11. ***Long-term Follow-up and Support:*** Given the chronic nature of personality disorders, long-term follow-up and support are crucial for maintaining stability and preventing relapse. Regular check-ins, ongoing therapy, and access to support networks can provide individuals with ongoing guidance, assistance, and resources.

It's important to note that the duration of treatment for personality disorders varies depending on individual needs and progress. Additionally, a multidisciplinary approach involving mental health professionals, such as psychiatrists, psychologists, and social workers, is often recommended to provide comprehensive and holistic care for individuals with personality disorders.

Conflict

Conflict as a mental disorder refers to a psychological condition where individuals experience an abnormal and distressing level of internal conflict that impairs their overall well-being and functioning. It involves an ongoing struggle between opposing thoughts, emotions, desires, or values, leading to significant psychological distress and difficulties in daily life. This type of conflict surpasses the ordinary conflicts people encounter and becomes a pervasive and debilitating aspect of their mental health.

Unlike typical conflicts that arise from everyday life situations, conflict as a mental disorder is characterized by the intensity, duration, and negative impact it has on an individual's thoughts, emotions, behaviours, and relationships. The internal struggle is marked by a sense of disharmony, confusion, and tension, making it challenging for individuals to find resolution or reach a state of equilibrium.

Conflict as a mental disorder can manifest in various ways, such as conflicting beliefs, desires, or goals, conflicting emotions, or a constant battle between different aspects of one's identity or values. These conflicts may be contradictory, irreconcilable, or perpetually unresolved, causing significant distress and interfering with an individual's ability to function effectively in their personal, social, and professional life.

The concept of conflict as a mental disorder highlights the complex nature of internal struggles and their impact on an individual's mental well-being. It emphasizes the need for intervention and treatment to address the distressing symptoms and help individuals navigate and resolve these conflicts in a healthier and more adaptive manner.

Identification Characteristics of Conflict

Identifying conflict as a mental disorder requires recognizing specific characteristics that distinguish it from ordinary conflicts. Conflict as a mental disorder refers to a psychological condition in which individuals experience persistent and intense internal struggles that significantly impact their mental well-being and overall functioning. These identification characteristics provide insights into the nature and effects of this disorder, allowing for a better understanding and appropriate intervention.

1. Internal Turmoil

- Individuals experiencing conflict as a mental disorder often exhibit persistent and intense internal turmoil.
- They struggle with contradictory thoughts, emotions, desires, or values, leading to a sense of disharmony and unrest within themselves.
- The internal conflicts create a continuous battle, making it challenging to find resolution or achieve a state of equilibrium.

2. Emotional Distress

- Conflict as a mental disorder is accompanied by significant emotional distress.
- Individuals may experience intense and conflicting emotions directly linked to their internal conflicts, such as anxiety, guilt, shame, anger, sadness, or frustration.

- The emotional distress caused by the conflicts contributes to the overall impairment and distress associated with the disorder.

3. Impaired Decision-making

- Individuals with conflict as a mental disorder often face difficulties in making decisions.
- The conflicting thoughts, desires, or values they experience create a state of cognitive dissonance, making it challenging to objectively weigh options and reach clear resolutions.
- The impairment in decision-making can lead to difficulties in various aspects of life, including personal relationships, work, and daily functioning.

4. Interpersonal Difficulties

- Conflict as a mental disorder can significantly impact an individual's interpersonal relationships.
- Individuals may struggle to communicate effectively, experience frequent misunderstandings or arguments, and find it challenging to establish and maintain healthy connections with others.
- The conflicts within themselves can spill over into their interactions with others, leading to strained relationships and social difficulties.

5. Persistent Conflict Themes

- Conflict as a mental disorder often involves recurring themes or patterns of internal conflicts.
- These conflicts may revolve around identity, relationships, self-worth, morality, or life goals, and persistently influence the individual's thoughts and emotions.
- The persistent nature of these conflict themes contributes to the chronicity and distress associated with the disorder.

6. Impaired Functioning

- Conflict as a mental disorder can significantly impair an individual's overall functioning.
- The distress caused by the conflicts can interfere with their ability to concentrate, perform daily tasks, pursue goals, or engage in activities they once enjoyed.
- The impairment in functioning affects various domains of life, including personal, social, academic, and professional areas.

7. Chronic Nature

- Conflict as a mental disorder tends to be chronic and persistent, with conflicts frequently reoccurring or remaining unresolved over an extended period.
- The conflicts are not easily resolved through simple decision-making or problem-solving techniques.
- The chronic nature of the conflicts differentiates them from temporary or situational conflicts.

8. Distorted Self-perception

- Internal conflicts can distort an individual's perception of themselves.
- They may experience a fragmented sense of self, struggle with understanding who they are, or experience confusion about their values and beliefs.
- The distorted self-perception contributes to the emotional distress and impaired self-esteem associated with the disorder.

9. Obsessive Rumination

- Individuals with conflict as a mental disorder often engage in obsessive rumination.
- They continuously and repetitively dwell on their internal conflicts, finding it difficult to let go of the thoughts and find resolution.
- The constant rumination exacerbates the distress and perpetuates the internal conflicts.

10. Physical Symptoms

- The intense and chronic nature of conflict as a mental disorder can manifest in physical symptoms.
- Individuals may experience headaches, digestive problems, muscle tension, insomnia, fatigue, or other psychosomatic symptoms resulting from the distress caused by internal conflicts.
- The physical symptoms further contribute to the overall impairment and distress associated with the disorder.

11. Avoidance Behaviours

- Some individuals may engage in avoidance behaviours as a coping mechanism for dealing with their internal conflicts.
- They may avoid situations, conversations, or decisions that trigger their conflicts, leading to limitations in their personal and professional life.
- Avoidance behaviours can perpetuate the conflicts and hinder the individual's progress towards resolution.

12. Impaired Self-identity

- Conflict as a mental disorder can impact an individual's self-identity.
- They may experience a fragmented sense of self, struggle with understanding who they are, or experience confusion about their values, interests, or goals.
- The impaired self-identity adds to the emotional distress and challenges associated with the disorder.

13. Impact on Self-Esteem

- Internal conflicts can significantly affect an individual's self-esteem.
- The contradictory thoughts and emotions may lead to self-criticism, feelings of inadequacy, or a persistent sense of failure, further exacerbating their emotional distress.

- The impact on self-esteem contributes to the overall impairment and reduced quality of life.

14. Social Isolation

- Individuals experiencing conflict as a mental disorder may withdraw socially or isolate themselves from others.
- The conflicts they experience can create a barrier to forming and maintaining meaningful connections with others, resulting in feelings of loneliness and social detachment.
- Social isolation further contributes to the distress and impairment associated with the disorder.

15. Functional Impairment across Domains

- Conflict as a mental disorder can impact various domains of an individual's life, including personal, social, academic, and professional areas.
- They may struggle to meet responsibilities, experience difficulties in academic or work settings, and find it challenging to engage in activities they once enjoyed.
- The impairment across different domains further highlights the significant impact of the disorder on an individual's overall functioning.

16. Co-occurring Mental Health Conditions

- Conflict as a mental disorder may commonly co-occur with other mental health conditions.
- Anxiety disorders, depression, or personality disorders may be present alongside the internal conflicts, intensifying the distress and complexity of the disorder.
- The presence of co-occurring conditions requires a comprehensive approach to address the various aspects of the individual's mental health.

It is important to remember that the identification characteristics of conflict as a mental disorder can vary in their presentation and intensity among individuals. A formal diagnosis and assessment by a qualified mental health professional are necessary to evaluate the specific symptoms and their impact on an individual's functioning and well-being. Top of Form

Causes of Conflict

The causes of conflict as a mental disorder are multifaceted and can arise from various factors, including developmental experiences, personality traits, environmental influences, cognitive processes, value conflicts, cultural and societal influences, as well as trauma and unresolved past experiences. Understanding these causes is crucial in comprehending the underlying factors that contribute to the development and persistence of conflict as a mental disorder. By exploring these causes, mental health professionals can gain insights into the complexities of this disorder and formulate effective treatment approaches.

Developmental Factors

- Inconsistent parenting styles, traumatic events, or disrupted attachment patterns during early childhood can contribute to the development of unresolved internal conflicts that persist into adulthood.
- Unresolved conflicts from childhood may resurface and intensify in later stages of life, leading to the manifestation of conflict as a mental disorder.

Personality Traits

- Certain personality traits can predispose individuals to conflict as a mental disorder. For example, perfectionistic tendencies can lead to conflicts between high standards and real-life circumstances, causing distress and dissatisfaction.
- Traits such as ambivalence, rigidity, or difficulties in adapting to change can also contribute to conflicts within oneself.

Environmental Factors

- Stressful life events, such as relationship conflicts, loss, trauma, or major life transitions, can trigger internal conflicts and contribute to the onset or worsening of conflict as a mental disorder.
- A lack of support systems or unhealthy social environments can intensify conflicts and impair an individual's ability to manage them effectively.

Cognitive Processes

- Cognitive biases, such as black-and-white thinking, overgeneralization, or catastrophizing, can perpetuate and intensify internal conflicts.
- These biases distort an individual's perception of conflicts, making them more difficult to resolve and contributing to distress.

Value Conflicts

- Conflicts arising from differing values or belief systems can contribute to conflict as a mental disorder. Contradictory or irreconcilable values can create significant distress and internal turmoil.
- Conflicting moral values, ethical dilemmas, or clashes between personal and societal expectations can give rise to this type of conflict.

Cultural and Societal Influences

- Cultural norms, expectations, and societal pressures can influence the development of conflict as a mental disorder.
- Conflicting cultural messages or expectations may lead to a profound sense of internal discord when they clash with an individual's personal beliefs or desires.

Trauma and Unresolved Past Experiences

- Traumatic experiences or unresolved conflicts from the past can contribute to the development of conflict as a mental disorder.

- Trauma disrupts an individual's sense of safety and coherence, leading to internal conflicts as they struggle to make sense of their experiences and integrate them into their lives.

Cultural and Familial Conditioning

- Cultural and familial conditioning can shape an individual's beliefs, values, and attitudes, which may contribute to internal conflicts.
- Conflicting cultural or familial expectations, societal norms, or rigid belief systems can create internal discord and lead to the development of this disorder.

Unmet Needs

- Unmet emotional, psychological, or relational needs can give rise to conflict as a mental disorder.
- When core needs for love, acceptance, belonging, autonomy, or security are not fulfilled, individuals may experience internal conflicts in their pursuit of fulfilling those needs.

Cognitive Dissonance

- Cognitive dissonance occurs when individuals hold conflicting beliefs, attitudes, or values.
- This conflict between their beliefs can lead to psychological discomfort and distress, fueling the development of conflict as a mental disorder.

Maladaptive Coping Mechanisms

- Maladaptive coping mechanisms, such as avoidance, suppression, or substance abuse, can contribute to the persistence of conflict as a mental disorder.
- These ineffective coping strategies prevent the resolution of conflicts, perpetuating distress and hindering healthy adaptation.

Genetic and Biological Factors

- While the exact genetic and biological factors contributing to conflict as a mental disorder are not fully understood, research suggests a potential role.
- Certain genetic predispositions or neurochemical imbalances may influence an individual's vulnerability to developing this disorder or exacerbating existing conflicts.

Learned Behaviour

- Learned behaviour from significant relationships or past experiences can influence the development of conflict as a mental disorder.
- Unhealthy patterns of conflict resolution or ineffective communication styles learned from family, peers, or societal models may contribute to the persistence of internal conflicts.

Perceived Threats to Identity

- Conflicts that arise from threats to an individual's core identity, such as gender, sexuality, or cultural identity, can contribute to conflict as a mental disorder.
- When internal conflicts emerge as a result of these threats, individuals may experience significant distress and struggle to reconcile conflicting aspects of their identity.

Understanding the causes of conflict as a mental disorder provides crucial insights into its origins and complexities. By recognizing these underlying factors, mental health professionals can develop tailored treatment approaches that address the specific needs of individuals experiencing this disorder. Through therapeutic interventions, individuals can gain resolution, alleviate distress, and restore harmony within themselves.

Treatments of Conflict

Treating conflict as a mental disorder requires a comprehensive and tailored approach that addresses the unique challenges individuals face when experiencing internal conflicts. The treatment aims to alleviate distress, promote resolution, and enhance overall well-being. By combining various therapeutic modalities and interventions, mental health professionals can assist individuals in managing and navigating their conflicts in a healthier and more adaptive manner. This discussion will explore the key treatment approaches used for conflict as a mental disorder, emphasizing the importance of personalized care.

1. Psychotherapy

- Psychotherapy, particularly cognitive-behavioural therapy (CBT), is a widely utilized treatment for conflict as a mental disorder.
- CBT helps individuals identify and challenge their conflicting thoughts, beliefs, and emotions, promoting insight and the development of more adaptive cognitive patterns.
- Through therapy sessions, individuals can learn coping strategies, problem-solving skills, and effective communication techniques to manage and resolve conflicts.

2. Medication

- In some cases, medication may be prescribed to manage symptoms associated with conflict as a mental disorder, especially when co-occurring conditions like anxiety or depression are present.
- Antidepressants, anti-anxiety medications, or mood stabilizers may be utilized to reduce distress and stabilize mood.
- Medication is often combined with psychotherapy to address both the underlying conflicts and associated symptoms.

3. *Mindfulness Practices*

- Mindfulness-based interventions have proven beneficial in managing conflict as a mental disorder.
- Techniques such as meditation, mindfulness-based stress reduction (MBSR), or mindfulness-based cognitive therapy (MBCT) cultivate present-moment awareness and non-judgmental acceptance of conflicting thoughts and emotions.
- By practising mindfulness, individuals can develop a greater sense of self-awareness and emotional regulation, fostering a more balanced response to internal conflicts.

4. *Supportive Interventions*

- Engaging in support groups or seeking support from loved ones can provide individuals with validation, empathy, and a sense of belonging.
- Supportive interventions create a safe space to share experiences, gain perspectives, and receive emotional support from others who can relate to similar internal struggles.

5. *Lifestyle Modifications*

- Adopting a healthy lifestyle can support overall well-being and contribute to managing conflict as a mental disorder.
- Regular exercise, adequate sleep, and a nutritious diet can enhance mood, reduce stress levels, and improve an individual's ability to cope with internal conflicts.
- Engaging in activities that promote relaxation and self-care, such as hobbies or creative outlets, can provide emotional nourishment.

6. *Emotion Regulation Techniques*

- Learning effective emotion regulation strategies is crucial in managing the intense emotions associated with internal conflicts.
- Therapeutic approaches like emotion-focused therapy (EFT) or dialectical behaviour therapy (DBT) help individuals identify and regulate emotions, allowing for a more adaptive response to internal conflicts.

7. *Self-reflection and Self-compassion*

- Encouraging self-reflection and self-compassion is essential in the treatment of conflict as a mental disorder.
- By fostering self-awareness and cultivating self-compassion, individuals can develop a more understanding and non-judgemental relationship with their internal conflicts, promoting healing and resolution.

8. *Integration of Conflicting Aspects*

- Therapeutic approaches that focus on integrating conflicting aspects of one's self or identity can be valuable in resolving internal conflicts.

- By exploring and reconciling contradictory beliefs, desires, or values, individuals can create a more cohesive sense of self and reduce the distress associated with conflict.

9. Relational Therapy

- Conflict as a mental disorder often impacts interpersonal relationships. Relational therapy or couples therapy can be instrumental in addressing conflicts within relationships and improving communication and understanding.

10. Narrative Therapy

- Narrative therapy involves exploring and reshaping the stories individuals tell themselves about their conflicts.
- Through the therapeutic process, individuals can gain a new perspective on their conflicts, reframe their narrative, and develop alternative, empowering narratives that promote resolution and personal growth.

11. Psychodynamic Therapy

- Psychodynamic therapy focuses on exploring unconscious conflicts and their origins.
- By delving into the underlying psychological dynamics, individuals can gain insight into the roots of their conflicts and work towards resolution through increased self-awareness and understanding.

12. Art Therapy

- Art therapy utilizes creative expression as a means of exploring and processing internal conflicts.
- Engaging in various art forms, such as painting, drawing, or sculpting, allows individuals to express and communicate their conflicting emotions and thoughts in a non-verbal and symbolic manner, facilitating insight and resolution.

13. EMDR Therapy

- Eye Movement Desensitization and Reprocessing (EMDR) therapy is often effective in addressing conflicts stemming from past traumatic experiences.
- EMDR helps individuals process unresolved traumatic memories and their associated conflicts, enabling healing and resolution of internal struggles.

14. Family Therapy

- In cases where conflicts within the family system contribute to an individual's internal conflicts, family therapy can be beneficial.
- Family therapy explores the family dynamics, communication patterns, and unresolved conflicts that may be influencing the individual's internal struggles, aiming to improve understanding, support, and conflict resolution within the family unit.

15. Cognitive Restructuring

- Cognitive restructuring techniques involve identifying and challenging distorted or negative thoughts related to the conflicts.
- Through cognitive restructuring, individuals learn to replace maladaptive thoughts with more realistic and balanced ones, reducing distress and facilitating resolution.

16. Gradual Exposure

- Gradual exposure is a therapeutic technique used to address avoidance behaviours related to internal conflicts.
- By gradually exposing individuals to the situations, thoughts, or emotions that evoke conflict, they can learn to confront and manage their conflicts more effectively, reducing avoidance and promoting resolution.

17. Psychosocial Education

- Providing individuals with psycho-education about conflict as a mental disorder can enhance their understanding and coping skills.
- Education about conflict resolution strategies, communication techniques, stress management, and emotional regulation can empower individuals in managing their conflicts and promoting resolution.

18. Holistic Approaches

- Holistic approaches, such as yoga, meditation, acupuncture, or massage therapy, can complement traditional treatment methods.
- These practices promote overall well-being, stress reduction, and self awareness, supporting individuals in managing and finding balance amidst their internal conflicts.

The treatment of conflict as a mental disorder necessitates a personalized and comprehensive approach that takes into account the unique challenges faced by individuals. By employing various therapeutic modalities and interventions, mental health professionals can support individuals in managing internal conflicts, promoting resolution, and enhancing overall well-being. The collaborative development of an individualized treatment plan, tailored to the specific needs of the individual, is crucial in addressing the complexities of conflict as a mental disorder.

7

Types of Mental Diseases

Psychoses and Neuroses

Psychoses and neuroses are two terms historically used in psychology to describe different types of mental disorders. However, it's important to note that the field of psychology has evolved, and these terms are less commonly used today. Instead, modern psychology typically categorizes mental disorders under the Diagnostic and Statistical Manual of Mental Disorders (DSM-5) or the International Classification of Diseases (ICD-10/ICD-11). Nevertheless, understanding the historical concepts of psychoses and neuroses can provide some insight into how mental disorders have been conceptualized over time.

Psychoses

- *Definition:* Psychoses refer to severe mental disorders characterized by a loss of contact with reality. Individuals with psychoses often experience delusions (false beliefs) and hallucinations (false perceptions), which can significantly impair their ability to function in daily life.
- *Examples:* Schizophrenia is a classic example of a psychotic disorder. People with schizophrenia may have hallucinations (e.g., hearing voices) and delusions (e.g., believing they have special powers) that are not based in reality.
- *Symptoms:* Symptoms of psychosis may include disorganized thinking and speech, social withdrawal, impaired emotional expression, and difficulty with activities of daily living.
- *Causes:* The exact causes of psychoses are not fully understood, but they are believed to involve a complex interplay of genetic, environmental, and neurobiological factors.

Neuroses

- *Definition:* Neuroses are milder forms of mental distress characterized by emotional and psychological symptoms. Unlike psychoses, individuals with neuroses do not lose touch with reality. Instead, they experience distressing emotions and behaviours that are more in line with everyday life.
- *Examples:* Conditions like generalized anxiety disorder, obsessive-compulsive disorder, and phobias were historically considered neuroses.
- *Symptoms:* Symptoms of neuroses may include excessive worry, irrational fears or phobias, compulsive behaviours, and various forms of emotional distress.

- *Causes:* Neuroses are often thought to be linked to stress, unresolved conflicts, and maladaptive coping mechanisms. They are generally considered less biologically based than psychoses.

Differences between Psychoses and Neuroses

Here's a tabular representation of the differences between psychoses and neuroses.

Characteristics	*Psychoses*	*Neuroses*
Reality Contact	Loss of contact with reality. Delusions and hallucinations are common.	Maintains contact with reality. May have irrational thoughts and fears, but awareness remains intact.
Severity	Severe; Profoundly impairs daily functioning.	Less severe; Typically does not lead to significant impairment in daily life.
Examples	Schizophrenia, schizoaffective disorder.	Generalized anxiety disorder, obsessive-compulsive disorder, phobias.
Treatment	Often requires antipsychotic medications, psychotherapy, and possibly hospitalization.	Responsive to psychotherapy (e.g., CBT), medication may not always be necessary.
Causation	Complex interplay of genetic, environmental, and neurobiological factors.	Often linked to stress, unresolved conflicts, and maladaptive coping mechanisms; less biologically based.

These distinctions help to provide a general understanding of the differences between psychoses and neuroses, the use of these terms has become less common in modern psychiatry.

Schizophrenia

Schizophrenia is a serious and chronic mental disorder characterized by disruptions in thinking, emotions, and behaviours. It often involves hallucinations, delusions, and impaired insight, leading to significant challenges in daily life and functioning.

Symptoms

Schizophrenia is a complex mental disorder characterized by a range of symptoms that affect a person's thinking, emotions, and behaviour. These symptoms can vary in severity and duration and often fall into several categories, including positive symptoms, negative symptoms, and cognitive symptoms.

Positive Symptoms

1. *Hallucinations*: A person with schizophrenia may experience auditory hallucinations, such as hearing voices that are not real. For example, they may hear voices commanding them to do things or making derogatory comments.
2. *Delusions*: Delusions are false beliefs that are firmly held, even when there is no evidence to support them. An example could be a paranoid

delusion where an individual believes that they are being followed or persecuted by government agents, despite no actual threat.

3. *Disorganized Thinking*: This symptom can manifest as incoherent speech or difficulty organizing thoughts. For instance, a person may jump from one unrelated topic to another during a conversation, making it challenging to follow their train of thought.

Negative Symptoms

1. *Affective Flattening*: Imagine a person with schizophrenia who shows little emotional expression. They might have a blank facial expression and seem unresponsive to joy, sadness, or anger.
2. *Anhedonia*: Someone with schizophrenia may lose interest in activities they once enjoyed. For example, they may have previously loved playing music or sports but no longer find pleasure in these activities.
3. *Avolition*: This could manifest as a lack of motivation or inability to complete daily tasks. For instance, a person with schizophrenia might struggle to maintain personal hygiene or find the energy to go to work or school.

Cognitive Symptoms

1. *Impaired Memory*: Individuals with schizophrenia may have difficulty remembering information. They may forget important dates, appointments, or even the names of close friends and family members.
2. *Attention Problems*: Maintaining focus and attention can be challenging for someone with schizophrenia. They may get easily distracted and find it hard to concentrate on tasks.
3. *Executive Functioning Issues*: Complex problem-solving and decision-making can be impaired. For instance, a person with schizophrenia might struggle to manage their finances or plan their daily activities effectively.
4. *Impaired Insight*: People with schizophrenia may lack awareness of their condition. They might not recognize that they have a mental illness and may resist seeking help or treatment. This lack of insight can make it challenging for them to manage their symptoms.

It's important to note that not all individuals with schizophrenia will experience all of these symptoms, and the severity can vary greatly from person to person. Diagnosis and treatment are typically based on the presence and combination of these symptoms, as well as their impact on the individual's daily life and functioning. Schizophrenia is a complex and often chronic condition that requires specialized care and support.

Causes of Schizophrenia

The exact causes of schizophrenia are not fully understood, but it is widely believed to result from a combination of genetic, environmental, and neurobiological factors. Researchers have made significant progress in understanding these factors, but the precise mechanisms remain complex and multifaceted. Here are some key factors that are thought to contribute to the development of schizophrenia:

1. *Genetics:* There is a strong genetic component to schizophrenia. Individuals with a family history of the disorder are at a higher risk of developing it themselves. While no single gene is responsible for schizophrenia, multiple genetic variations, or a combination of genes, may increase susceptibility. The risk is higher among close relatives of individuals with schizophrenia, and identical twins of affected individuals have a higher concordance rate than fraternal twins.
2. *Neurobiological Factors:* Neuroimaging studies have revealed structural and functional differences in the brains of individuals with schizophrenia. These include abnormalities in brain structure, such as enlarged ventricles and reduced gray matter volume in certain regions. Imbalances in neurotransmitters, particularly dopamine and glutamate, are believed to play a role in the development of psychotic symptoms.
3. *Environmental Factors:* Certain environmental factors have been associated with an increased risk of schizophrenia, including:
   - *Prenatal Exposure*: Adverse prenatal factors, such as maternal malnutrition, infections, and stress during pregnancy, may increase the risk.
   - *Birth Complications*: Complications during birth, such as hypoxia (lack of oxygen), have been linked to an elevated risk.
   - *Childhood Trauma*: Experiencing trauma or severe stress during childhood may contribute to the development of schizophrenia in some cases.
   - *Cannabis Use*: There is evidence to suggest that heavy cannabis use during adolescence may increase the risk of developing schizophrenia, particularly in individuals with a genetic predisposition.
4. *Brain Development:* Abnormal brain development during fetal and early childhood stages has been proposed as a contributing factor. Disruptions in neural connectivity and synaptic pruning processes may play a role.
5. *Stress:* Chronic or severe stress can trigger the onset of schizophrenia or exacerbate symptoms in individuals already predisposed to the disorder.
6. *Substance Abuse:* The use of certain psychoactive substances, particularly stimulants or hallucinogens, can induce symptoms resembling schizophrenia. Substance abuse can also worsen the course of the illness.

It's important to note that the development of schizophrenia is likely the result of interactions between these various factors. Not everyone with genetic susceptibility or exposure to environmental risk factors will develop schizophrenia, and the disorder can manifest differently from person to person.

Early intervention and comprehensive treatment are essential for managing schizophrenia and improving outcomes for individuals affected by this complex mental health condition.

Treatments of Schizophrenia

The treatment of schizophrenia typically involves a combination of approaches aimed at managing symptoms, improving overall functioning, and helping individuals lead fulfilling lives. It's important to note that schizophrenia is a chronic condition, and treatment often needs to be ongoing. Here are some of the primary treatments and interventions for schizophrenia:

Antipsychotic Medications

- Antipsychotic medications, also known as neuroleptics, are the cornerstone of schizophrenia treatment. They help manage the positive symptoms of the disorder, such as hallucinations and delusions.
- There are two main categories of antipsychotics: typical (first-generation) and atypical (second-generation) antipsychotics. Atypical antipsychotics are often preferred due to their lower risk of extrapyramidal side effects (movement-related side effects).
- Medication choice is tailored to the individual's specific symptoms and may require some trial and error to find the most effective and tolerable option.
- Compliance with medication is crucial for symptom control. Long-acting injectable antipsychotic formulations may be used for individuals who have difficulty with daily pill regimens.

Psychotherapy

- Cognitive-behavioural therapy (CBT) and supportive psychotherapy can help individuals with schizophrenia manage their symptoms, cope with stress, and improve their insight into the disorder.
- Cognitive remediation therapy may be used to address cognitive deficits associated with schizophrenia, helping individuals improve their thinking and problem-solving abilities.

Family Education and Support

- Involving family members in treatment can be highly beneficial. Family psychoeducation programmes can help loved ones understand schizophrenia, enhance communication, and provide support for both the affected individual and their family.

Rehabilitation Services

- Vocational rehabilitation programmes help individuals with schizophrenia gain job skills and find employment opportunities.
- Social skills training can improve interpersonal interactions and relationships.
- Psychosocial rehabilitation programmes focus on enhancing daily living skills, including managing finances and maintaining housing.

Community Support

- Assertive Community Treatment (ACT) teams provide intensive, community-based support, including medication management, therapy, and assistance with daily living.
- Supportive housing programmes offer safe and stable housing for individuals with schizophrenia.

Hospitalization

- In severe cases or during acute psychotic episodes, hospitalization may be necessary to ensure safety, stabilize symptoms, and adjust medication.

Self-help Strategies

- Encouraging individuals with schizophrenia to engage in self-help strategies, such as adhering to medication regimens, maintaining a regular daily routine, and avoiding substance abuse, is essential for long-term management.

Early Intervention Programmes

- Early intervention services aim to identify and treat schizophrenia in its early stages, potentially improving long-term outcomes.

It's important to approach schizophrenia treatment on an individual basis, as the disorder varies in its presentation and response to treatment from person to person. Collaborative, multidisciplinary care involving psychiatrists, psychologists, social workers, and other mental health professionals is often necessary to provide comprehensive support. Treatment plans should be regularly reviewed and adjusted based on the individual's progress and changing needs. With the right treatment and support, many individuals with schizophrenia can lead productive and fulfilling lives.

Manic Depressive Disorder

Manic Depressive Disorder, more commonly known as Bipolar Disorder, is a mental health condition characterized by extreme mood swings between manic episodes and depressive episodes. Let's explore this disorder with some examples to better understand its manifestations:

Example 1-Manic Episode

Rani, a 32-year-old woman with Bipolar I Disorder, experiences a manic episode. During this time, she feels euphoric and has boundless energy. She:

- Stays awake for days, needing only a few hours of sleep but feeling fully rested.
- Rapidly talks about her plans to start multiple businesses, convinced they will all succeed.
- Makes impulsive purchases, such as expensive electronics, without considering her budget.
- Embarks on a spontaneous road trip, disregarding her responsibilities at work.
- Becomes easily irritable and agitated if anyone tries to intervene or suggest that her ideas might be unrealistic.

Example 2-Depressive Episode

A few weeks later, Rani enters a depressive episode. During this time, she feels profoundly sad and lethargic. She:

- Struggles to get out of bed in the morning and often spends most of the day in her pajamas.
- Loses interest in her hobbies and socializing, withdrawing from friends and family.
- Experiences significant changes in her appetite, leading to weight loss.
- Can't concentrate on even simple tasks and feels overwhelmed by everyday responsibilities.
- Frequently thinks about death and contemplates suicide as a way to escape her emotional pain.

Example 3-Bipolar II Hypomania

Arnab, a 28-year-old man with Bipolar II Disorder, experiences hypomanic episodes, which are milder than full-blown manic episodes. During a hypomanic episode, he:

- Feels unusually upbeat and energetic, often accomplishing a lot in a short time.
- Engages in impulsive behaviours like spending money recklessly but without severe financial consequences.
- Becomes more talkative and sociable than usual, enjoying the company of friends.
- Has a reduced need for sleep but still gets a few hours of rest each night.
- While showing increased productivity, Mike's behaviour doesn't escalate to the extreme levels seen in full manic episodes.

Example 4-Cyclothymic Disorder

Krishna, a 40-year-old man, has Cyclothymic Disorder. He experiences frequent mood swings but doesn't have full-blown manic or depressive episodes. Krishna:

- Has periods of increased energy and creativity, during which he takes on numerous projects.
- Experiences phases of mild irritability and restlessness but doesn't engage in impulsive or risky behaviours.
- Goes through times of mild sadness and introspection but never reaches the depths of severe depression.
- Despite these mood fluctuations, Krishna's symptoms don't meet the criteria for Bipolar I or Bipolar II Disorder.

Manic Depressive Disorder can vary widely from person to person, and the intensity and frequency of manic and depressive episodes can differ significantly. It's essential to note that these examples only scratch the surface of the complexity of Manic Depressive Disorder, and a qualified mental health professional is best suited to diagnose and provide appropriate treatment for individuals experiencing these mood swings. Treatment may involve medication, therapy, and lifestyle adjustments to help individuals manage their symptoms and lead more stable lives.

Symptoms of Manic Depressive Disorder

Manic Depressive Disorder, also known as Bipolar Disorder, is characterized by distinct periods of manic or hypomanic episodes and depressive episodes. Here are the symptoms associated with each phase:

Symptoms of Manic Episodes

1. *Elevated Mood*: A persistently elevated, euphoric, or irritable mood is a hallmark of manic episodes.
2. *Increased Energy*: Individuals experience a surge in energy levels and may feel overly active and restless.
3. *Reduced Need for Sleep*: They can go for days with little or no sleep without feeling fatigued.
4. *Racing Thoughts*: Thoughts may race, and individuals may have difficulty concentrating on one topic.
5. *Rapid Speech*: Speech becomes rapid, with thoughts pouring out quickly.
6. *Grandiose Beliefs*: Individuals may develop grandiose beliefs about their abilities, talents, or importance.
7. *Impulsivity*: There's a propensity for impulsive and risky behaviours, such as reckless spending, substance abuse, or engaging in unprotected sexual activities.
8. *Distractibility*: An increased distractibility can make it challenging to focus on tasks.
9. *Increased Goal-Directed Activity*: Individuals may undertake numerous activities, often with grand plans, but struggle to complete them.
10. *Irritability*: Irritability and agitation are common, especially when others attempt to intervene or challenge their ideas.
11. *Decreased Judgement*: Impaired judgement can lead to decisions with potentially severe consequences.

Symptoms of Depressive Episodes

1. *Persistent Sadness*: A pervasive feeling of sadness, hopelessness, or emptiness characterizes depressive episodes.
2. *Fatigue*: Individuals experience significant fatigue and a lack of energy.
3. *Sleep Disturbances*: Sleep patterns may change, leading to either insomnia or excessive sleeping.
4. *Appetite Changes*: Appetite may decrease or increase, often resulting in significant weight loss or gain.
5. *Difficulty Concentrating*: Concentration and decision-making become challenging.
6. *Loss of Interest*: A marked loss of interest or pleasure in previously enjoyable activities.

7. *Feelings of Worthlessness*: Individuals may feel excessively guilty or worthless.
8. *Thoughts of Death*: Recurrent thoughts about death, suicide, or suicide attempts may occur.
9. *Physical Symptoms*: Some people experience physical symptoms like aches and pains without a clear medical cause.
10. *Withdrawal*: Individuals may withdraw from social activities and isolate themselves from friends and family.

It's important to note that not all individuals with Manic Depressive Disorderwill experience all of these symptoms, and the severity and duration of episodes can vary. Additionally, some individuals may have a milder form of Manic Depressive Disorderknown as Bipolar II, which is characterized by hypomanic episodes (less severe than full mania) and depressive episodes. Diagnosis and treatment of Manic Depressive Disordershould be conducted by qualified mental health professionals who can assess an individual's specific symptoms and tailor an appropriate treatment plan, which may include medication, psychotherapy, and lifestyle adjustments. Early diagnosis and effective treatment can help individuals with Manic Depressive Disordermanage their condition and lead more stable lives.

Causes of Manic Depressive Disorder

The exact causes of Manic Depressive Disorder, also known as Bipolar Disorder, are not fully understood, but it is believed to result from a combination of genetic, neurobiological, and environmental factors. Here are some key factors that are thought to contribute to the development of Manic Depressive Disorder:

1. *Genetics:* There is a strong genetic component to Manic Depressive Disorder. Individuals with a family history of the disorder are at a higher risk of developing it themselves. Researchers have identified specific genes that may be associated with an increased susceptibility to Manic Depressive Disorder, but the genetic factors involved are complex and not fully elucidated.
2. *Neurobiological Factors:* Abnormalities in brain structure and function are often observed in individuals with Manic Depressive Disorder. Imbalances in neurotransmitters, which are chemical messengers in the brain, such as dopamine, serotonin, and norepinephrine, are thought to play a role in mood regulation. Changes in the functioning of neural circuits that regulate mood, emotion, and impulse control are also implicated.
3. *Neurochemical Imbalances:* Dysregulation of certain neurotransmitters, particularly serotonin and dopamine, is believed to contribute to mood swings in Manic Depressive Disorder. High levels of dopamine during manic episodes and low levels during depressive episodes may be involved in extreme mood shifts.

4. *Hormonal Changes:* Hormonal imbalances or changes, particularly in thyroid function, can trigger mood disturbances that resemble Manic Depressive Disordersymptoms. However, these are not primary causes but can exacerbate the condition in individuals already predisposed to it.
5. *Environmental Factors:* Stressful life events, trauma, and significant life changes can act as triggers for the onset of Manic Depressive Disorderin individuals who are genetically predisposed. These environmental factors can disrupt mood regulation and contribute to the emergence of manic or depressive episodes.
6. *Substance Abuse:* Substance abuse, including alcohol and drug use, can exacerbate or trigger episodes of Manic Depressive Disorder. Substance use can interact with the brain's neurochemistry and make mood symptoms more severe.
7. *Brain Structure and Function:* Structural abnormalities in certain brain regions, such as the prefrontal cortex and amygdala, have been observed in individuals with Manic Depressive Disorder. These brain regions play a role in emotional regulation and may contribute to mood instability.
8. *Psychological Factors:* While not a primary cause, psychological factors such as personality traits, coping styles, and early life experiences can influence how individuals with a genetic predisposition to Manic Depressive Disordermanifest symptoms and respond to treatment.

It's important to note that the interplay of these factors can be complex and may vary from person to person. Manic Depressive Disorderis a complex and multifaceted condition, and its development is likely influenced by a combination of these genetic, neurobiological, and environmental factors. A thorough evaluation by a mental health professional is essential for accurate diagnosis and the development of an effective treatment plan tailored to the individual's specific needs.

Treatments of Manic Depressive Disorder

The treatment of Manic Depressive Disorder, also known as Bipolar Disorder, typically involves a combination of medication, psychotherapy (talk therapy), and lifestyle management. The goal of treatment is to stabilize mood, reduce the frequency and severity of manic and depressive episodes, and improve the individual's overall quality of life. Treatment plans may vary based on the type and severity of Manic Depressive Disorder and the individual's specific needs. Here are some common treatments:

1. *Medication*

- *Mood Stabilizers*: Mood stabilizing medications are the primary treatment for Manic Depressive Disorder. Lithium is a commonly prescribed mood stabilizer that helps control manic and depressive episodes. Other mood stabilizers include valproic acid (Depakote) and lamotrigine (Lamictal).

- *Antipsychotic Medications*: Some atypical antipsychotic medications, like quetiapine (Seroquel) or olanzapine (Zyprexa), are prescribed to help manage symptoms during manic or mixed episodes.
- *Antidepressants*: In some cases, antidepressant medications may be used cautiously during depressive episodes, but they are often used in combination with a mood stabilizer to prevent a switch into mania.
- *Medication Adjustment*: Medications may need to be adjusted periodically based on symptom changes and side effects. Regular follow-up with a healthcare provider is essential.

2. Psychotherapy (Talk Therapy)

- *Cognitive-Behavioural Therapy (CBT)*: CBT can help individuals with Manic Depressive Disorder identify and manage problematic thought patterns and behaviours. It can also assist in coping with stress and preventing relapses.
- *Interpersonal and Social Rhythm Therapy (IPSRT)*: IPSRT focuses on stabilizing daily routines and improving interpersonal relationships, which can help regulate mood in individuals with Manic Depressive Disorder.
- *Family-Focused Therapy*: Involving family members in therapy can help improve communication, support, and understanding of the disorder within the family system.

3. Electroconvulsive Therapy (ECT): In severe cases of Manic Depressive Disorder where medications and psychotherapy have not been effective, electroconvulsive therapy may be considered. ECT involves the controlled induction of seizures under anesthesia and is often used as a last resort.

4. Lifestyle Management

- *Stress Reduction*: Learning stress management techniques, such as mindfulness, meditation, and relaxation exercises, can help individuals with Manic Depressive Disorder manage stress, which can trigger episodes.
- *Sleep Hygiene*: Maintaining a regular sleep schedule and ensuring adequate sleep is crucial in managing Manic Depressive Disorder. Sleep disturbances can trigger mood swings.
- *Alcohol and Drug Avoidance*: Substance abuse can worsen Manic Depressive Disorder symptoms, so avoiding alcohol and recreational drugs is essential.
- *Regular Exercise*: Physical activity can help regulate mood and reduce depressive symptoms.
- *Healthy Diet*: A balanced diet with regular meals can help stabilize mood and energy levels.

5. Support Groups: Participating in support groups or seeking peer support can provide individuals with a sense of community and understanding from others who have experienced similar challenges.

*6. **Regular Monitoring:*** Ongoing monitoring by a mental health professional is crucial to assess treatment progress, manage medication side effects, and make adjustments as needed.

It's important to note that treatment for Manic Depressive Disorder should be individualized based on the specific needs and preferences of each person. It may take time to find the most effective combination of treatments, and a collaborative approach involving the individual, their healthcare provider, and support network is essential for managing the condition effectively. Early diagnosis and consistent treatment can greatly improve the quality of life for individuals living with Manic Depressive Disorder.

Paranoia

Paranoia is a mental health condition characterized by irrational and persistent feelings of fear, distrust, suspicion, and the belief that others are plotting against or trying to harm the person. These beliefs are often unfounded and not based on credible evidence, leading to significant distress and impaired functioning in daily life. Paranoia can vary in severity, from mild to severe, and may be a symptom of various mental health disorders.

Here are some key features and examples of paranoia:

1. *Suspicion of Others:* People with paranoia often have an intense distrust of others, including friends, family members, coworkers, or even strangers. They may believe that others have hidden motives or are part of a conspiracy against them. For example, someone with paranoia might think that their colleagues are deliberately sabotaging their career or that their spouse is plotting to leave them.
2. *Exaggerated Perceptions of Threat:* Paranoia can lead individuals to perceive threats where none exist or to interpret innocent actions as malicious. For instance, someone might believe that a casual comment made by a friend is a veiled insult or that a passerby on the street is following them.
3. *Secrecy and Isolation:* Paranoia often causes individuals to withdraw from social interactions, as they fear that others are watching or judging them. They may become increasingly secretive about their thoughts and actions, isolating themselves from friends and family.
4. *Unfounded Beliefs and Delusions:* Paranoia can be accompanied by delusional thinking, where individuals firmly hold false beliefs despite evidence to the contrary. These beliefs can be bizarre and irrational. For example, a person might believe that they have a microchip implanted in their brain by a government agency to monitor their thoughts.
5. *Emotional Distress:* Paranoia can cause significant emotional distress, including anxiety, fear, anger, and sadness. These emotions may be triggered by perceived threats or situations that confirm the individual's paranoid beliefs.

6. *Interference with Daily Life:* Paranoia can interfere with a person's ability to work, maintain relationships, and engage in everyday activities. This can lead to job loss, strained relationships, and social isolation.
7. *Underlying Causes:* Paranoia can be a symptom of various mental health conditions, including paranoid personality disorder, schizophrenia, delusional disorder, or severe anxiety disorders. Substance abuse, sleep deprivation, and certain medical conditions can also contribute to paranoid symptoms.

It's essential to note that not all suspicious thoughts or feelings of distrust are indicative of paranoia. In some cases, these emotions may be reasonable responses to actual threats or past experiences of betrayal. However, when these feelings become chronic, irrational, and significantly impact one's life, professional help should be sought.

Symptoms of Paranoia

Paranoia is characterized by a range of symptoms that revolve around irrational and persistent mistrust, suspicion, and fear of others. These symptoms can vary in intensity and may be indicative of an underlying mental health condition. Here are some common symptoms associated with paranoia:

1. *Excessive Suspicion*: A hallmark symptom of paranoia is an unwarranted and intense suspicion of others. Individuals may become preoccupied with the belief that people are plotting against them or trying to harm them in some way.
2. *Distrust*: Paranoia often involves a deep and pervasive distrust of others, even those who have been close or trusted for a long time. Individuals may believe that friends, family members, coworkers, or authority figures are untrustworthy or have hidden agendas.
3. *Misinterpretation of Intentions*: Paranoia can lead individuals to misinterpret the intentions of others. Innocent actions or comments may be perceived as hostile or threatening. For example, a simple greeting from a colleague may be seen as a veiled insult.
4. *Perceived Conspiracies*: Some individuals with paranoia may believe in elaborate and unfounded conspiracy theories involving government agencies, secret organizations, or powerful figures. They may think they are being surveilled or targeted by these conspiracies.
5. *Delusional Beliefs*: Paranoia can be accompanied by delusional thinking, where individuals hold firmly to false beliefs despite a lack of evidence. These beliefs may be bizarre and irrational. For instance, someone might believe that they have special powers or are the subject of experiments.
6. *Hypervigilance*: People with paranoia are often hypervigilant, constantly on guard, and alert to potential threats. They may scan their environment for signs of danger or suspicious behaviour.

7. *Social Isolation*: Due to their mistrust and fear of others, individuals with paranoia often isolate themselves from friends and family. They may avoid social gatherings or cut ties with loved ones.
8. *Anger and Hostility*: Paranoia can lead to heightened anger and hostility, especially when individuals perceive others as a threat. They may become confrontational, argumentative, or even aggressive in response to perceived slights or provocations.
9. *Emotional Distress*: People with paranoia frequently experience intense emotions such as anxiety, fear, and anger. These emotions can be triggered by perceived threats or situations that confirm their paranoid beliefs.
10. *Interference with Daily Life*: Paranoia can significantly impact a person's ability to function in daily life. It may affect their work, relationships, and overall well-being, leading to job loss, strained family ties, and social isolation.

It's important to note that paranoia can be a symptom of various underlying mental health conditions, including paranoid personality disorder, schizophrenia, delusional disorder, or severe anxiety disorders. Substance abuse, sleep deprivation, and certain medical conditions can also contribute to paranoid symptoms. If you or someone you know is experiencing symptoms of paranoia that are interfering with daily life, it's essential to seek professional help. Early intervention and appropriate treatment, which may include therapy and medication, can help manage and improve the symptoms of paranoia. A mental health professional can provide an accurate diagnosis and develop a tailored treatment plan.

Causes of Paranoia

Paranoia can have various causes, and it often arises from a complex interplay of genetic, environmental, psychological, and neurological factors. Understanding the causes of paranoia can help in its diagnosis and treatment. Here are some of the key factors that may contribute to the development of paranoia:

1. *Underlying Mental Health Conditions*
   - *Schizophrenia*: Paranoia is a common symptom of schizophrenia, a severe mental disorder characterized by distorted thinking, hallucinations, and disorganized behaviour.
   - *Delusional Disorders*: Certain types of delusional disorders, such as paranoid delusional disorder, involve persistent and irrational beliefs in the malevolent intentions of others.
   - *Paranoid Personality Disorder*: This personality disorder is characterized by a long-standing pattern of distrust and suspicion of others, often beginning in early adulthood.
2. *Trauma and Stress:* Traumatic experiences, such as physical or emotional abuse, can contribute to the development of paranoia. These experiences can lead individuals to develop a heightened sense of vigilance and mistrust.

3. *Genetics:* There is evidence to suggest that genetics plays a role in the susceptibility to paranoid thinking. Individuals with a family history of schizophrenia or other psychotic disorders may be at a higher risk of developing paranoid symptoms.
4. *Substance Abuse:* The use of certain drugs, including hallucinogens, amphetamines, and marijuana, can induce paranoid symptoms. Substance-induced paranoia is often temporary but may persist in some cases.
5. *Neurobiological Factors:* Abnormalities in brain structure and function, such as imbalances in neurotransmitters like dopamine, have been linked to paranoia. These neurobiological factors can be associated with various mental health disorders.
6. *Social Isolation:* Prolonged social isolation or loneliness can lead to increased suspiciousness and paranoia. A lack of social support and interaction may exacerbate existing paranoid tendencies.
7. *Cultural and Environmental Factors:* Cultural and societal factors can influence the expression of paranoia. In some cultures, beliefs in witchcraft or malevolent spirits may contribute to paranoid thinking.
8. *Personality Traits:* Certain personality traits, such as high levels of mistrust or suspiciousness, can predispose individuals to develop paranoid thoughts and beliefs.
9. *Medical Conditions:* Some medical conditions, such as neurological disorders, infections, or brain injuries, can result in changes in thinking and behaviour that may include paranoia.

It's important to note that paranoia is a symptom that can occur in various mental health disorders, and it can also be a temporary response to stress or trauma. Accurate diagnosis and treatment typically involve a thorough evaluation by a mental health professional, who can determine the underlying cause and develop an appropriate treatment plan. Treatment options may include psychotherapy, medication, or a combination of both, depending on the specific diagnosis and individual needs. Early intervention is often crucial in managing and improving the symptoms of paranoia.

Treatments of Paranoia

The treatment of paranoia primarily depends on its underlying cause and severity. It's important to note that paranoia is often a symptom of an underlying mental health condition, and addressing the root cause is essential. Here are some common approaches to treating paranoia:

1. *Psychotherapy*
    - *Cognitive-Behavioural Therapy (CBT)*: CBT is often used to treat paranoia. It helps individuals identify and challenge irrational thoughts and beliefs, replacing them with more realistic and balanced ones. It also teaches coping strategies to manage anxiety and reduce paranoid thinking.

- *Individual Psychotherapy*: Talk therapy with a trained mental health professional can provide a safe space for individuals to explore their thoughts, emotions, and beliefs. It can help uncover the underlying causes of paranoia and develop healthier ways of thinking and coping.

2. *Medication:* In some cases, medication may be prescribed to alleviate the symptoms of paranoia. The choice of medication depends on the underlying condition. Commonly used medications may include antipsychotic drugs for conditions like schizophrenia or mood stabilizers for disorders with paranoid features.
3. *Supportive Services:* Peer support groups or community-based mental health programmes can offer individuals with paranoia a sense of belonging and understanding. These services can help reduce social isolation and provide valuable coping strategies.
4. *Family Therapy:* In cases where paranoia affects family dynamics, family therapy can be beneficial. It helps family members understand the condition, improve communication, and develop strategies to support their loved one effectively.
5. *Stress Management and Coping Skills:* Learning stress management techniques and healthy coping skills can be essential for individuals with paranoia. These skills can help reduce anxiety and prevent the escalation of paranoid thoughts.
6. *Lifestyle Changes:* Maintaining a healthy lifestyle, including regular exercise, a balanced diet, and sufficient sleep, can contribute to overall mental well-being and potentially reduce paranoia.
7. *Substance Abuse Treatment:* If substance abuse is a contributing factor to paranoia, seeking treatment for addiction is crucial. Addressing substance use issues can improve mental health outcomes.
8. *Education and Psycho-Education:* Providing individuals and their families with information about the condition can enhance understanding and reduce stigma. Psycho-Education can empower individuals to manage their symptoms and seek timely treatment.
9. *Long-term Management:* For individuals with chronic conditions like schizophrenia or delusional disorders, long-term management and adherence to treatment plans are essential. Regular follow-up with mental health professionals can help monitor symptoms and adjust treatment as needed.

It's important to remember that treatment for paranoia should be individualized and tailored to the specific needs and circumstances of the person experiencing it. Early intervention and consistent support can significantly improve the prognosis for individuals with paranoia. Additionally, a collaborative approach involving mental health professionals, family members, and the affected individual can be highly effective in managing and reducing paranoid symptoms.

Delusional Disorder

Delusional Disorder, also known as Paranoid Disorder, is a mental health condition characterized by the presence of persistent and false beliefs (delusions) that are held with a high level of conviction despite evidence to the contrary. These delusions are not explained by another mental disorder, such as schizophrenia, and they do not significantly impair the individual's overall functioning. Delusional Disorder is relatively rare, and individuals with this condition often appear normal and well-adjusted in all other aspects of their life.

There are several subtypes of Delusional Disorder, including:

1. *Erotomanic Type:* In this subtype, individuals believe that someone, often of higher social status, is in love with them. They may interpret ordinary actions and gestures from the supposed admirer as evidence of their affection, even when there is no basis for such beliefs. For example, someone with this type of delusion may believe that a famous actor is secretly in love with them because they received a fan letter.
2. *Grandiose Type:* Individuals with this subtype have an exaggerated sense of self-importance and may believe they possess special powers, talents, or knowledge. They might think they are a genius or that they have a unique mission in life, despite no objective evidence to support these beliefs. For instance, someone might believe they are the reincarnation of a historical figure.
3. *Persecutory Type:* Individuals with this subtype believe they are being conspired against, harassed, or persecuted by others. They often interpret benign events as malicious in nature and may think that they are being spied on or targeted in some way, even when there is no concrete reason to believe so.
4. *Jealous Type:* In this subtype, individuals have delusions that their partner is unfaithful or disloyal, despite no evidence to support these suspicions. This can lead to relationship difficulties and conflict.
5. *Somatic Type:* People with this subtype are convinced they have a physical illness or defect, even when medical examinations consistently show no such problem. They may frequently seek medical attention, which can be frustrating for healthcare professionals.
6. *Mixed Type:* This subtype involves a combination of delusional themes that do not fit into one specific category.

Examples of Delusional Disorder

1. *Erotomanic Delusion*: Sourav is convinced that a famous celebrity is in love with him and sends him secret messages through their TV appearances and social media posts. He believes they will eventually be together, despite never having met the celebrity in person.
2. *Grandiose Delusion*: Aksah believes he is the world's greatest inventor, even though he has never invented anything of note. He is convinced that

he holds the key to solving all of humanity's problems and that everyone should listen to him and follow his ideas.

3. *Persecutory Delusion*: Riya believes that her coworkers are secretly plotting to get her fired. She thinks they are spreading rumours about her and monitoring her every move, even though there is no evidence to support these claims.
4. *Somatic Delusion*: Rekha is convinced that she has a rare and deadly disease, even though numerous medical tests have shown she is perfectly healthy. She spends a significant amount of time seeking medical opinions and treatments for her imagined illness.

It's important to note that individuals with Delusional Disorder often do not recognize that their beliefs are irrational or untrue, which can make treatment challenging. Treatment typically involves psychotherapy, particularly cognitive-behavioural therapy (CBT), and sometimes medication to address associated symptoms such as anxiety or depression. If you or someone you know is struggling with Delusional Disorder, it's crucial to seek professional help for an accurate diagnosis and appropriate treatment.

Symptoms of Delusional Disorder

Delusional Disorder is a mental health condition characterized by the presence of false and unshakable beliefs, known as delusions, which persist despite contradictory evidence. These delusions are typically bizarre or implausible and are the hallmark feature of the disorder. Unlike some other mental illnesses, individuals with Delusional Disorder often maintain their cognitive and functional abilities in most aspects of their lives.

The symptoms of Delusional Disorder can manifest differently depending on the specific subtype of the disorder:

1. *Erotomanic Type:* People with this subtype firmly believe that someone of higher social status is deeply in love with them, even when there is no factual basis for this belief. They may interpret ordinary interactions or gestures as evidence of this imagined affection.
2. *Grandiose Type:* In this subtype, individuals hold grandiose delusions, believing that they possess extraordinary talents, knowledge, or powers. They often have an inflated sense of self-importance and may express these beliefs in a pompous or arrogant manner.
3. *Persecutory Type:* Those with this subtype are convinced that they are the targets of conspiracies, harassment, or persecution by others. They tend to misinterpret neutral actions or remarks as hostile, leaving them feeling constantly threatened.
4. *Jealous Type:* Individuals with this subtype experience delusions related to infidelity or disloyalty within their romantic relationships. They may firmly believe that their partner is unfaithful, even in the absence of any concrete evidence.

5. *Somatic Type:* The primary symptom in this subtype is the unfounded belief in having a severe physical illness or defect despite repeated medical evaluations indicating otherwise. This can lead to frequent doctor visits and unnecessary medical tests.
6. *Mixed Type:* This subtype involves a combination of delusions that don't fit neatly into one specific category. For instance, a person might simultaneously believe they have a unique mission in life and are the victims of a sinister plot.

Other common aspects and symptoms of Delusional Disorder include:

Lack of Insight: People with Delusional Disorder often cannot recognize the irrationality of their beliefs and are resistant to changing them, even when presented with contrary evidence.

Emotional Distress: Delusions can cause significant emotional distress, anxiety, and preoccupation with false beliefs.

Normal Functioning in Other Areas: Despite their delusions, individuals with Delusional Disorder can typically manage their daily responsibilities, such as work, family, and social interactions, except when these tasks directly involve their delusional beliefs.

It's important to understand that the specific content and nature of delusions can vary widely among individuals with Delusional Disorder. Treatment typically involves psychotherapy, particularly cognitive-behavioural therapy (CBT), and, in some cases, medication to alleviate associated symptoms like anxiety or depression. Effective treatment can help individuals improve their quality of life and work with a mental health professional to challenge and modify their delusional beliefs.

Causes of Delusional Disorder

The exact causes of Delusional Disorder are not fully understood, and it is likely that a combination of genetic, biological, psychological, and environmental factors contribute to the development of this condition. Here are some potential factors that may play a role in the onset of Delusional Disorder:

1. *Genetic Factors:* There is evidence to suggest that genetic predisposition may increase the risk of developing Delusional Disorder. Individuals with a family history of psychotic disorders, including schizophrenia and Delusional Disorder, may be more susceptible to developing this condition themselves.
2. *Biological Factors:* Abnormalities in brain structure or function have been implicated in Delusional Disorder. Changes in neurotransmitter systems, such as dopamine and serotonin, have also been associated with psychotic disorders, including Delusional Disorder. These neurotransmitters play a role in regulating mood, perception, and thought processes.
3. *Psychological Factors:* Certain personality traits and coping strategies may make some individuals more vulnerable to Delusional Disorder.

For example, individuals with high levels of suspicion, social isolation, or a tendency to overinterpret events may be more prone to developing delusional beliefs.

4. *Environmental Factors:* Stressful life events or traumatic experiences can sometimes trigger the onset of Delusional Disorder or exacerbate existing symptoms. These events may disrupt an individual's ability to process reality accurately and contribute to the development of delusional beliefs.
5. *Cultural and Societal Influences:* Cultural and societal factors can shape the content and nature of delusions. For example, cultural beliefs or societal norms may influence the themes of delusions in some individuals. Delusions can also be influenced by exposure to certain media or cultural narratives.
6. *Substance Abuse:* The use of substances such as alcohol, drugs, or even prescription medications can sometimes trigger or exacerbate symptoms of Delusional Disorder. Substance-induced delusional disorder may occur during substance intoxication or withdrawal.
7. *Neurological Conditions:* In some cases, Delusional Disorder may be associated with certain neurological conditions or brain injuries. Damage to specific brain regions can lead to alterations in perception and thought processes, potentially contributing to the development of delusions.

It's important to note that while these factors may increase the risk of developing Delusional Disorder, they do not guarantee its occurrence. The precise interplay of these factors can vary from person to person, and the development of Delusional Disorder is a complex and multifaceted process.

Treatments of Delusional Disorder

The treatment of Delusional Disorder typically involves a combination of psychotherapy, medication, and support to help individuals manage their symptoms and improve their quality of life. The specific treatment approach may vary depending on the subtype and severity of the disorder, as well as the individual's unique needs. Here are the primary treatment modalities for Delusional Disorder:

1. *Psychotherapy*
    - *Cognitive-Behavioural Therapy (CBT)*: CBT is often considered the most effective form of psychotherapy for Delusional Disorder. It aims to help individuals identify and challenge irrational beliefs and thought patterns associated with their delusions. Through a collaborative and structured approach, individuals learn to reevaluate their beliefs, develop coping strategies, and reduce distress related to their delusions.
    - *Supportive Psychotherapy*: Supportive therapy focuses on providing emotional support and helping individuals cope with the challenges associated with their delusions. It does not aim to challenge delusional beliefs directly but instead focuses on improving overall well-being and functioning.

- *Family Therapy*: In some cases, family therapy can be beneficial, particularly when family members are involved in the individual's care. Family therapy can help improve communication, understanding, and support within the family unit.

2. *Medication*
   - *Antipsychotic Medications*: Antipsychotic medications are often prescribed to manage the symptoms of Delusional Disorder. These medications can help reduce the intensity of delusions, as well as associated symptoms such as anxiety or agitation. Typical and atypical antipsychotics may be used, depending on the individual's response and side effects.
   - *Antidepressant Medications*: In some cases, antidepressant medications, particularly selective serotonin reuptake inhibitors (SSRIs), may be prescribed to address any co-occurring mood disorders, such as depression or anxiety, that can accompany Delusional Disorder.
   - *Mood Stabilizers*: Mood stabilizers like lithium may be used when there is evidence of mood instability or fluctuations in addition to delusional symptoms.
3. *Hospitalization or Inpatient Care:* In severe cases where individuals are at risk of harming themselves or others due to their delusions or associated behaviours, hospitalization in a psychiatric facility may be necessary. This can provide a safe and controlled environment for stabilization and treatment.
4. *Community Support and Education:* Support groups and educational programmes can help individuals and their families better understand Delusional Disorder, manage the condition, and connect with others facing similar challenges.
5. *Addressing Underlying Factors:* Identifying and addressing any underlying factors contributing to the development or exacerbation of delusions is essential. This may include addressing substance abuse issues, traumatic experiences, or other co-occurring mental health conditions.
6. *Long-term Management:* Delusional Disorder often requires long-term management and support. Regular follow-up appointments with mental health professionals, medication management, and ongoing therapy can help individuals maintain stability and manage their symptoms effectively.

It's important to note that individuals with Delusional Disorder often have limited insight into the irrationality of their beliefs, which can make treatment challenging. Building trust and rapport with a mental health professional and involving family members or a support network can be essential for treatment success. Effective treatment can help individuals with Delusional Disorder reduce the severity of their symptoms, improve their functioning in daily life, and enhance their overall well-being. Early intervention and consistent care are key factors in achieving positive outcomes for individuals with this disorder.

Phobia

A phobia is an intense and irrational fear of a specific object, situation, or activity. People with phobias experience overwhelming anxiety and distress when confronted with the source of their fear, even if the threat is minimal or non-existent. Phobias can significantly disrupt a person's daily life and well-being, leading them to go to great lengths to avoid their triggers. Here are some common types of phobias along with examples:

1. *Specific Phobias*
    - *Arachnophobia*: Fear of spiders. Individuals with arachnophobia may experience extreme anxiety or panic attacks when they see a spider, even if it's harmless.
    - *Acrophobia*: Fear of heights. This phobia can make it challenging for individuals to visit high places like tall buildings or mountains.
2. *Social Phobia (Social Anxiety Disorder)*
    - *Social Phobia*: Also known as social anxiety disorder, it involves an intense fear of social situations, such as public speaking, meeting new people, or attending parties. Individuals with social phobia often fear judgement or humiliation.
3. *Agoraphobia*
    - *Agoraphobia*: This involves a fear of being in situations or places from which escape might be difficult or embarrassing. Common triggers include crowded spaces, public transportation, or open spaces.
4. *Claustrophobia*
    - *Claustrophobia*: Fear of confined spaces. People with claustrophobia may experience panic attacks when inside elevators, small rooms, or tunnels.
5. *Glossophobia*
    - *Glossophobia*: Fear of public speaking. This can hinder one's ability to speak in front of an audience, even in relatively small or informal settings.
6. *Emetophobia*
    - *Emetophobia*: Fear of vomiting. Individuals with emetophobia may go to great lengths to avoid situations or foods they fear could cause them to vomit.
7. *Trypophobia*
    - *Trypophobia*: Fear of clusters of small holes or irregular patterns. Although not officially recognized as a specific phobia in the Diagnostic and Statistical Manual of Mental Disorders (DSM-5), many people report experiencing distress or discomfort when exposed to such images.
8. *Blood-Injection-Injury Phobia*
    - *Blood-Injection-Injury Phobia*: This phobia involves an intense fear of medical procedures involving injections, blood, or injury. Some individuals may faint when confronted with these triggers.

9. *Flying Phobia (Aviophobia)*
    - *Aviophobia*: Fear of flying. It can lead to individuals avoiding air travel, even if it's necessary for work or personal reasons.
10. *Dentophobia*
    - *Dentophobia*: Fear of dentists and dental procedures. This phobia can prevent individuals from seeking necessary dental care, leading to dental health problems.

Phobias can vary in severity, and treatment options include cognitive-behavioural therapy (CBT), exposure therapy, medication, and relaxation techniques. If you or someone you know is struggling with a phobia that is interfering with daily life, it's important to seek help from a mental health professional who can provide guidance and support in managing and overcoming the fear.

Symptoms of Phobia

Phobias are characterized by a set of symptoms, both physical and psychological, that are triggered when an individual encounters the specific object, situation, or activity they fear. These symptoms can vary in intensity but are typically intense and distressing. The most common symptoms of phobias include:

1. *Overwhelming Fear:* A phobia is marked by an intense and irrational fear that is out of proportion to the actual danger posed by the phobic stimulus. This fear can be all-consuming and distressing.
2. *Anxiety:* Individuals with phobias often experience heightened levels of anxiety when confronted with the source of their fear. This can include symptoms such as restlessness, a racing heart, sweating, trembling, and a sense of impending doom.
3. *Panic Attacks:* Phobias can trigger panic attacks, which are sudden and intense episodes of fear or extreme discomfort. Panic attack symptoms may include shortness of breath, chest pain, dizziness, nausea, and a feeling of being detached from reality.
4. *Avoidance Behaviour:* Phobic individuals often go to great lengths to avoid the phobic stimulus. They may rearrange their daily routines, make significant lifestyle changes, or refuse to participate in certain activities to prevent encountering their fear.
5. *Anticipatory Anxiety:* Just the thought of encountering the phobic stimulus can cause anticipatory anxiety in individuals with phobias. This anxiety can start days or even weeks before the feared event or situation.
6. *Physical Symptoms:* Phobias can manifest with various physical symptoms, such as increased heart rate, rapid breathing, sweating, trembling, nausea, and muscle tension.
7. *Difficulty Functioning:* Phobias can interfere with daily life and functioning. For example, someone with a fear of flying may avoid travel, potentially impacting their work or social life. This avoidance can lead to social isolation or significant life disruptions.

8. *Inability to Relax:* Individuals with phobias may find it challenging to relax or calm down, even when they are not directly exposed to the phobic stimulus.
9. *Distorted Thinking:* Phobias can lead to distorted or irrational thinking patterns. For example, someone with a phobia of dogs might believe that every dog is dangerous and will attack them, even if there is no evidence to support this belief.
10. *Depression and Mood Changes:* Over time, the stress and limitations caused by phobias can contribute to the development of depression or other mood disorders.

It's important to note that the severity of phobia symptoms can vary from person to person. While some individuals may experience mild anxiety and avoidance behaviour, others may have more severe symptoms that significantly impact their quality of life. If you or someone you know is experiencing symptoms of a phobia, it is advisable to seek help from a mental health professional who can provide an accurate diagnosis and recommend appropriate treatment options, which often include therapy and, in some cases, medication.

Causes of Phobia

The exact causes of phobias are not fully understood, and they are likely to result from a combination of genetic, environmental, and psychological factors. Here are some potential causes and contributing factors that are associated with the development of phobias:

1. *Genetics:* There is evidence to suggest that a genetic predisposition may play a role in the development of phobias. If someone in your family has a phobia, you may be at a higher risk of developing one as well.
2. *Brain Structure and Function:* Some studies have found differences in the brain structures and functioning of individuals with phobias. These differences may contribute to an increased vulnerability to developing phobias.
3. *Traumatic Experiences:* Traumatic or distressing experiences related to the phobic stimulus can lead to the development of phobias. For example, if someone has a traumatic experience involving a dog (e.g., a dog bite) as a child, they may develop a specific phobia of dogs.
4. *Learned Behaviour:* Phobias can be learned through observational learning or by hearing about or witnessing the fearful reactions of others. For example, if a child observes a family member reacting with extreme fear to spiders, they may develop a fear of spiders themselves.
5. *Negative Conditioning:* A negative or traumatic event associated with a specific object or situation can lead to the development of a phobia. This is known as classical conditioning. For instance, if someone experiences a panic attack in an elevator, they may develop a phobia of elevators.

6. *Cultural and Environmental Factors:* Cultural and societal influences can contribute to the development of phobias. Certain cultures may emphasize specific fears or superstitions that can lead to the development of phobias in susceptible individuals.
7. *Stress and Anxiety:* High levels of stress and anxiety can make individuals more susceptible to the development of phobias. Stress can lower one's tolerance for coping with fear, making them more prone to developing intense and irrational fears.
8. *Personality Factors:* Certain personality traits, such as a tendency toward anxiety or neuroticism, may increase the likelihood of developing phobias.
9. *Parental Modeling:* If parents or caregivers exhibit phobic behaviours or attitudes, children may be more likely to develop similar fears.

It's important to note that not everyone exposed to these factors will develop a phobia, and phobias can vary widely in terms of their specific triggers and severity. Additionally, the development of a phobia may involve a combination of these factors rather than a single cause.

Treatments of Phobia

Phobias are treatable, and there are several effective approaches to help individuals manage and overcome their phobias. The choice of treatment may depend on the specific phobia, its severity, and the individual's preferences. Here are some common treatments for phobias:

1. *Cognitive-Behavioural Therapy (CBT):* CBT is one of the most widely used and effective treatments for phobias. In CBT, individuals work with a therapist to identify and challenge the irrational thoughts and beliefs that underlie their phobia. They learn coping strategies and relaxation techniques to manage anxiety and gradually confront their fears through exposure therapy.
2. *Exposure Therapy:* Exposure therapy is a key component of CBT and is particularly effective for specific phobias. It involves gradually exposing the individual to the phobic stimulus in a controlled and systematic manner. Over time, the exposure helps desensitize the person to the feared object or situation, reducing their anxiety response.
3. *Systematic Desensitization:* This is a type of exposure therapy that involves creating a hierarchy of feared situations or objects and gradually exposing the individual to them in a progressive manner, starting with the least anxiety-provoking situation and moving up to the most anxiety-provoking. Relaxation techniques are often used to manage anxiety during exposure.
4. *Virtual Reality Exposure Therapy:* In some cases, virtual reality technology is used to create a controlled and safe environment for exposure therapy. This can be particularly useful for phobias related to specific situations like flying or driving.

5. *Medication:* Medication may be prescribed in some cases to help manage the symptoms of phobias, particularly when the anxiety is severe or when the phobia is accompanied by other mental health conditions like generalized anxiety disorder or panic disorder. Medications such as selective serotonin reuptake inhibitors (SSRIs) or benzodiazepines may be used, but they are typically not considered first-line treatments and are often used in combination with therapy.
6. *Self-help Strategies:* Individuals with milder phobias may benefit from self-help strategies, such as self-guided exposure exercises, relaxation techniques, and mindfulness practices. Books, online resources, and apps are available to assist individuals in managing their phobias independently.
7. *Group Therapy:* Group therapy sessions can provide a supportive environment for individuals with phobias to share their experiences, learn from others, and practice exposure techniques in a group setting.
8. *Hypnotherapy:* Some individuals find hypnotherapy helpful in addressing phobias. Hypnotherapy aims to help individuals access their subconscious and modify their responses to phobic stimuli.
9. *Biofeedback:* Biofeedback techniques can help individuals learn to control physiological responses to anxiety and stress, such as heart rate and muscle tension. These techniques can be used as part of a comprehensive treatment plan for phobias.
10. *Mindfulness-Based Stress Reduction (MBSR):* MBSR techniques can help individuals develop awareness of their thoughts and emotions and reduce reactivity to anxiety-provoking situations. While not a primary treatment for phobias, mindfulness practices can complement other therapeutic approaches.

It's important to consult with a mental health professional to determine the most appropriate treatment for your specific phobia. Phobias can be highly distressing and can significantly impact an individual's quality of life, so seeking help early can lead to effective management and symptom relief.

Hysteria

"Hysteria" is a term that has been historically used to describe a range of psychological and physical symptoms, often occurring in clusters, and typically affecting women. The concept of hysteria has evolved significantly over time and has been associated with various cultural, medical, and psychological interpretations. Here's an overview of hysteria:

1. *Historical Context:* The term "hysteria" comes from the Greek word 'Hystera,' which means uterus. In ancient Greece, it was believed that hysteria was specific to women and was linked to disturbances or imbalances in the female reproductive system.
2. *Historical Perceptions:* Throughout history, hysteria has been associated with a variety of symptoms, including emotional disturbances, physical

ailments, and neurological symptoms. These symptoms were often misunderstood and attributed to a wandering uterus or other supernatural causes.
3. *Changing Views:* Hysteria was considered a common "diagnosis" for women during the 19th century when it was thought to result from a lack of emotional control or sexual frustration. Treatments included hysterectomies, bed rest, and other ineffective and harmful interventions.
4. *Psychoanalytic Theory:* Sigmund Freud played a significant role in shifting the understanding of hysteria. He proposed that hysteria had its roots in unresolved psychological conflicts and that the symptoms represented a form of unconscious communication. This led to the development of psychoanalysis as a treatment approach.
5. *Modern Understanding:* In contemporary psychiatry and psychology, the term "hysteria" has largely fallen out of use in favour of more specific diagnoses. Many of the symptoms once associated with hysteria are now classified under various psychiatric disorders, such as somatic symptom disorders, conversion disorder, or dissociative disorders.
6. *Conversion Disorder:* Conversion disorder, in particular, is a diagnosis that encompasses symptoms once attributed to hysteria. It involves the presence of physical symptoms, such as paralysis or blindness, that cannot be explained by medical conditions but are believed to have a psychological origin.
7. *Gender Bias:* It's important to note that the historical concept of hysteria had a strong gender bias, as it was primarily associated with women. This bias has been widely criticized, and contemporary approaches to understanding and treating psychosomatic symptoms emphasize a more gender-neutral perspective.

In summary, hysteria is a historical term that has been used to describe a range of psychological and physical symptoms, often affecting women, but it has evolved significantly in terms of its understanding and treatment. Contemporary medicine and psychology now rely on more specific diagnoses and therapeutic approaches to address the underlying psychological factors contributing to such symptoms.

Symptoms of Hysteria

Historically, 'Hysteria' was a term used to describe a wide range of physical and psychological symptoms, often affecting women. However, it's important to note that in modern psychiatry, the concept of hysteria has been largely replaced by more specific diagnoses, such as conversion disorder or somatic symptom disorder. These disorders can manifest with a variety of symptoms that are believed to have a psychological origin. Here are some examples of symptoms that might have been associated with hysteria in the past or that may be present in individuals with conversion disorder or somatic symptom disorder:

1. *Conversion Symptoms*
   - *Motor Symptoms*: These can include paralysis (e.g., inability to move a limb), muscle weakness, tremors, or difficulty coordinating movements.
   - *Sensory Symptoms*: Individuals may experience sensory disturbances such as blindness, deafness, or numbness in various parts of the body.
   - *Seizures*: Some individuals may have episodes that resemble epileptic seizures but lack the characteristic electrical abnormalities seen in epilepsy.
2. *Somatic Symptoms*
   - *Pain*: Individuals with hysteria or related disorders may report chronic or acute pain in various parts of their bodies, often with no clear medical explanation.
   - *Gastrointestinal Distress*: Symptoms such as nausea, vomiting, diarrhea, or abdominal pain may be present without an identifiable physical cause.
   - *Cardiovascular Symptoms*: Rapid heart rate (tachycardia), palpitations, or chest pain might occur.
3. *Sensory and Perceptual Disturbances*
   - *Visual Symptoms*: These can range from blurred vision to tunnel vision or even complete blindness.
   - *Hearing Problems*: Auditory disturbances, including hearing loss or auditory hallucinations, may occur.
   - *Paresthesia*: Abnormal sensations like tingling, pins and needles, or a crawling feeling on the skin can be reported.
4. *Difficulty Swallowing (Dysphagia)*
   - Individuals might experience the sensation of something being stuck in their throat or have difficulty swallowing without any structural or physical cause.
5. *Loss of Consciousness or Dissociation*
   - Some individuals may experience episodes of loss of consciousness or altered states of consciousness, often triggered by stress or emotional distress.
6. *Non-Epileptic Seizures (NES)*
   - These are seizures that resemble epileptic seizures but do not have the characteristic electrical abnormalities seen in epilepsy. They are often associated with psychological factors.
7. *Hallucinations or Delusions*
   - In some cases, individuals may experience hallucinations (perceiving things that are not present) or delusions (false beliefs) that are related to their physical symptoms.

It's important to emphasize that individuals experiencing these symptoms are not consciously 'faking' or 'making up' their conditions. These symptoms are believed to be a way of expressing psychological distress or conflict, often unconsciously. Accurate diagnosis and appropriate treatment typically involve a thorough evaluation by medical professionals to rule out other potential causes and a collaborative approach that may include psychotherapy to address the underlying psychological factors.

Causes of Hysteria

The term 'hysteria' has been largely replaced in modern psychiatry by more specific diagnoses, such as conversion disorder, somatic symptom disorder, or dissociative disorders. These conditions involve the presence of physical symptoms that cannot be explained by a known medical condition and are believed to have psychological origins. While the precise causes of these conditions can be complex and multifaceted, several factors may contribute to the development of symptoms associated with hysteria or its modern equivalents. Here are some potential causes:

1. *Psychological Factors*
   - *Stress and Emotional Distress*: High levels of stress, trauma, or emotional distress can play a significant role in the development of conversion or somatic symptoms. These symptoms may serve as a way for the individual to cope with or express their emotional turmoil.
2. *Underlying Mental Health Conditions*
   - *Anxiety and Depression*: Conditions such as generalized anxiety disorder or major depressive disorder can contribute to the development of physical symptoms. The mind may convert emotional distress into physical complaints.
3. *History of Trauma*
   - *Past Trauma*: Individuals who have experienced physical, emotional, or sexual trauma in their past may be more susceptible to developing somatic or conversion symptoms as a way of dealing with unresolved trauma.
4. *Personality Factors*
   - *High Levels of Anxiety or Neuroticism*: Individuals with certain personality traits, such as high levels of anxiety or neuroticism, may be more prone to developing somatic symptoms when faced with stressors.
5. *Cultural and Social Influences*
   - *Socio-cultural Factors*: Cultural and societal beliefs about illness and health can influence the way symptoms are expressed. Some cultures may have specific idioms of distress that manifest as physical symptoms.
6. *Environmental Stressors*
   - *Life Events*: Significant life events, such as job loss, divorce, or the death of a loved one, can trigger the onset of somatic symptoms.
7. *Unconscious Psychological Conflicts*
   - *Conflict Resolution*: Conversion symptoms may arise as a way for the unconscious mind to resolve internal psychological conflicts that the individual may not be consciously aware of.

8. *Modeling and Suggestion*
    - *Social Learning*: In some cases, individuals may develop conversion symptoms after observing or hearing about similar symptoms in others. Suggestion from family members or healthcare providers can also play a role.
9. *Genetic and Biological Factors*
    - While the primary causative factors are psychological, genetic predisposition or certain neurobiological vulnerabilities may influence an individual's susceptibility to developing conversion or somatic symptoms.

It's important to emphasize that individuals experiencing these symptoms are not consciously fabricating their condition but rather are often unaware of the psychological processes underlying their physical complaints. Diagnosis and treatment typically involve a comprehensive evaluation by healthcare professionals to rule out any underlying medical conditions and the use of psychotherapy to explore and address the psychological factors contributing to the symptoms. A multidisciplinary approach that includes collaboration between mental health professionals and medical specialists is often necessary to provide appropriate care.

Treatments of Hysteria

The treatment of hysteria, or more accurately, conditions like conversion disorder, somatic symptom disorder, or dissociative disorders, has evolved significantly over time as our understanding of these conditions has improved. It's important to note that modern psychiatric and psychological practice focuses on evidence-based treatments aimed at addressing the underlying psychological factors contributing to the symptoms. Here are some common approaches to treating these conditions:

1. *Psychological Therapies*
    - *Psychotherapy*: Psychotherapy, especially cognitive-behavioural therapy (CBT) and psychodynamic therapy, is often the primary treatment for conditions related to hysteria. These therapies help individuals identify and address the psychological conflicts and emotional distress underlying their physical symptoms.
    - *Mindfulness-Based Therapies*: Mindfulness-based approaches, such as Mindfulness-Based Stress Reduction (MBSR) or Dialectical-Behaviour Therapy (DBT), can help individuals become more aware of their emotions, thoughts, and bodily sensations, which can be useful in managing symptoms.
    - *Exposure Therapy*: This approach can be helpful when symptoms are related to anxiety or phobias. It involves gradual exposure to the situations or stimuli that trigger the symptoms, helping individuals learn to manage their reactions.

2. *Medication*
    - *Antidepressants or Anxiolytics*: In some cases, medications such as selective serotonin reuptake inhibitors (SSRIs) or benzodiazepines may be prescribed to manage coexisting anxiety or depression that often accompanies these conditions.
3. *Physical Therapy and Rehabilitation*
    - For individuals with physical symptoms like paralysis or mobility issues, physical therapy and rehabilitation can be beneficial. These therapies help improve physical functioning and may complement psychological treatments.
4. *Education and Psycho-education*
    - Educating the individual about their condition and helping them understand the psychological factors contributing to their symptoms can be an essential part of treatment. This can reduce fear and anxiety about the symptoms and improve cooperation in therapy.
5. *Supportive Care*
    - Providing a supportive and empathetic environment is crucial. This can include involving family members in treatment, addressing any secondary gains (unintended benefits, such as attention or avoidance of responsibilities) that may be reinforcing the symptoms, and offering emotional support.
6. *Hypnosis and Suggestion*
    - In some cases, hypnotherapy or suggestion techniques may be used as adjunctive treatments to help individuals gain insight into their symptoms or alleviate specific symptoms.
7. *Multidisciplinary Approach*
    - Collaboration between mental health professionals (psychiatrists, psychologists, therapists) and medical specialists (neurologists, gastroenterologists, etc.) is often necessary to provide a comprehensive evaluation and ensure that any underlying medical conditions are ruled out.
8. *Long-term Follow-up*
    - These conditions can have a variable course, and long-term follow-up may be necessary to monitor progress, address any relapses, and provide ongoing support.

It's essential to tailor treatment to the individual's specific needs and circumstances, as the factors contributing to these conditions can vary widely. Moreover, building a therapeutic alliance based on trust and understanding is often crucial, as individuals with these conditions may be experiencing significant distress and may be initially resistant to accepting psychological explanations for their symptoms. Patience and a holistic approach to treatment are key in helping individuals manage and overcome conditions related to hysteria.

Neurasthenia

Neurasthenia is a historical term that was once used in the field of psychiatry and psychology to describe a condition characterized by chronic fatigue, mental and physical exhaustion, and a range of other somatic (physical) and psychological symptoms. The term "neurasthenia" literally means "nerve weakness" and reflects the historical belief that this condition was related to a breakdown or depletion of the nervous system's energy reserves. However, it's important to note that neurasthenia is no longer recognized as a valid diagnosis in modern psychiatric practice.

Symptoms of Neurasthenia

Many of the symptoms once associated with neurasthenia are now understood and diagnosed within the framework of various specific mental and physical health conditions. Here are some of the symptoms that were commonly associated with neurasthenia:

1. *Chronic Fatigue*: Neurasthenia was often characterized by persistent and unexplained fatigue. Individuals with neurasthenia typically reported feeling tired or exhausted much of the time, regardless of rest or sleep.
2. *Muscle Weakness*: Weakness or a feeling of physical debilitation was a common symptom. Neurasthenic individuals often felt like they lacked the physical strength to engage in routine activities.
3. *Irritability*: Irritability and mood swings were frequently observed. People with neurasthenia might become easily agitated, frustrated, or irritable, often in response to minor stressors.
4. *Anxiety and Worry*: Excessive worry, anxiety, and nervousness were common features. Neurasthenic individuals could experience a constant state of apprehension and nervous tension.
5. *Headaches*: Chronic headaches, sometimes described as tension headaches, were often reported by those with neurasthenia.
6. *Digestive Problems*: Gastrointestinal symptoms, such as nausea, indigestion, and abdominal discomfort, were associated with neurasthenia.
7. *Sleep Disturbances*: Sleep difficulties, including insomnia or excessive daytime sleepiness, were common complaints among individuals with neurasthenia.
8. *Sensory Sensitivities:* Hypersensitivity to sensory stimuli, such as sensitivity to light, noise, or touch, was sometimes noted.
9. *Difficulty Concentrating*: Neurasthenic individuals often struggled with concentration and focus, which could affect their work or daily activities.
10. *Heart Palpitations*: Some people with neurasthenia reported heart palpitations, which may have been related to their heightened state of anxiety.
11. *Emotional Distress*: Emotional distress, including feelings of despair, hopelessness, or frustration, was often associated with the chronic nature of the condition.

It's important to emphasize that while these symptoms were once attributed to neurasthenia, they are now understood and diagnosed within the context of various specific mental and physical health conditions. For example, chronic fatigue syndrome (CFS), anxiety disorders, mood disorders, somatic symptom disorders, and other medical conditions canbe present with symptoms similar to those once described as neurasthenia. Modern psychiatric and medical practice emphasizes precise diagnosis and evidence-based treatment approaches tailored to the specific condition and needs of the individual.

Causes of Neurasthenia

Neurasthenia was once used to describe a condition characterized by chronic fatigue, mental and physical exhaustion, and a range of other symptoms. It's important to note that neurasthenia is not considered a valid or recognized diagnosis in modern psychiatric practice. Instead, the symptoms once associated with neurasthenia are now understood and diagnosed within the framework of various specific mental and physical health conditions. Nevertheless, during its historical use, several factors were proposed as potential causes or contributors to neurasthenia:

1. *Stress and Overwork*: One of the prevailing theories was that chronic stress, especially related to the demands of modern life, was a significant cause of neurasthenia. It was believed that individuals who were mentally and physically overtaxed by the stresses of daily life were more susceptible to developing this condition.
2. *Sedentary Lifestyle*: A sedentary lifestyle, characterized by minimal physical activity and extended periods of sitting or inactivity, was thought to contribute to neurasthenia. Lack of exercise and outdoor activity was believed to weaken the body and nerves.
3. *Social and Cultural Factors*: Rapid societal changes, urbanization, and the fast-paced nature of modern industrialized societies were thought to play a role in the development of neurasthenia. It was suggested that individuals were not adapted to the demands of the modern world.
4. *Environmental Factors*: Factors such as noise pollution, overcrowding, and environmental toxins were also considered as potential contributors to neurasthenia.
5. *Genetic and Hereditary Factors*: Some proponents of the time believed that there could be a hereditary or genetic component to neurasthenia, making certain individuals more susceptible to its development.
6. *Dietary Habits*: Poor dietary habits, including inadequate nutrition and irregular eating patterns, were considered potential causes of neurasthenia.
7. *Infectious Agents*: At one point, some researchers explored the possibility of infectious agents, such as bacteria or viruses, being linked to neurasthenia. However, this theory did not gain widespread acceptance.

8. *Psychological Factors*: Psychological factors, including personality traits like perfectionism and excessive worrying, were thought to contribute to neurasthenia. Additionally, traumatic life events or emotional stressors were believed to play a role.
9. *Hormonal Factors*: Some physicians suggested that hormonal imbalances could be responsible for the symptoms of neurasthenia, though this theory lacked substantial scientific evidence.

It's important to emphasize that the concept of neurasthenia fell out of favour in modern psychiatry and psychology due to its lack of specificity and empirical basis. Today, the symptoms once associated with neurasthenia are understood within the context of more specific and well-defined mental and physical health conditions, such as anxiety disorders, mood disorders, chronic fatigue syndrome, and somatic symptom disorders. Contemporary healthcare professionals focus on evidence-based approaches to diagnosis and treatment, addressing the unique needs of each individual.

Treatments of Neurasthenia

During its historical use in the late 19th and early 20th centuries, various treatments were employed to address the symptoms associated with neurasthenia. These treatments were often based on the understanding and beliefs of the time, and many of them have been replaced by more evidence-based approaches. Here are some of the treatments that were commonly used for neurasthenia:

1. *Rest Cure*: A popular treatment for neurasthenia was the "rest cure", which involved extended periods of bed rest or seclusion. Patients were often isolated from stressors, given minimal mental stimulation, and encouraged to rest and relax. This approach aimed to replenish the perceived depleted nerve energy.
2. *Hydrotherapy*: Water treatments, such as cold baths, hot baths, and various hydrotherapy techniques, were used as part of neurasthenia treatment. Hydrotherapy was believed to have a calming effect on the nervous system.
3. *Dietary Changes*: Some physicians recommended dietary modifications, including dietary restrictions or changes in nutrition. It was thought that a balanced diet could help restore physical and mental health.
4. *Exercise and Fresh Air*: Gentle exercises and outdoor activities, such as walking or gardening, were often encouraged to promote physical fitness and well-being. Fresh air and exposure to natural surroundings were believed to have a restorative effect.
5. *Massage and Manipulative Therapies*: Massage and other forms of bodywork were used to relieve muscle tension and promote relaxation. Manipulative therapies, such as osteopathy, were also employed to address physical symptoms.

6. *Psychotherapy*: Psychotherapy, in its early and less formalized forms, was sometimes used to address the psychological symptoms of neurasthenia. Talk therapy and supportive counseling were aimed at reducing anxiety and improving mental well-being.
7. *Medications*: Various medications were prescribed, although the understanding of pharmacology and psychopharmacology was limited compared to modern standards. These medications might have included sedatives, tonics, and drugs believed to address specific symptoms.
8. *Electrotherapy*: In some cases, electrotherapy, such as the use of electrical currents, was employed as a treatment for neurasthenia. This approach aimed to stimulate or relax the nervous system.
9. *Psychological Interventions*: Early forms of psychological interventions, such as suggestion and hypnosis, were used to address symptoms like anxiety, sleep disturbances, and concentration difficulties.

It's important to note that many of these historical treatments lacked a solid empirical basis and were based on the limited scientific understanding of the time. As a result, they have been largely replaced by evidence-based treatments for specific mental and physical health conditions. In contemporary mental healthcare, treatments are tailored to the individual's specific diagnosis and needs, and they are informed by rigorous scientific research and clinical trials.

8

Therapies

Psychodrama

Psychodrama therapy is a dynamic and experiential form of psychotherapy that uses action methods, role-playing, and group dynamics to help individuals explore and resolve emotional and psychological issues. Developed by Jacob L. Moreno in the early 20th century, psychodrama therapy is rooted in the belief that individuals can gain insight and healing by reenacting and processing their past experiences and current challenges in a supportive and structured group setting. Below, psychodrama therapy with key points is elaborated:

Theoretical Foundation

- *Role Theory*: Central to psychodrama is the concept of roles. Moreno believed that individuals play various roles in their lives, and conflicts and issues often arise from these roles.
- *Sociometry*: Moreno also developed sociometry, a method for measuring social relationships and interactions. Psychodrama incorporates sociometric exercises to explore group dynamics and interpersonal relationships.

Psychodrama Process

- *Warm-up*: A psychodrama session typically begins with a warm-up phase where participants gather in a circle and share their thoughts, feelings, and concerns. This helps establish trust and build a sense of community within the group.
- *Role-play*: The heart of psychodrama involves role-playing. A participant, referred to as the "protagonist", selects a specific issue or conflict they want to explore. The protagonist then enacts the chosen scenario, with other group members taking on roles of significant people in their life. This role-play is often spontaneous and unscripted.
- *Action and Interaction*: As the role-play unfolds, participants engage in interactions and dialogue, bringing the scenario to life. The therapist, known as the "director", guides the process, helping participants delve deeper into their emotions and experiences.
- *Sharing and Reflection*: After the role-play, there is a sharing and reflection phase. Participants discuss their experiences, emotions, and insights gained during the session. This discussion helps integrate the learning from the role-play into their lives.

Therapeutic Goals

- *Catharsis*: Psychodrama aims to facilitate catharsis, allowing participants to release repressed emotions and tension, which can be therapeutic and lead to emotional healing.
- *Insight and Self-awareness*: Through role-playing and introspection, individuals gain insight into their own behaviours, motivations, and patterns of interaction.
- *Conflict Resolution*: Participants can work through unresolved conflicts and traumas within the controlled setting of psychodrama, leading to resolution and personal growth.
- *Improved Communication*: Psychodrama provides a platform for practising and enhancing interpersonal skills, as participants engage in role-play and communication within the group.

Applications of Psychodrama Therapy

- *Individual Therapy*: Psychodrama can be used in one-on-one therapy sessions to address specific issues and traumas.
- *Group Therapy*: It is often conducted in group settings, allowing participants to learn from each other's experiences and provide support.
- *Addiction Treatment*: Psychodrama is effective in addiction therapy, helping individuals explore the underlying emotional issues driving their addictive behaviours.
- *Trauma Resolution*: Many trauma survivors find psychodrama therapy helpful in processing and healing from traumatic experiences.
- *Personal Growth and Development*: Psychodrama is used for personal development, helping individuals improve their self-esteem, self-awareness, and interpersonal skills.

Ethical Considerations

- Psychodrama therapy should be conducted by trained and certified professionals to ensure the safety and well-being of participants.
- Informed consent is essential, and participants should be fully aware of the nature, purpose, and potential outcomes of the therapy.

Effectiveness

- Numerous studies and anecdotal evidence suggest that psychodrama therapy can be highly effective in addressing a wide range of psychological and emotional issues.
- It offers a unique and experiential approach to therapy that can complement more traditional forms of psychotherapy.

In summary, psychodrama therapy is a dynamic and engaging therapeutic approach that leverages role-play, group dynamics, and action methods to help individuals gain insight, process emotions, and work toward personal growth and healing. It has found applications in various therapeutic settings and can be a powerful tool for individuals seeking to understand and address their psychological and emotional challenges.

Play Therapy

Play therapy is a specialized form of psychotherapy primarily designed for children. It utilizes play as a means for children to express themselves, communicate their feelings, and work through emotional and behavioural issues. Play therapists, often trained mental health professionals, provide a safe and structured environment where children can engage in therapeutic play activities. Here's an elaborate discussion of play therapy with key points:

Theoretical Foundation

- *Psychodynamic Theory*: Play therapy is rooted in psychodynamic principles. It draws from the work of Freud and Erikson, emphasizing the importance of early childhood experiences and unconscious processes in shaping behaviour.
- *Attachment Theory*: Play therapy incorporates attachment theory, recognizing the significance of secure attachments in a child's emotional development.
- *Developmental Psychology*: Play therapy aligns with developmental psychology, tailoring therapeutic techniques to the child's age, cognitive abilities, and emotional development.

Play Therapist's Role

- *Trained Professionals*: Play therapists are mental health professionals who undergo specialized training in play therapy techniques.
- *Observation*: Therapists carefully observe the child's play, paying attention to themes, patterns, and expressions that emerge during the sessions.
- *Non-directive Approach*: Play therapists typically employ a non-directive or child-centered approach. This means that they allow the child to lead the play, intervening minimally to provide support and structure when needed.
- *Creating a Safe Space*: Therapists create a secure and nonjudgmental space where the child feels comfortable expressing themselves.

Types of Play Therapy

- *Child-centered Play Therapy (CCPT)*: In CCPT, children are given the freedom to choose from a variety of toys and materials to express themselves. The therapist's role is to provide a supportive environment.
- *Directive Play Therapy*: In this approach, therapists may introduce specific activities or themes to address particular issues, such as art therapy or sandplay therapy.
- *Filial Play Therapy*: This approach involves training parents or caregivers to become active participants in their child's therapeutic play sessions.

Therapeutic Goals

- *Emotional Expression*: Play therapy allows children to express their emotions, fears, and anxieties in a non-verbal way.
- *Problem Solving*: Through play, children can explore and find solutions to problems or conflicts they may be experiencing.
- *Improved Communication*: It helps children develop better communication skills, both verbally and non-verbally.
- *Emotional Regulation*: Play therapy supports the development of emotional regulation skills, helping children manage their emotions more effectively.
- *Healing from Trauma*: Play therapy can be particularly effective in helping children process and heal from traumatic experiences.

Applicability

- Play therapy is primarily used with children aged 3 to 12, but it can also be adapted for adolescents and adults in certain cases.
- It is utilized in various settings, including schools, clinics, hospitals, and private practices.
- Play therapy is suitable for a wide range of issues, including anxiety, depression, trauma, behavioural problems, and developmental delays.

Ethical Considerations

- Play therapists must maintain a strict code of ethics, ensuring the safety, confidentiality, and well-being of their child clients.
- Informed consent is obtained from parents or legal guardians, and they are often involved in the therapeutic process.

Effectiveness

- Research suggests that play therapy can be highly effective, especially for children who may struggle to express themselves through traditional talk therapy.
- Outcomes may include improved behaviour, better emotional regulation, increased self-esteem, and enhanced social skills.

In conclusion, play therapy is a valuable and specialized form of psychotherapy designed to meet the unique emotional and developmental needs of children. It provides a safe and supportive environment for children to express themselves, work through emotional challenges, and develop essential life skills. Play therapists play a crucial role in helping children build resilience and achieve positive emotional and behavioural outcomes.

Behaviour Modification Therapy

Behaviour Modification Therapy, also known as Behaviour Therapy or Behaviourism, is a therapeutic approach that focuses on changing and improving specific behaviours by using empirically-based techniques and principles of learning and conditioning. It is grounded in the belief that behaviours are learned and can be unlearned or modified through systematic interventions. Behaviour Modification Therapy is often used to address a wide range of psychological and behavioural issues. Here is an elaborate discussion of Behaviour Modification Therapy with key points:

Theoretical Foundation

- *Behaviourism*: Behaviour Modification Therapy is rooted in behaviourist theories, particularly the work of B.F. Skinner and John B. Watson. Behaviourism emphasizes observable behaviours and the idea that behaviour is a product of environmental stimuli and reinforcement.

Core Concepts

- *Operant Conditioning*: Behaviour Modification Therapy utilizes operant conditioning principles, where behaviours are shaped through the consequences they produce. Reinforcement (positive or negative) and punishment are used to strengthen or weaken behaviours.
- *Behaviour Analysis*: Therapists carefully analyze target behaviours, identifying antecedents (triggers) and consequences (reinforcers or punishers) to understand the behavioural function.
- *Functional Assessment*: A functional assessment is conducted to determine why a behaviour occurs. This involves identifying the specific purpose or function of the behaviour in the individual's life.

Therapeutic Techniques

- *Positive Reinforcement*: Desirable behaviours are reinforced with rewards or positive consequences to increase their frequency. This might involve praise, tokens, or other incentives.
- *Negative Reinforcement*: Unwanted behaviours are reduced by removing or avoiding aversive stimuli when the desired behaviour is performed.
- *Extinction*: This technique involves the withholding of reinforcement for a problem behaviour, leading to its eventual reduction or elimination.
- *Punishment:* Punishment is used sparingly and carefully, typically as a last resort, to decrease undesirable behaviours. It involves introducing an aversive consequence when the problem behaviour occurs.
- *Token Economy*: Token systems are often used, especially in educational or institutional settings, where individuals earn tokens for appropriate behaviours that can later be exchanged for rewards.

Therapeutic Goals

- *Behaviour Change*: The primary goal is to modify or replace maladaptive or undesirable behaviours with more adaptive ones.
- *Skill Development*: Behaviour Modification Therapy can teach individuals new skills or coping strategies to address specific issues.

- *Self-management*: Clients are encouraged to learn self-control and self-regulation techniques to maintain desired behaviours independently.
- *Generalization*: Therapists aim to ensure that the learned behaviours are generalized to various settings and contexts.

Applicability

- Behaviour Modification Therapy is used in various settings, including clinical therapy, schools, institutions, and even self-help contexts.
- It is effective in addressing a wide range of behavioural issues, such as phobias, anxiety disorders, substance abuse, attention-deficit/hyperactivity disorder (ADHD), and conduct disorders.

Ethical Considerations

- Therapists using behaviour modification techniques must adhere to ethical guidelines and prioritize the well-being and dignity of their clients.
- Informed consent is obtained from clients, and they are informed about the goals, methods, and potential risks and benefits of the therapy.

Effectiveness

- Behaviour Modification Therapy has a strong empirical basis and is considered highly effective, especially for addressing specific, observable behaviours.
- Its structured and systematic approach makes it suitable for both short-term and long-term therapy.

Limitations

- Behaviour Modification Therapy may not address underlying psychological or emotional issues, as it primarily focuses on observable behaviours.
- The use of punishment can have ethical and unintended side effects, making it necessary to use it with caution.

In summary, Behaviour Modification Therapy is a structured and evidence-based approach that aims to modify behaviours by using principles of learning and conditioning. It is effective for addressing specific behavioural issues and is widely used in various therapeutic and educational settings. However, it is essential for therapists to balance the use of reinforcement and punishment while considering the ethical implications and potential consequences of their interventions.

Cognitive Therapy

Cognitive therapy, also known as cognitive-behavioural therapy (CBT), is a widely practised form of psychotherapy that focuses on identifying and changing negative thought patterns and behaviours that contribute to emotional distress and psychological problems. Developed by Aaron T. Beck in the 1960s, cognitive therapy is based on the premise that our thoughts, beliefs, and perceptions significantly influence our emotions and behaviour. Here is an elaborate discussion of cognitive therapy with key points:

Theoretical Foundation

- *Cognitive Theory*: Cognitive therapy is grounded in cognitive psychology, which suggests that our thoughts, interpretations, and beliefs about events are critical determinants of our emotional reactions and behaviours.
- *Automatic Thoughts*: Beck introduced the concept of automatic thoughts, which are spontaneous and often irrational thoughts that occur in response to situations and trigger emotional responses.

Core Concepts

- *Cognitive Restructuring*: Cognitive therapy aims to identify and challenge irrational or negative thought patterns and replace them with more balanced and rational beliefs.
- *Self-monitoring*: Clients are encouraged to monitor their thoughts and feelings to gain insight into their cognitive patterns and emotional triggers.
- *Behavioural Activation*: Cognitive therapy often includes behavioural components to encourage clients to engage in activities that are consistent with their desired emotions and values.

Therapeutic Techniques

- *Socratic Questioning*: Therapists use open-ended questions to help clients examine and challenge their automatic thoughts and beliefs. This encourages self-reflection and cognitive restructuring.
- *Thought Records*: Clients are asked to keep a record of their automatic thoughts, emotions, and associated behaviours. This tool is used to identify patterns and explore alternative interpretations.
- *Homework Assignments*: Clients often have homework assignments that involve practising new cognitive and behavioural strategies between sessions.

Therapeutic Goals

- *Cognitive Restructuring*: The primary goal is to help clients identify and change irrational and negative thought patterns that contribute to emotional distress.
- *Emotion Regulation*: Cognitive therapy teaches clients how to manage and regulate their emotions more effectively.
- *Behavioural Change*: Clients learn to modify maladaptive behaviours by addressing the thoughts and beliefs that drive them.
- *Skill Development*: Clients acquire coping skills and strategies for managing stress, anxiety, depression, and other emotional challenges.

Applicability

- Cognitive therapy is highly versatile and is used to treat a wide range of psychological disorders, including depression, anxiety disorders, eating disorders, post-traumatic stress disorder (PTSD), and more.
- It is suitable for children, adolescents, and adults and can be delivered in individual or group therapy settings.

Ethical Considerations

- Cognitive therapists adhere to ethical guidelines that prioritize the well-being, autonomy, and confidentiality of clients.
- Informed consent is obtained from clients, outlining the nature and goals of the therapy.

Effectiveness

- Cognitive therapy has a strong empirical basis and is considered one of the most effective forms of psychotherapy for various psychological disorders.
- Research has demonstrated its effectiveness in both the short-term and long-term treatment of a wide range of mental health issues.

Limitations

- Cognitive therapy may not address underlying psychological issues or traumas that contribute to negative thought patterns.
- It may require active participation and effort from clients, which can be challenging for some individuals.

In summary, cognitive therapy is a goal-oriented and evidence-based approach that targets the interplay between thoughts, emotions, and behaviours. It is effective in helping individuals identify and change irrational thought patterns, improve emotional regulation, and develop coping skills. Cognitive therapy has a broad range of applications and is widely used in clinical psychology to treat various mental health conditions.

Humanistic Therapy

Humanistic therapy, also known as humanistic-existential therapy, is a psychological approach to therapy that emphasizes the individual's capacity for self-awareness, personal growth, and self-actualization. This therapeutic approach emerged as a reaction to the limitations of behaviourism and psychoanalysis. Humanistic therapy focuses on the holistic well-being of individuals and encourages them to explore their feelings, thoughts, and behaviours in a nonjudgmental and empathetic environment. Here is an elaborate discussion of humanistic therapy with key points:

Theoretical Foundation

- *Humanistic Psychology*: Humanistic therapy is rooted in humanistic psychology, which emerged in the mid-20th century as a response to Behaviourism and psychoanalysis. Prominent humanistic psychologists include Abraham Maslow and Carl Rogers.
- *Self-actualization*: Central to humanistic therapy is the concept of self-actualization, which refers to the innate drive within individuals to fulfill their potential and become the best version of themselves.

Core Concepts

- *Client-centered Therapy*: Humanistic therapy is often associated with client-centered therapy, developed by Carl Rogers. This approach places the client at the center of the therapeutic process, emphasizing the importance of empathy, unconditional positive regard, and genuineness from the therapist.
- *Holistic Perspective*: Humanistic therapy considers the whole person, taking into account their emotions, thoughts, behaviours, and experiences within their social and cultural context.
- *Existential Perspective*: Existential themes, such as freedom, choice, responsibility, and the search for meaning, are often explored in humanistic therapy.

Therapeutic Techniques

- *Empathetic Listening*: Therapists in humanistic therapy provide active and empathetic listening, creating a safe and nonjudgemental space for clients to express themselves.
- *Reflection and Clarification*: Therapists use reflective techniques to help clients gain insight into their thoughts and feelings. This may involve restating or summarizing what the client has said to encourage self-exploration.
- *Unconditional Positive Regard*: Therapists offer genuine acceptance and unconditional positive regard for clients, fostering a sense of worth and self-acceptance.
- *Gestalt Techniques*: Some humanistic therapists incorporate gestalt techniques that focus on increasing self-awareness by exploring and experiencing the present moment.

Therapeutic Goals

- *Self-actualization*: The primary goal is to facilitate self-actualization, helping clients become more authentic and in touch with their true selves.
- *Enhanced Self-esteem*: Humanistic therapy aims to boost self-esteem and self-worth by helping clients recognize and embrace their strengths and weaknesses.
- *Improved Self-concept*: Clients work on developing a more accurate and positive self-concept by shedding negative self-judgments and unrealistic expectations.
- *Increased Personal Growth*: Humanistic therapy encourages personal growth and a greater sense of purpose and meaning in life.

Applicability

- Humanistic therapy is applicable to a wide range of issues, including anxiety, depression, low self-esteem, relationship problems, and personal development.
- It can be used with individuals, couples, families, and groups, making it versatile in various therapeutic contexts.

Ethical Considerations

- Ethical guidelines in humanistic therapy emphasize the importance of client autonomy, confidentiality, informed consent, and the therapist's commitment to nonjudgmental acceptance.

Effectiveness

- While humanistic therapy lacks the extensive empirical research base of some other therapeutic approaches, many clients report positive outcomes in terms of increased self-awareness, self-acceptance, and personal growth.
- Effectiveness may vary depending on the client's needs, the therapist's skills, and the specific therapeutic techniques used.

Limitations

- Critics argue that humanistic therapy can lack structure, which may be challenging for clients who prefer more directive approaches.
- It may not be suitable for clients with severe mental health issues or those who require more structured and symptom-focused interventions.

In conclusion, humanistic therapy is a client-centered and empathetic approach that prioritizes the individual's capacity for self-actualization, personal growth, and self-discovery. By providing a safe and accepting therapeutic environment, humanistic therapy aims to help clients explore their thoughts, emotions, and behaviours, ultimately fostering a greater sense of self-acceptance and personal fulfillment.

Psychoanalytic Method

Free Association, Transference and Dream Analysis

The psychoanalytic method encompasses several key techniques and concepts, including free association, transference, and dream analysis. Developed by Sigmund Freud, these methods are fundamental to the practice of psychoanalysis and aim to explore the unconscious mind, uncover unresolved conflicts, and gain insight into a person's thoughts, emotions, and behaviours. Here's an elaborate discussion of each of these components with key points:

1. Free Association

Definition

Free association is a psychoanalytic technique in which the patient is encouraged to express thoughts, feelings, and memories as they come to mind, without censorship or judgement. The therapist observes and analyzes the patient's associations for patterns and hidden meanings.

Purposes

- *To access the unconscious*: By allowing the patient to speak freely, psychoanalysts believe that repressed or unconscious thoughts and emotions can surface.

- *To identify resistance*: The therapist pays attention to moments when the patient hesitates or avoids discussing specific topics, which may indicate areas of resistance and potential unconscious material.

Process
- The patient lies on a couch or sits comfortably in a relaxed position.
- The therapist provides minimal guidance, encouraging the patient to "say whatever comes to mind".
- The therapist listens attentively and notes any recurring themes, emotions, or significant words or images.

Analysis
- The therapist analyzes the patient's associations to identify unconscious conflicts, hidden desires, and unresolved issues.
- Patterns in the patient's associations are explored, and connections between past experiences and current symptoms are examined.

2. Transference

Definition
Transference is a psychoanalytic concept that refers to the patient's unconscious transfer of feelings, attitudes, and reactions from significant figures in their past (e.g., parents) onto the therapist. These feelings can be positive, negative, or ambivalent.

Purposes
- *To gain insight*: Transference provides a window into the patient's internal world, revealing unresolved emotional conflicts and past relationship dynamics.
- *To work through past issues*: By experiencing and discussing transference reactions with the therapist, patients have the opportunity to work through and resolve unresolved feelings and conflicts.

Examples
- *Positive transference*: The patient may see the therapist as a nurturing or supportive figure, similar to a parent.
- *Negative transference*: The patient may become angry, critical, or resentful toward the therapist, reflecting unresolved conflicts with authority figures.

Analysis
- The therapist observes and interprets transference reactions, helping the patient understand their emotional responses within the therapeutic relationship.
- Transference is a central focus of psychoanalytic therapy, as it provides valuable insights into the patient's inner world and the dynamics of their relationships.

3. Dream Analysis

Definition

Dream analysis is a psychoanalytic technique that involves exploring the content and symbolism of a patient's dreams. Freud believed that dreams are a pathway to the unconscious mind and can reveal repressed thoughts and desires.

Purposes

- To access unconscious material: Dreams often contain symbolic representations of unconscious conflicts and desires that may be difficult to access during waking life.
- To gain insight: Analyzing dreams can help patients and therapists uncover hidden meanings, unresolved issues, and emotional conflicts.

Process

- The patient is asked to recall and describe their dreams during therapy sessions.
- The therapist and patient work together to analyze the dream's symbols, themes, and emotions.
- The therapist assists the patient in making connections between dream content and their waking life experiences.

Analysis

- Symbols in dreams are interpreted in the context of the patient's personal experiences and emotions.
- Dream analysis can lead to important insights into the patient's unconscious conflicts, desires, and fears.

In summary, the psychoanalytic method involves several key components, including free association, transference, and dream analysis, all of which aim to explore the unconscious mind and gain insight into the patient's psychological dynamics. These techniques play a central role in psychoanalysis and provide a framework for understanding and resolving unconscious conflicts and emotional issues.

9

Coping Strategies for Stressful Situation

Stress and Stressors

Stress and stressors are concepts that play a significant role in psychology and have a profound impact on an individual's physical and mental well-being. Stress refers to the body's response to challenging or threatening situations, while stressors are the specific events or factors that trigger this response.

Stress

Stress is a physiological and psychological response to perceived or real threats, challenges, or demands, often referred to as stressors.

Biological Basis

Stress triggers the body's "fight or flight" response, involving the release of stress hormones like cortisol and adrenaline. These hormones prepare the body to react quickly in a potentially dangerous situation.

Types of Stress

- *Acute Stress*: Short-term stress response to immediate challenges.
- *Chronic Stress*: Ongoing stress due to long-term problems or situations.
- *Eustress*: Positive stress, such as excitement or motivation that can enhance performance.
- *Distress*: Negative stress, which can lead to physical and psychological health issues.

Effects of Stress

- *Physical Effects*: Stress can lead to physical symptoms like headaches, muscle tension, increased heart rate, and gastrointestinal problems.
- *Emotional Effects*: It can cause anxiety, depression, irritability, and mood swings.

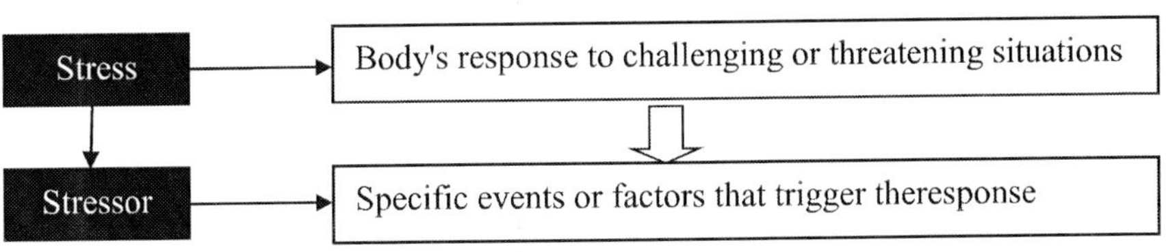

Figure 9.1: *Stress and Stressors*

- *Cognitive Effects:* Stress can impair memory, concentration, and decision-making abilities.
- *Behavioural Effects*: People may resort to unhealthy coping mechanisms like overeating, substance abuse, or withdrawal from social activities.

Coping Strategies

Individuals use various coping mechanisms to manage stress, such as relaxation techniques, exercise, social support, and seeking professional help.

Stressors

Stressors are the specific events, situations, or factors that trigger the stress response in an individual.

Types of Stressors

- *Environmental Stressors*: These include natural disasters, pollution, noise, and traffic.
- *Life Events*: Major life changes like marriage, divorce, job loss, or the death of a loved one can be significant stressors.
- *Daily Hassles*: Everyday irritations like traffic jams, work deadlines, or financial worries can accumulate and cause stress.
- *Workplace Stressors*: Factors such as job demands, long working hours, conflicts with colleagues, and job insecurity can lead to workplace stress.
- *Psychological Stressors*: These are related to thoughts and perceptions, like unrealistic expectations, negative self-talk, or chronic worry.

Perception of Stressors

Not everyone reacts to the same stressor in the same way. An individual's perception and interpretation of a stressor play a crucial role in determining its impact.

Cumulative Stress

Stressors can accumulate over time, with one stressor adding to the burden of existing stressors. This cumulative stress can have more severe effects on health and well-being.

Resilience

Some individuals are more resilient and better able to cope with stressors due to factors like a strong support system, effective coping strategies, and a positive mindset.

Managing Stressors

Strategies for managing stressors include problem-solving, time management, setting realistic goals, and seeking social support.

In conclusion, stress and stressors are integral aspects of human life. While stress is a natural response to challenges, excessive or chronic stress can have detrimental effects on physical and mental health. Understanding stressors and learning effective coping strategies are essential for maintaining well-being in an increasingly stressful world.

Personal and Environmental Stresses

Personal and environmental stresses are two broad categories of stressors that individuals encounter in their lives. These stressors can have significant effects on an individual's physical and mental well-being.

Personal Stress

Personal stressors are stress-inducing factors that arise from within an individual's own life circumstances, choices, and experiences. These stressors are often closely tied to an individual's thoughts, emotions, and actions. Here are some key points to consider:

1. *Life Events*: Personal stressors can arise from major life events such as marriage, divorce, childbirth, the death of a loved one, or significant career changes. These events can bring about both positive and negative stress.
2. *Daily Hassles*: Everyday irritations, frustrations, and inconveniences, such as traffic jams, financial worries, household chores, or work-related stressors, can accumulate and contribute to personal stress.
3. *Psychological Factors*: Internal stressors include negative thought patterns, perfectionism, unrealistic expectations, and excessive worrying. These cognitive factors can significantly impact an individual's stress levels.
4. *Emotional Factors*: Personal stress can result from intense emotions like anger, fear, sadness, or anxiety. Emotional reactions to various life situations can amplify stress.
5. *Behavioural Factors*: Unhealthy coping mechanisms such as overeating, smoking, alcohol or drug abuse, or social withdrawal can be personal stressors in themselves and can exacerbate other stressors.
6. *Resilience and Coping*: Personal stressors are not universally distressing. One's ability to cope with these stressors depends on their resilience, social support network, and the strategies they employ to manage stress.
7. *Long-term Impact*: Prolonged exposure to personal stressors without effective coping strategies can lead to chronic stress, which may contribute to physical health issues like cardiovascular disease, as well as mental health problems like depression and anxiety.

Environmental Stress

Environmental stressors, on the other hand, are external factors or conditions in an individual's surroundings that contribute to stress. These stressors often exist independently of an individual's choices or actions and can be more difficult to control. Here are some key points:

1. *Natural Disasters*: Environmental stressors can include natural events like earthquakes, hurricanes, floods, wildfires, and extreme weather conditions. These events can cause physical danger, property damage, and emotional trauma.
2. *Pollution and Toxins*: Environmental stressors also encompass exposure to environmental pollutants, chemicals, and toxins, whether in the air, water, or food supply. These exposures can lead to health concerns and stress.
3. *Noise and Crowding*: Urban living and crowded environments can be environmental stressors due to noise pollution, congestion, and a lack of personal space. These factors can contribute to feelings of overwhelm and irritation.
4. *Workplace Environment*: Factors within the workplace, such as demanding job roles, long working hours, conflict with colleagues, and job insecurity, are environmental stressors that can affect an individual's well-being.
5. *Socio-economic Conditions*: Poverty, economic instability, discrimination, and inequality are environmental stressors that can have long-lasting effects on mental and physical health.
6. *Access to Resources*: The availability of resources like healthcare, education, and social support can vary by location and impact an individual's ability to cope with environmental stressors.
7. *Adaptation and Mitigation*: In some cases, individuals and communities can adapt to or mitigate environmental stressors through disaster preparedness, environmental conservation efforts, and policy changes.

In summary, personal and environmental stressors both contribute to the overall stress experienced by individuals. While personal stressors are often connected to an individual's mindset, emotions, and behaviours, environmental stressors are external factors in the surrounding world. Both types of stressors can have a profound impact on an individual's physical and mental health, highlighting the importance of effective coping strategies and support systems to manage and reduce stress.

Coping Strategies for Stress

Coping strategies for stress are techniques and behaviours that individuals use to manage and mitigate the impact of stressors on their physical and mental well-being. Developing effective coping strategies is essential for reducing stress and maintaining a healthy lifestyle. Here are several coping strategies, elaborated with key points:

1. *Identifying Stressors*: Recognize and understand the specific stressors in your life. Identifying the sources of stress is the first step in effectively addressing them.

2. *Mindfulness and Relaxation Techniques*: Practise mindfulness meditation, deep breathing exercises, progressive muscle relaxation, or yoga to calm the mind and reduce physiological stress responses.
3. *Time Management*: Prioritize tasks and set realistic goals to avoid feeling overwhelmed. Create a daily or weekly schedule to allocate time for work, leisure, and self-care.
4. *Healthy Lifestyle Choices*: Maintain a balanced diet, exercise regularly, and get enough sleep. Physical health and fitness can significantly impact your ability to cope with stress.
5. *Social Support*: Seek support from friends, family, or support groups. Talking to someone you trust can provide emotional relief and different perspectives on your stressors.
6. *Problem-solving Skills*: Develop problem-solving techniques to address the root causes of stress. Analyze issues, brainstorm solutions, and implement action plans.
7. *Cognitive Restructuring*: Challenge and reframe negative thought patterns and irrational beliefs that contribute to stress. Replace them with more rational and positive thinking.
8. *Seeking Professional Help*: Consult with a mental health professional or counselor when stress becomes overwhelming or persistent. Therapy can provide valuable tools and insights.
9. *Set Realistic Expectations*: Avoid setting overly high or unattainable goals for yourself. Realistic expectations can reduce perfectionism and performance-related stress.
10. *Engage in Hobbies and Leisure Activities*: Make time for activities you enjoy, as they can provide a sense of accomplishment, relaxation, and a break from stressors.
11. *Limit Technology and Screen Time*: Reduce exposure to stress-inducing news or social media, especially before bedtime, to improve sleep quality and reduce anxiety.
12. *Positive Social Interactions*: Surround yourself with positive and supportive individuals. Engaging in social activities can boost mood and reduce feelings of isolation.
13. *Progressive Muscle Relaxation*: Practise techniques like tensing and relaxing muscle groups to release physical tension and promote relaxation.
14. *Humour and Laughter*: Find humour in everyday situations, watch a comedy, or spend time with people who make you laugh. Laughter can be a powerful stress reliever.
15. *Self-compassion*: Be kind and understanding to yourself. Avoid self-criticism and negative self-talk, which can exacerbate stress.
16. *Express Emotions*: Share your feelings through creative outlets like art, writing, or music. Expressing emotions can provide relief and a sense of catharsis.

17. *Set Boundaries*: Learn to say "no" when necessary. Setting healthy boundaries can prevent over-commitment and reduce stress from excessive obligations.
18. *Plan for the Future*: Create a vision for the future and set long-term goals. Having a sense of purpose can help you navigate and endure stressful times.
19. *Mindful Consumption*: Be mindful of what you consume, not only in terms of food but also regarding information, media, and substances like alcohol or caffeine.
20. *Gratitude Practice*: Regularly reflect on the things you are grateful for. Focusing on positive aspects of your life can counterbalance stress.

Remember that coping strategies may vary from person to person, and it's essential to experiment with different techniques to determine which ones work best for you. Additionally, seeking professional guidance when needed is a crucial part of effective stress management. Building a repertoire of coping strategies can help you navigate life's challenges and maintain overall well-being.

10

Application of Psychological Tool

Palsane and Sharma's Study Habits Inventory Scale — Tool's Name

Introduction

The process of acquiring knowledge and skills within the context of formal education is fundamentally complex and characterized by multiple interconnected aspects. Numerous psychologists have made efforts to clarify this phenomenon by employing their unique viewpoints. The definition of 'Learning' as provided by the Oxford Dictionary andThesaurus (2007) refers to the act of acquiring knowledge through the process of study. Academic pursuit pertains to the process of acquiring knowledge through diligent and focused study endeavours. The term 'Learning' as defined by the Longman Dictionary of Contemporary English (2004) pertains to '*The acquisition of knowledge through the activities of reading and studying*'. On the other side "*Habit is defined as something that you do regularly or usually, often without thinking about it because you have done it so many times before*". The definitions described above propose that the attainment of knowledge and skills is the primary goal of the educational process. Essentially, one might argue that learning involves the development and improvement of efficient study habits and skills. It is crucial to acknowledge that habits are not innate abilities comparable to intelligence; rather, they are generally cultivated, learned, nourished, and consolidated by consistent efforts.

"*Poor habits of study not only retard school progress but develop frustration, destroy initiative and confidence and make prominent the feeling of worthlessness towards himself and the subject of study whereas effective methods ensure success, happiness and sense of accomplishment*" — Smith, Sammuel and Field (1948).

Study habits encompass the systematic and consistent approaches utilized to enhance and refine one's cognitive skills through frequent exercise and practise. Students employ these strategies to systematically approach their academic endeavours, and these methods have become conventional as a result of their widespread implementation and repetition. The aforementioned factor is widely recognized as a crucial element that has a profound impact on pupils' academic success. Psychologists and educators argue that the development of efficient study habits plays a crucial role in facilitating the acquisition of knowledge and wisdom. The methodical cultivation of information, language competence, and personal growth of an individual is widely regarded as a highly effective strategy. The cultivation of effective study habits is contingent upon a multitude of aspects, including but not limited to focus, motivation, astute observation, adaptation to the academic environment, and the establishment of social connections.

According to Husen and others in the International Encyclopedia of Education (1994) defines the term study habit as *'Study habitats and strategies refer to activities carried out by a learner during the learning process for the purpose of improving learning.*'Rao (1965) posited that the development of proficient study habits may engender intrinsic motivation. Undoubtedly, the development of efficient study practices provides learners with the chance to partake in extended study sessions. Research has shown that an extended duration of study has a beneficial effect on academic achievement within educational environments, consequently promoting a heightened inclination to participate in additional learning activities. As a result, the iterative process of heightened academic engagement and subsequent progress serves to bolster the learner's overall scholastic attainment. Hence, the development of efficient study practices not only enhances academic achievement but also exerts a substantial influence on students' motivation and overall satisfaction.

Hence, it can be deduced that the acquisition of particular mechanical processes and skills is of utmost importance in achieving success throughout all disciplines and facets of schooling. The study habits exhibited by students play a crucial role and possess the capacity to exert a substantial impact on attaining elevated levels of academic success. The cultivation of effective study habits and skills is crucial for achieving efficient learning outcomes (Jamuar, 1961). Tuli (1981) and Kaur andLekhi (1995) argue that the cultivation of effective study habits is crucial for academic success. One of the primary factors that play a crucial role in academic underachievement is the presence of inadequate study habits (Panchalingappa, 1995; Dhaliwal, 1971; Jain, 1967; Jha, 1970; Vanarase, 1970; Kapoor, 1987 and Singh, 1984).

The acquisition of knowledge is not exclusively contingent upon the instructor, but rather necessitates the involvement of multiple elements on the part of the learners. These aspects encompass their ability to successfully manage their time, establish a study plan, sustain concentration, practise note-taking, engage in mental revision, and utilize both comprehensive and segmented learning strategies. Therefore, one could propose that the act of studying constitutes a manifestation of self-directed learning. Nevertheless, it is crucial to acknowledge that this does not suggest that students ought to be completely autonomous in their quest for knowledge.

According to Secondary Education Commission (1952-53) *'The underachievers need some form of special help or remedial education and guidance to overcome their difficulties and achieve up to the maximum of their potential. To plan remedial education and guidance programme for underachievers we need to know about the factors related to and their possible contribution towards underachievement.'*

Therefore, the process of engaging in academic learning is a complex undertaking, prompting educators to see study habits and attitudes as influential elements in shaping an individual's academic successes or challenges. This perspective is grounded in the acknowledgment that the acquisition of knowledge is facilitated by the process of studying. The development of study habits can be shaped by a multitude of circumstances that exert an influence on the individual. The existence of common elements can influence the formation of both efficacious and inefficacious study practices.

Objectives

1. To find out the participants' study habits in various areas.
2. To find out the study the type of habits the participants have.
3. To understand the participants' attention and help them accordingly to the problems they are facing.
4. Teachers get the information easily through this.
5. Through this inventory we get the opportunity to understand participants' study habit level.

Methodology

(i) Sample and Sampling

The present study was conducted among 50 undergraduate students who were studying 4th Semester in 'Education Honours Course' in the session 2021-22 at Dukhulal Nibaran Chandra College, Aurangabad, Murshidabad, affiliated to University of Kalyani, Nadia, West Bengal.

The researcher utilized the 'Convenience Sampling Method' to pick the participants for the study. Convenience sampling is a non-probability sampling method in which the researcher chooses participants based on their convenience and ease of access. In this case, the researcher had selected undergraduate students who were readily available and accessible at the mentioned college. The sampling procedure entailed the researcher's selection of participants based on their accessibility and closeness to the investigator. The researcher had approached students who were studying in the 'Education Honours Course' at DukhulalNibaran Chandra College and conveniently available at the college campus. The participants were selected based on their willingness to participate and their convenience.

(ii) Description of Tool

Name of Inventor: This study habit inventory manual was first developed by M.N. Palsane of Pune University in 1977 and later the one that has been used for study inventory was developed by Sadhna Sharma of Agra and Palsane in 1989.

Dimensions

The assessment of students' study habits should encompass the subsequent domains:

(i) Budgeting Time

The strategic allocation of study time is of utmost significance. The implementation of a time plan facilitates the allocation of study periods and other activities in accordance with the specific requirements of the individual. One effective approach to time management is to maintain a comprehensive log of daily activities over the course of one week in a journal. By effectively managing their time, students can enhance their academic performance and engage in extracurricular activities more efficiently.

(ii) Physical Conditions for Study

The influence of physical factors on study habits is significant. An ideal environment for studying should possess qualities of tranquility and little noise. The cleanliness of the area should be ensured, along with the provision of enough illumination and ventilation. It is imperative that furniture possesses a high level of comfort. It is imperative to ensure the presence of adequate illumination. The study table should be maintained in a clean and organized manner, with just essential items such as papers, pens, pencils, and books present.

(iii) Reading Ability

The ability to read is a fundamental talent in all areas of academic inquiry. The components encompassed under this domain encompass a range of criteria, such as a robust lexicon, rapid reading pace, adept comprehension skills, autonomous selection of suitable reading materials, and proficient information retrieval abilities. It is vital for individuals to endeavour to cultivate a strong memory by retaining the exact significance of words. The velocity at which one reads is moreover a significant determinant. The act of reading silently consistently yields a higher reading speed compared to reading aloud. It is imperative to modulate the pace of reading in accordance with the significance of the subject matter. Technical stuff typically demands a greater amount of time compared to non-technical content. It is imperative for an individual to endeavour to comprehend the content he is perusing. The individual should endeavour to retain the concepts assimilated during the act of reading and possess the ability to succinctly encapsulate the primary notions.

(iv) Taking Notes

The act of note-taking in an educational setting is a significant cognitive process that contributes to the acquisition and retention of knowledge. The act of taking notes from a book can significantly enhance one's learning efforts. There exist various methods for recording information. It is possible for individuals to replicate the entirety of a book. One may choose to choose transcribe significant paragraphs or alternatively, opt to transcribe the headings, sub-headings, and essential paragraphs of importance in order to create an outline. Paraphrasing in one's own words and summarizing is regarded to be the greatest manner of making one's notes. The consolidation of class notes and textbook materials is a commendable approach to creating a comprehensive set of notes. The establishment of a habitual practise of note-taking can be facilitated through regular engagement.

(v) Factors in Learning Motivation

In addition to cognitive aptitude, the inclination to acquire knowledge is a significant factor to be taken into account. Individuals who possess a genuine desire in acquiring knowledge have the potential to acquire new information rapidly and maintain it over an extended period. There exist variations among individuals in their aptitude for acquiring knowledge. It is widely acknowledged that individuals have the capacity to enhance their performance through additional exertion. The integration of both competitive and cooperative elements fosters a conducive environment for effective learning. Learning is enhanced when individuals engage in group settings.

(vi) Memory

Enhancing memory entails the acquisition of improved learning abilities. The distribution of learning periods is deemed more favourable compared to continuous or massed learning. The more effectively we acquire knowledge, the greater our capacity for long-term retention. The process of over-learning has been found to enhance long-term retention of information.

(vii) Taking Examinations

The majority of our assessments consist of essay-style examinations, wherein students are presented with a limited number of questions and are expected to provide comprehensive written responses. It is advisable to construct a comprehensive outline and systematically organize the concepts, adhering to a coherent structure of exposition. It is recommended to utilize straightforward wording. The discussion of separate themes should be organized into distinct paragraphs. The appropriate placement of headings and sub-headings is crucial. Significant words and phrases may be emphasized.

a) Preparation for Examination

It is advisable to allocate additional time and focus towards addressing one's areas of weakness. It is advisable to have a structured timetable for academic studies. Individuals that adhere to consistent study habits are already adequately prepared for the examination. Maintaining a composed, collected, and relaxed demeanor towards the examination is crucial and can only be attained via thorough preparation.

b) Use of Examination Results

Through the analysis of the outcomes, individuals are able to identify their areas of strength and weakness. The provision of feedback regarding outcomes can serve as a source of motivation and guidance for an individual, influencing their level of effort and focus.

(viii) Health

Establishing and adhering to consistent and healthful patterns of eating, engaging in physical activity, pursuing recreational activities, and obtaining sufficient sleep are integral to preserving optimal physical well-being and promoting a stable mental state, both of which are crucial for attaining success in academic examinations.

Number of Test Items: This inventory contains 45 items.

Reliability

The determination of inventory reliability is accomplished through the utilization of two distinct methodologies.

(i) The test-retest method was employed to determine the reliability coefficient, which yielded a value of 0.88. This assessment was conducted on a sample of 200 male college students, with a time interval of fourweeks between the two administrations of the test. The study determined that the dependability coefficient for a sample of 60 females studying in intermediate classes, measured over a period of threemonths, was 0.67.
(ii) The split-half technique was employed on a sample of 150 male students from intermediate and undergraduate classes. The resulting coefficient of correlation between odd and even items was determined to be 0.56.

Validity

In addition to possessing strong face validity, the inventory also exhibits other validity coefficients, as outlined below:

Validity Coefficients of Study Habits Inventory

(a) Table 1: *With External Criterion (Similar type of Study Habit Inventories)*

Sl. No.	*Name of Other Tests*	*N*	*Validity Coefficient*
1.	Study Habit Inventory—Mukhopadhyaya and Sansanwal	80	0.69
2.	Test of Study Habits and Attitudes—C.P. Mathur	80	0.67
3.	Study Habit Inventory—B. V. Patel	80	0.74
4.	Study Involvement Inventory—Asha Bhatnagar	80	0.83

(b) Table *2: With other Variable Measures*

Sl. No.	*Name of Other Tests*	*N*	*Validity Coefficient*
1.	Verbal Achievement Motivation Test—V. P. Bhargava	50	0.46
2.	Scholastic Achievement (Total Marks in Annual Examination)	50	0.42
3.	Level of Aspiration—Shah and Bhargava	50	0.58
4.	Reading Comprehension Test—Ahuja and Ahuja	50	0.76

The validity coefficients presented above demonstrate that the inventory exhibits a satisfactory level of validity when compared to other inventories of a similar nature and related measures developed by other authors. Furthermore, the inventory has a substantial association with other variables that impact study habits and academic achievement.

Scoring Procedure

The scoring technique is rather straightforward. A score of 2 is assigned for responses indicating 'Always' or 'Mostly', while scores of 1 and 0 are allocated for responses indicating 'Sometimes' and 'Never', respectively.

Table 3: *Scoring Pattern of Study Habits Inventory*

Sl. No.	*Response*	*Score*
1.	Always or Mostly	2
2.	Sometimes	1
3.	Never	0

The scoring weightage for statement numbers 6, 9, 13, 15, 24, 26, 34, 36, 37, 41, and 42 is reversed, with a weightage of 0, 1, and 2 assigned to the responses 'always', 'sometimes', and 'never', respectively. The highest achievable score is 90 for each individual. A higher score is indicative of exemplary study habits.

Norms

The subsequent data represents the established standards observed among students of both male and female genders enrolled in educational programmes ranging from intermediate to postgraduate levels.

Table 4: *Norms to Interpret Study Habits on the basis of Scores Obtained by Participants*

Percentile Level	*Boys (Scores)*	*Girls (Scores)*	*Category*	*Interpretation*
100	75	78	A	Excellent Study Habits
90	74	73		
80	64	68		
75	62	67	B	Good Study Habits
70	61	65		
60	60	64	C	Average Study Habits
50	59	63		
40	57	60		
30	55	58	D	Unsatisfactory Study Habits
25	54	57		
20	53	56	E	Very Unsatisfactory Study Habits
10	50	53		

Data Analysis

Table 5: *Scores Obtained by Participants in Different Areas of Study Habits*

Sl. No.	*Areas*	*Number of items*	*Maximum Scores for Total Participants*	*Total Marks Obtained*
1.	Budgeting time	1, 2, 3, 4, 32	10×50=500	318
2.	Physical conditions for study	5, 6, 7, 8, 9, 43	12×50=600	408
3.	Reading ability	10, 13, 14, 15, 16, 17, 22, 28	16×50=800	621
4.	Taking notes	11, 18, 19	06×50=300	174
5.	Factors in learning motivation	20, 21, 23, 24, 25, 40	12×50=600	371
6.	Memory	12, 26, 27, 37	08×50=400	266
7.	Taking examinations	29, 30, 31, 33, 34, 35, 36, 38, 39, 42	20×50=1000	704
8.	Health	41, 44, 45	06×50=300	206

Table 6: *Participants Involved in the Study*

Name of the Department	*Number of Participants*		
	Girls	*Boys*	*Total*
Department of Education, Dukhulal Nibaran Chandra College, Aurangabad, Murshidabad	30	20	50

Nature of Distribution of Study Habits Scores

The scores acquired from the study habits inventory were arranged in a frequency distribution for the entire sample, as well as for the sub-samples of male and female students from the Department of Education. The specific details can be found in the tables provided below:

Table 7: *Frequency Distribution of Study Habits Scores*

Sl. No.	*Class Interval*	*Girls*			*Boys*			*Total Students*		
		F	*C.F.*	*% of C.F.*	*F*	*C.F.*	*% of C.F.*	*F*	*C.F.*	*% of C.F.*
1.	50-55	01	01	3.33	01	01	5.00	02	02	4.00
2.	56-61	11	12	4.00	08	09	45.00	19	21	42.00
3.	62-67	16	28	93.33	10	19	95.00	26	47	94.00
4.	67-72	02	30	100	01	20	100	03	50	100
Total		**30**			**20**			**50**		

Based on the analysis of the data presented in Table 7, it can be inferred that the study habits scores of students exhibit a central tendency, with a progressive decline towards the extremes, irrespective of gender. This pattern is observed among both male and female students, as well as the entire student population. This finding also indicates that the study habits of the participants

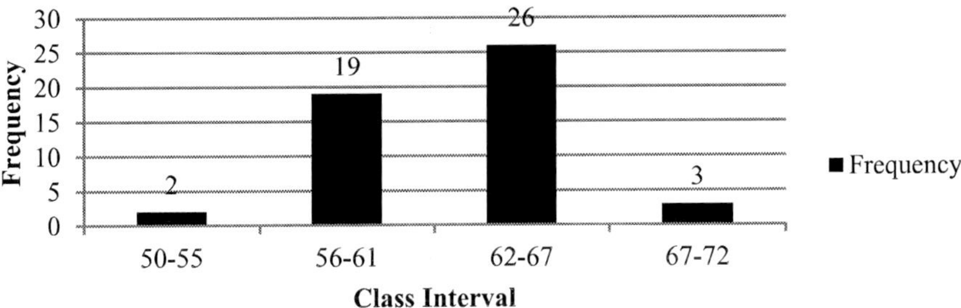

Figure 10.1: *Frequency Distribution of Study Habits Scores*

in the sample tend to be moderate. The aforementioned observation is further supported by the visual depiction (Fig. 10.1) illustrating the distribution pattern of study habits scores.

Table 8: *Interpretation of Study Habits on the Basis of Obtained Scores of Participants*

Participants	*Obtained Scores*	*Gender (Boys/Girls)*	*Percentile Level*	*Category*	*Interpretation*
1	61	G	50	C	Average Study Habits
2	63	G	50	C	Average Study Habits
3	65	G	70	B	Good Study Habits
4	61	G	50	C	Average Study Habits
5	62	G	50	C	Average Study Habits
6	63	G	50	C	Average Study Habits
7	63	G	50	C	Average Study Habits
8	64	G	60	C	Average Study Habits
9	65	G	70	B	Good Study Habits
10	65	G	70	B	Good Study Habits
11	64	G	60	C	Average Study Habits
12	65	G	70	B	Good Study Habits
13	64	G	60	C	Average Study Habits
14	64	G	60	C	Average Study Habits
15	67	B	90	A	Excellent Study Habits
16	68	G	80	A	Excellent Study Habits
17	68	G	80	A	Excellent Study Habits
18	63	G	50	C	Average Study Habits
19	63	G	50	C	Average Study Habits
20	63	G	50	C	Average Study Habits
21	63	B	80	A	Excellent Study Habits
22	62	B	75	B	Good Study Habits
23	62	B	75	B	Good Study Habits
24	63	B	80	A	Excellent Study Habits
25	62	B	75	B	Good Study Habits
26	62	B	75	B	Good Study Habits
27	58	G	30	D	Unsatisfactory Study Habits
28	58	G	30	D	Unsatisfactory Study Habits
29	61	G	50	C	Average Study Habits
30	61	G	50	C	Average Study Habits

Participants	Obtained Scores	Gender (Boys/Girls)	Percentile Level	Category	Interpretation
31	62	B	75	B	Good Study Habits
32	63	B	80	A	Excellent Study Habits
33	59	G	40	C	Average Study Habits
34	59	G	40	C	Average Study Habits
35	59	G	40	C	Average Study Habits
36	57	G	25	D	Unsatisfactory Study Habits
37	60	G	40	C	Average Study Habits
38	59	B	50	C	Average Study Habits
39	58	B	50	C	Average Study Habits
40	58	B	50	C	Average Study Habits
41	58	B	50	C	Average Study Habits
42	56	B	40	C	Average Study Habits
43	57	B	40	C	Average Study Habits
44	53	G	10	E	Very Unsatisfactory Study Habits
45	50	B	10	E	Very Unsatisfactory Study Habits
46	57	B	40	C	Average Study Habits
47	57	B	40	C	Average Study Habits
48	66	B	90	A	Excellent Study Habits
49	63	B	80	A	Excellent Study Habits
50	64	G	60	C	Average Study Habits

Table-8 indicates that majority (28) of the participants have average study habits. Table-8 also shows that total eight (8) participants have excellent study habits and nine (9) participants have good study habits. In spite of that Table-8 also highlights that total three (3) participants have unsatisfactory study habits and total two (2) participants have very unsatisfactory study habits.

Table 9: *Comparison of Study Habits between Girls and Boys*

Category	Interpretation	Girls		Boys	
		Frequency	%	Frequency	%
A	Excellent Study Habits	2	6.67	6	30.00
B	Good Study Habits	4	13.33	5	25.00
C	Average Study Habits	20	66.67	8	40.00
D	Unsatisfactory Study Habits	3	10.00	Nil	Nil
E	Very Unsatisfactory Study Habits	1	3.33	1	5.00
Total		30	100	20	100

Table 9 indicates that 30% boys haveexcellent study habits and only 6.67% girls have excellent study habits in this study. 20% boys havegood study habits and only 13.33% girls have good study habits in this study. 40% boys haveaverage study habits, whereas 66.67% girls have average study habits in this study. 10% girls have unsatisfactory study habits in this study.5% boys havevery unsatisfactory study habits, whereas 3.33% girls have very

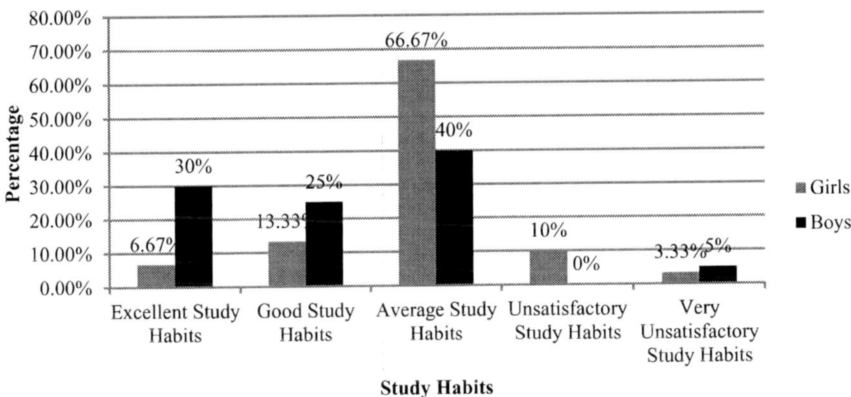

Figure 10.2: *Comparison of Study Habits between Girls and Boys*

unsatisfactory study habits in this study. Therefore, it can be said that boys have slightly better study habits in comparison to girls in this study. The pictorial representation (Fig. 10.2) of comparison of study habits between girls and boys also confirms this observation.

Educational Implications

1. By conducting this study, investigator will be able to know the study habits of the students.
2. From this study, students can be aware about their study habits and they can be actively involved themselves in the learning process.
3. It can help teachers and students to improve teaching-learning process.
4. It helps teachers to attain the knowledge of individual differences in the classroom.
5. Regular study habits help students to improve memory and to achieve good marks.

Conclusion

Thus after the test we can say that the majority (28) of the participants have average study habits. The study also revealed that boys have slightly better study habits in comparison to girls. The participants should try to improve their exam skills and make the experience more pleasurable and fruitful. They can do it by following regular study habits. Thus they will be able to give examinations without any stress. The study habit inventory can be used by the teacher as well as counselor for giving proper guidance to the students.

References

Dhaliwal, A.S. (1971). *A Study of Some Factors Contributing to AcademicSuccess and Failure among High School Students — Personality Correlates ofAcademic Underachievement.* Ph.D. Psy., AMU.

Husen & others (1994): The International Encyclopaedia of Education. Second edition, vol. 10, 5829.

Husen & others (1994): The International Encyclopaedia of Education. Second edition, vol. 06, 3293.

Jain, S.K. (1967). *Study Habits and academic achievement attainment in U.P.* Doctoral Theses, Psychology, Agra Univ.

Jamuar, K.K. (1961). *Investigation of some psychological factors underlying the study habits of college students'.* Ph.D. Education, Patna Univ.

Jha, V. (1970). *An Investigation into some factors related to achievement inscience by students in Secondary Schools.* Doctoral Theses, Edu., Patna Univ.

Kapoor, R. (1987). *Study of Factors Responsible for High and Low Achievement at the Junior High School Level.* Ph.D. Edu. Awadh Univ.

Kaur, G.P. & Lekhi, V. (1995). *Intelligence, achievement motivation and study habits as correlates of academic achievement.* Buch, M.B., vol. 4(2).

Longman Dictionary of Contemporary English (2004). International Edition. Printed in India by Gopsons Papers Limited, New Delhi.

Oxford Dictionary & Thesaurus (2007). Published in United States by Oxford University Press Inc., New York.

Palsane, M.N. & Sharma, A. (1989). *Study Habits Inventory* (English Version). Agra: National Psychological Corporation.

Panchalingappa, N. (1995). *An Investigation into the Causes of Underachievement in Secondary School Mathematics.* Ph.D. Edu., Kamataka Univ.

Rao, A.M.S. (1965). *A Diagnostic study of Reading difficulties of students in High School.* Ph.D. Psy., Mysore Univ.

Secondary Education Commission. (1953). *Report of the Secondary Education Commission 1952-1953.* Govt. of India.

Singh, H. (1984). *A Survey of the Study Habits of High, Middle and Low Achievers Adolescents in Relation to their Sex, Intelligence and Socioeconomic Status,* Ph.D. Edu., H.P Univ.

Smith, Samuel, & Field, L. (1948). *An Outline of Best Methods of Study.* New York: Bamess and Noble Inc.

Tuli, M.R. (1981). Study habits as correlates of achievement in Mathematics. *Journal of Educational Psychology,* vol. 38(3), 137-140.

Vanarase, S.J. (1970). *Ability and Scholastic Underachievement.* Ph.D. Psy. Poona Univ.

Bibliography

American Psychiatric Association (2000). *Diagnostic and Statistical Manual of Mental Disorders*. Fourth Edition Text Revision (DSM-IV-TR). Washington DC: American Psychiatric Association.

American Psychiatric Association. (1994). *Diagnostic and Statistical Manual of Mental Disorders* (4th ed.). American Psychiatric Publishing.

American Psychiatric Association. (2013). *Diagnostic and Statistical Manual of Mental Disorders* (5th ed.). American Psychiatric Publishing.

Andreasen, N.C. (1999). *The Creating Brain: The Neuroscience of Genius*. Plume.

Burns, D.D. (1980). *Feeling Good: The New Mood Therapy*. Harper.

Comer, R.J. (2014). *Abnormal Psychology*. Worth Publishers.

Corey, G. (2016). *Theory and Practice of Counseling and Psychotherapy*. Cengage Learning.

Freud, S. (1961). *Civilization and Its Discontents*. W.W. Norton & Company.

Goleman, D. (1995). *Emotional Intelligence: Why It Can Matter More Than IQ*. Bantam.

Greenberger, D., & Padesky, C.A. (1995). *Mind Over Mood: Change How You Feel by Changing the Way You Think*. The Guilford Press.

Jahoda, M. (1958). *Current Concepts of Positive Mental Health*. Basic Books.

Kandel, E.R. (1999). "Biology and the future of psychoanalysis: A new intellectual framework for psychiatry revisited."*The American Journal of Psychiatry*, 156(4), 505-524.

Kessler, R.C., & Wang, P.S. (2008). "The descriptive epidemiology of commonly occurring mental disorders in the United States."*Annual Review of Public Health*, 29, 115-129.

Kraepelin, E. (1919) "Dementia praecox and paraphrenia." In: *Textbook of Psychiatry*, 8th Edition. Barclay, E.S., Translated, Livingston, Edinburgh.

Lazarus, R.S., & Folkman, S. (1984). *Stress, Appraisal, and Coping*. Springer Publishing Company.

Linehan, M.M. (1993). *Cognitive-Behavioural Treatment of Borderline Personality Disorder*. Guilford Press.

Pilgrim, D. (2015). *Key Concepts in Mental Health*. SAGE Publications.

Seligman, M.E.P. (2011). *Flourish: A Visionary New Understanding of Happiness and Well-being*. Atria Books.

World Health Organization. (2001). The World Health Report 2001: Mental Health: New Understanding, New Hope. World Health Organization.

World Health Organization. (2018). International Classification of Diseases for Mortality and Morbidity Statistics (11th Revision). World Health Organization.

World Health Organization. (1992). International Statistical Classification of Diseases and Related Health Problems, 10th Revision (ICD-10). World Health Organization.